Rehabilitation and Probation
in England and Wales, 1876–1962

History of Crime, Deviance and Punishment

Series Editor:
Anne-Marie Kilday, Professor of Criminal History,
Oxford Brookes University, UK

Editorial Board:
Neil Davie, University of Lyon II, France
Johannes Dillinger, University of Maine, Germany
Wilbur Miller, State University of New York, USA
Marianna Muravyeva, University of Helsinki, Finland
David Nash, Oxford Brookes University, UK
Judith Rowbotham, Nottingham Trent University, UK

Academic interest in the history of crime and punishment has never been greater and the *History of Crime, Deviance and Punishment* series provides a home for the wealth of new research being produced. Individual volumes within the series cover topics related to the history of crime and punishment, from the later medieval to modern period and in both Europe and North America, and seek to demonstrate the importance of this subject in furthering understanding of the way in which various societies and cultures operate. When taken together, the works in the series will show the evolution of the nature of illegality and attitudes towards its perpetration over time and will offer their readers a rounded and coherent history of crime and punishment through the centuries. The series' broad chronological and geographical coverage encourages comparative historical analysis of crime history between countries and cultures.

Published:
Policing the Factory, Barry Godfrey
Crime and Poverty in 19th-Century England, Adrian Ager
Print Culture, Crime and Justice in Eighteenth-Century London, Richard Ward

Forthcoming:
The Policing of Belfast 1870–1914, Mark Radford (2015)
Deviance, Disorder and Music in Modern Britain and America,
Cliff Williamson (2015)
Crime, Regulation and Control during the Blitz,
Peter Adey, David J. Cox and Barry Godfrey (2015)
The Forefathers of Terrorism, Johannes Dillinger (2015)
Private Policing in Modern America, Wilbur Miller (2016)
Feminist Campaigns against Child Sexual Abuse, Daniel J. R. Grey (2016)

Rehabilitation and Probation in England and Wales, 1876–1962

Raymond Gard

Bloomsbury Academic
An imprint of Bloomsbury Publishing Plc

B L O O M S B U R Y

LONDON · OXFORD · NEW YORK · NEW DELHI · SYDNEY

Bloomsbury Academic

An imprint of Bloomsbury Publishing Plc

50 Bedford Square
London
WC1B 3DP
UK

1385 Broadway
New York
NY 10018
USA

www.bloomsbury.com

BLOOMSBURY and the Diana logo are trademarks of Bloomsbury Publishing Plc

First published 2014
Paperback edition first published 2016

© Raymond Gard, 2014

British Library Cataloguing-in-Publication Data
A catalogue record for this book is available from the British Library.

ISBN: HB: 978-1-4725-2632-8
PB: 978-1-4742-8274-1
ePDF: 978-1-4725-2233-7
ePub: 978-1-4725-3260-2

Library of Congress Cataloging-in-Publication Data
Gard, Raymond L., 1961-
Rehabilitation and probation in England and Wales, 1876–1962 / Raymond Gard.
pages cm
Includes bibliographical references and index.
ISBN 978-1-4725-2632-8 (hardback) – ISBN 978-1-4725-3260-2 (epub) –
ISBN 978-1-4725-2233-7 (epdf) 1. Criminals–Rehabilitation–England–History.
2. Criminals–Rehabilitation–Wales–History. 3. Probation–England–History.
4. Probation–Wales–History. I. Title.
HV9346.A5G37 2014
364.6'3094209041 – dc23
2014014861

Series: History of Crime, Deviance and Punishment

Typeset by Integra Software Services Pvt. Ltd.
Printed and bound in Great Britain

Contents

Introduction

In many respects this work is a relatively straightforward history of probation between 1876 and 1962. The dates are significant as they coincide with the appointment of the first police court missionary in Britain and the publication of the Home Office review of probation usually referred to as the Morrison Report (Home Office 1962). The former was the descendent of the modern-day probation officer, and the 1962 Report, so the work will argue, represents a high point of probation. High point in this case is in terms of numbers of probation orders, the range of the work that probation officers did, the political support the organization and its methods enjoyed, and its own self-confidence.

Most recent surveys of criminal justice and the more specific literature on probation agree that probation reached something of a zenith or highpoint sometime in the 1960s or early 1970s. At this time probation enjoyed substantial political support such that when the work of the divorce courts was expanded it was probation officers who were considered the correct people to work with the courts. When the prison aftercare and welfare were expanded, again probation officers were considered the correct people to take on those roles (see Mair and Burke 2012). It was more than this; confidence in probation practice was shared not only by officers but their political masters and arguably the general public. Vanstone refers to it as 'the heyday of treatment' (Vanstone 2007: 94). A belief that the rehabilitation of criminals was achievable and the correct aim of all criminal justice agencies was almost taken for granted at this time. Indeed, every prison gate had a notice posted on it stating their aim was the rehabilitation of the criminal sent to them.

Anyone interested in probation or for that matter criminal justice over the last thirty years can't fail to have noticed how that has changed. Most recent writing on criminal justice comment on the huge changes in the field that began at some point in the 1970s. The dates often vary but a shift to a new punitiveness is usually noted. There is already a fascinating and wide ranging literature on the 'new consensus'. Downes and Morgan (1994) are a very good place to start but Garland's (2001) book covers a similar phenomenon but takes a different approach and particularly alerts us to the fact that similar occurred in the USA at this time.

Not only did the political consensus on rehabilitation and penal policy break down but confidence in probation and particularly probation practice was severely dented. Research in the 1970s into the effectiveness of rehabilitative social casework as practised by probation officers was found to be ineffective in reducing reoffending. In practice and policy terms the carpet was taken from underneath probation's feet. Research into probation effectiveness had begun to attract attention in the 1960s but it is often said that it was Martinson's (1974) celebrated essay that discovered that 'nothing works'. However, things have moved on and more recent research has begun to uncover that some things do work and debate in the 1980s and later in probation has moved to 'what works'. Large-scale research projects conducted by the Home Office (see Nuttall et al 1998) and local research from within the probation service itself (see Deering et al 1996, for example) have shown that some things do work. This research into probation effectiveness has meant that cognitive behavioural approaches have become very popular within the probation service (Worrall 1997: 113) which have led to 'a new mood of optimism' (Worrall 1997: 114). Effectiveness became the key word and the programmes based on a cognitive behavioural understanding of human nature, epitomized by Priestly and Maguire (1985), became very influential.

At a policy level probation has not recovered. Not only has the political context in which probation and criminal justice generally operate changed enormously but probation policy has also shifted over the last twenty or thirty years. The influence of the responsible government department has loomed large over this area. For example, Worrall's survey of probation notes:

> In the past probation areas have enjoyed relative autonomy to developed their own policies but the service has become increasingly centralised, particularly since the publication by the Home Office in 1984 of the Statement of National Objectives and Priorities. (Worrall 1997: 66)

May (1991) also notes changes in the Home Office and probation relationship and the far more interventionist role that the Home Office plays in the work of probation officers. He writes that these changes 'have left the service in a state of flux regarding its purpose and peculiarly vulnerable to blinkered and politically inspired change' (May 1991: 177). Both these works were published in the 1990s but that centralizing trend has not stopped. Since then probation has been reorganized a number of times and is now part of the National Offender Management Service (NOMS). It is no longer managed by the Home Office but the newly created Ministry of Justice whose latest proposal is to contract out much of the probation service's work to the private and voluntary sectors (see Guilfoyle 2013).

The aim of this work is to chart the arrival of the so-called golden age of probation, or more generally rehabilitation and probation. There is a substantial body of literature that debates recent criminal justice shifts and looks at the politics, policy and practice of criminal justice and some that deal specifically with probation (see Whitehead and Statham 2006). This work intends to show that change, debate and controversy are not new in probation; the importance of the Home Office, shifting understandings of delinquency, its causes and how we should respond to it are also not new. The aim of this work is to shed some light on those controversies and changes as probation and rehabilitation in probation reached their heyday.

This study uses the terms 'politics', 'policy' and 'practice' throughout. Politics refers to the social and political context in which probation operated; policy refers to the rules, legal framework and even management of probation. Practice refers to the working methods used by probation officers and their methods of working with offenders. The work will argue that the three are inextricably linked and are a product of their time and place. It will also show how all three move; there is a subtext of change running throughout the work. All three aspects of probation moved enormously in the time period covered; illuminating, even explaining, those changes is the aim of the work.

In terms of probation practice the work also looks at contemporary understandings of social work and psychology and how they impacted on the practice of probation officers and the earlier police court missionaries. Again there is an emphasis on change and how these disciplines move over the ninety years in question. The term 'discourse' is used regularly when discussing social work and psychology and there is a large body of work and much teaching offered that uses this term. In the criminal justice field much of the inspiration comes from Foucault (1991) and he would doubtless be spinning in his grave if he were to see the way the term is used here. It is no more than a tool, a device to explain a body of knowledge that defines a problem and then offers a solution to that problem. In this work that problem is criminality, or on occasion delinquency, and the tools offered are social work and psychology. The key point is that these disciplines move and change at the same time that politics and policy change. The work will also identify key strands within the discourses and so show the social work and psychological discourses operating within probation practice but also elements or strands of those discourses, competing, rising and falling over time. Again we return to this idea of change.

The original inspiration for this work came from reading David Garland's (1985) account of the creation of, what he terms, the penal welfare complex between roughly 1906 and 1912. His focus is on the social, political and cultural context of the creation of something remarkably new, that is a range of penal institutions dealing primarily with the young offender and focused on the reformation and welfare of that offender. These institutions included the Borstal, the children's courts and probation and all was done within a two-year period. He identifies four discourses competing within the field for the attention of policy makers and practitioners within these new institutions. This work makes an attempt to take a similar approach but focuses on only one area, namely probation, and follows its trajectory over a ninety-year period. Garland's time frame was much narrower but he covered a far wider range of institutions and practices.

Further help came in the form of Tim May's (1991) research in which he spent a good deal of time talking to probation officers and middle managers in the probation service about their work and then went on to produce an eminently readable account of probation politics, policy and practice. It may well have been pure coincidence but May's research coincided with the probation service grappling with a major reform of their work. At the time wide ranging Home Office intervention in probation officers' day-to-day practice had been introduced and further was being mooted in the form of National Standards (see Home Office 1988 and 1992) at the same time that proposals to change the whole structure and language of probation were being made in what was to become *The Criminal Justice Act 1991*. Of course he had the enormous advantage of being able to talk to the people involved, middle managers and those on the ground actually doing the work.

The difficulty with an historical approach is having access to the people; those devising policy and those actually responsible for implementing it, effectively to give voice to those people. In order to do that a number of archives have been consulted in the preparation of this work. These are sources which taken together can give a picture of probation practice. The obvious place to start is the journal of the National Association of Probation Officers, known as *Probation*. This was first published in 1929 and much of it is now available online (see Annison 2009 for more on this) and it includes regular contributions from working probation officers or those working with probation officers. There is also a tradition of probation officers and the earlier police court missionaries writing personal accounts and memoirs of their work. These can often be quite idiosyncratic but nonetheless reveal much. There are then contemporary textbooks about probation and more general contemporary works about criminal justice.

The Church of England Temperance Society archive is held at the Galleries of Justice in Nottingham and this includes reports and minute books from various meetings of the London and Southwark Branches of the Church of England Temperance Society which in turn reveal much about the methods and beliefs of the early police court missionaries and later missionary probation officers. Contemporary works on psychology and social work proved to be useful, as did a small archive that used to be held at the Institute for the Study Treatment of Delinquency (ISTD). This includes the correspondence, notes and minute books of the ISTD in its very early days. These sources all help to add to the picture of probation practice as they show contemporary social work and psychological services impacting on the daily practice of probation officers.

As for the policy aspect of the work, a number of government and Home Office reports and documents were produced in the time period under consideration and these have been consulted. However, the Home Office files of the time held at the National Archive in Kew were incredibly revealing and really bring to life policy and political debate regarding probation. Those consulted in this work were in the main the day-to-day operating files of the Children's and later Probation Branch at the Home Office, files usually from the HO45 and HO144 series. However, some of the Metropolitan Police files in the MEPO1 and MEPO2 series also prove to be revealing. Occasionally these files were closed under the so-called '100 year rule' but application to the Records Office at the Home Office under the *Public Records Act 1958* gave access to them. Thus by using a range of published contemporary work and archive material it became possible to give voice to those devising policy and implementing that policy and to those actually working as probation officers. Importantly they show some of the debate around probation policy that is often missed in accounts of probation's history.

There are already a number of books that look at the history and development of the probation service. Two of the most recent are Vanstone's (2007) history of the theory and practice of probation and Mair and Burke's (2012) description of the probation service, past and present. Both the works referred to take the story up to the present day; this work focuses on the rise of probation or what might be called a modern probation service. The word 'rehabilitation' is used in the title but in a rather general sense. It is used as a term to describe the aim of probation officers, police court missionaries and missionary probation officers – that is helping offenders to turn away from crime or in modern parlance reducing the risk of reoffending. It is used in a general sense to stress the fact that methods changed and that policy changed but both remained under this general umbrella of the rehabilitation of the offender. Throughout the period covered in this work probation was not seen primarily as a punishment or restriction of liberty.

The work is divided into a number of time slots. However, the first two chapters overlap with the first chapter focusing on the mission to the police court of the late nineteenth century. This is a story that continues well into the 1930s but it predates the first probation officers. The second chapter focuses on the appointment of the first probation officers following the *Probation of Offenders Act 1907*. However, to do that it needs to look at earlier probation acts and the lead-up to the 1907 Act. The contention of this work is that the police court mission and the 1907 Act are quite distinct and need a separate history, hence the two chapters. Later chapters in the work tend to focus on roughly ten-year periods and one key piece of legislation. Chapter 3 deals with the *Criminal Justice Act 1925* and argues that this was hugely significant for probation. It therefore looks at the reasons for the changes and the consequences of the legislation. Chapter 4 deals with the *Children and Young Persons Act 1933* which shaped the way that the state dealt with children for many years to come; it also had significant implications for probation. This chapter also detects a major shift in probation practice influenced very much by changing attitudes to juvenile delinquency. The *Criminal Justice Act 1948* is covered in the next chapter and this work will argue that this legislation and its consequences created the administrative framework of a probation service that was to survive well into the 1980s. The final chapter focuses on the period through the 1950s to the publication of the Morrison Report in 1962. It discusses the arrival of psycho-dynamic social casework that was to shape probation practice, in fact social work generally, in the 1950s. It was an impact that was to survive well into the 1980s.

The ultimate aim of this work is to produce a history that shows probation's development to be messy, uneven and contested and to reveal some of the debate and some of the controversy of the time. There is a tendency in many of the earlier histories of probation to take the 'steady march to enlightenment' view of probation's history. It is a weakness spotted by Young, who wrote:

> The past is seen as inexorably leading along a pre-determined pathway that terminates in the natural state of welfare society. Similarly the history of probation – its reform, expansion and 'institutionalisation' – mark the signposts that make clear the way to any who happen to wander. (Young 1976: 4)

He is very damming of what he terms 'whig' histories, as is Wiener, who in a review of Radzinowicz and Hood's mammoth study of the criminal law in England and Wales wrote, 'in the end, it always presses on towards the light' (Wiener 1987: 95).

Our story ends with a well-established distinctly modern probation service enjoying political support and approval amongst many who worked in or were connected with the criminal justice process. Most officers were qualified, comparatively well paid, enjoyed a good deal of public and political approval and their methods were generally agreed to be effective – what many have referred to as probation's zenith. The route there was anything but even, planned and uncontroversial, and there were many dead ends, diversions and alternatives not taken up. It would be easy to get the impression from reading much of the literature about probation that controversy, conflict and debate are new to the service and signify the end of a long period of consensus. This work aims to bring some of those older controversies into the light. In the meantime, to follow the route taken we need to go back to the middle of the nineteenth century, which is where our story starts.

1

The Mission to the Police Court: 1876–1907

There is a substantial and growing body of literature that deals with histories of crime and responses to crime (see, for example, Foucault 1991, Hay, D. 1975, Ignatieff 1978, Melossi and Pavarini 1981, Radzinowicz and Hood 1986) and most agree that there was a major change in the treatment of the criminal which occurred some time in the middle of the nineteenth century. Some leave the impression that these major changes were completed by the late nineteenth century and from this point onward there occurred a steady march towards a modern system of penalties in place by the late 1970s. This work will argue that there were later changes of equal importance which are crucial in understanding the creation of a modern system of probation. However, it would be to mislead the reader if these later changes were not placed in the context of those made in the middle of the nineteenth century.

What this means in practice is that although the *Probation of Offenders Act of 1907* created the first probation officers in the UK, its introduction was not only rooted in changes that had occurred in the mid-nineteenth century but was also a product of concerns both social and political current in 1907. Therefore, to understand the arrival of probation officers in England and Wales, both the historical antecedents and contemporary concerns of 1907 need to be considered.

To begin to account for the *Probation of Offenders Act of 1907* we need to go (very briefly) back to the middle of the nineteenth century. The system of punishments operating at the start of the nineteenth century are described by Hay so: 'It was a bloody penal code, an astute ruling class who manipulated it to their advantage, and a people schooled in the lessons of Justice, Terror and Mercy' (Hay, D. 1975: 63). This was the period of a ruling class dominated by a propertied landed gentry and an aristocracy. Large cities were rare and local ties and obligations were strong, particularly to the local landowner for whom many worked and were reliant on for food and shelter. Obedience, Hay argues, was assured through a law based on terror. He points out that between 1688 and 1820 there was an increase from 50 to 200 of offences which attracted the death penalty. Despite this, 'the number of executions for offences against property remained relatively stable, especially after 1750' (Hay, D. 1975: 22). The reason for this, he argues, was that the use of mercy ran through the whole legal process and created personal obligations between all those connected with it. As prosecutions were private and could usually only be afforded by the rich, the obligations created tended to be between rich prosecutor and poor defendant. Thus social stability was achieved between the classes. In respect of the death penalty Hay points out that only about a half were actually carried out, here mercy was applied via the pardon. Hay writes that equilibrium was thus achieved whereby 'The law made enough examples to inculcate fear, but not so many as harden or repel a populace that had to assent, in some measure at least, to the rule of property' (Hay, D. 1975: 57).

As the century progressed, major changes occurred which have been well documented in a number of historical works. Of these, the work of Foucault (1991) is a useful point at which to start. He focuses on the creation of a system of punishment whose central plank was the prison but crucially a new type of prison. He writes:

> By the end of the eighteenth and the beginning of the nineteenth century, the gloomy festival of punishment was dying out, though here and there it flickered momentarily into life. (Foucault 1991: 8)

He argues that punishment prior to this date had focused on the body of the offender, often expressed in terms of the death penalty. The new set of punishments focused on the segregation of the criminal in the new prisons of the time, the aim of which was to change the behaviour of the criminal.

The arrival of the new style of prison coincided, Foucault argues, with other less tangible changes in the system of punishments. He argues:

> During the 150 or 200 years that Europe has been setting up its new penal systems, the judges have gradually, by means of a process that goes back very far indeed, taken to judging something other than crimes, namely the 'soul' of the criminal. (Foucault 1991: 19)

He continues:

> A corpus of knowledge, techniques, 'scientific' discourses is formed and becomes entangled with the power to punish. (Foucault 1991: 23)

Foucault identifies two key aims of the new system of punishments; these were surveillance and normalization. Although he describes other aims, these two are particular pertinent to this work. In respect of surveillance he refers to both the surveillance of the prisoner and the prison guards in the new prisons, the object of which was the control of both groups. The normalization programme was given a particularly important place in what Foucault terms the 'disciplinary apparatus'. He writes:

> But the supervision of normality was firmly encased in a medicine or a psychiatry that provided with a 'scientificity'; it was supported by a judicial apparatus which, directly or indirectly gave it legal justification. Thus, in the shelter of these two considerable protectors, and, indeed, acting as a link between them, or a place of exchange, a carefully worked out technique for the supervision of norms has continued to develop right up to the present day. (Foucault 1991: 296)

In other words, the treatment of the criminal, which is the focus of this work, traces its origins to the surveillance and normalization programme initiated in the prisons of the middle of the nineteenth century.

In fact Cohen (1979, 1983) borrows many of Foucault's ideas when he describes a panoptican effect being created in the community in the latter half of the twentieth century. He sees the argument being circular with the growth of the prisons in the middle of the nineteenth century being followed by a decarceration movement begun in the 1960s. Significantly though he sees this decarceration as the prison simply moving into the community via a system of community corrections. He argues that the boundaries between the two have become blurred and asks, 'when is a prison a prison and a community a community?' (Cohen 1979: 346). A 'punitive city' is therefore created, he writes:

> The new move into the community is merely a continuation of the overall pattern established in the nineteenth century. The proliferation of new experts and professionals, the generation of specialized domains of scientific knowledge, the creation of complicated classification systems, the establishment of a network of agencies surrounding the court and the prison – all these developments marked the beginning a century ago of the widening of the 'carcereal circle' or 'carcereal archipelgo'. (Cohen 1979: 360)

Thus he brings Foucault into the late twentieth century seeing evidence of similar changes today.

Ignatieff (1978) argues that in the mid-nineteenth century powerful groups of the time had two key problems. The first was the end of the availability of transportation as a meaningful penalty (so felons had to be accommodated in Britain) coupled with much interest in the poor conditions within the old goals and bridewells highlighted by reformers such as John Howard and later Elizabeth Fry. The influence of Unitarian philosophers like Bentham and John

Stuart Mill along with the non-conformist religions led to the arrival of the possibility of the reformation of the criminal and a possible but partial solution. The second dilemma was an increasingly radical and troublesome working class (concentrated in the new industrial cities). Whilst on one hand the franchise was extended via the *Reform Act of 1832*, 'the advent of democracy was characterised by an increased intolerance toward "deviant minorities"' (Ignatieff 1978: 212). At the same time as improvements were made to living conditions in the new cities, 'No attempt to raise the housing, educational, or sanitary standards of the poor was made without an accompanying attempt to colonise their minds' (Ignatieff 1978: 214). Therefore, both the urban working classes and prisoners were 'discovered' and incorporated into what Foucault called a 'normalisation programme'. That is, for different reasons, both groups had to be rendered safe or acceptable to the rest of the population, particularly the propertied and powerful.

Melossi and Pavarini (1981), though adopting an explicitly Marxist approach to their history, also identify similar important shifts over the same period of time. Early in the work they write that theirs is 'the analysis of the connection between the genealogy of capitalism and the genealogy of the penal institution' (Melossi and Pavarini 1981: 4). They therefore also identify the middle of the nineteenth century as a period of change focusing on the rapid industrial expansion of the time and the reform of the Poor Laws in 1834. They describe numerous 'segregated institutions' created at the time one of which was the Panopticon. However, 'Over and above their specific functions, one overall aim united them: control over a rising proletariat' (Melossi and Pavarini 1981: 42).

Interestingly, Melossi and Pavarini add a further dimension to their study when they identify another shift in capitalism at the end of the nineteenth and early twentieth century. One consequence of which was:

> The new strategy was towards dispersion, towards the exclusion and pervasion of control. Individuals are no longer locked up: they are got at where they are *normally* locked up: outside the factory, in society as a whole. Propaganda, the mass media, a new and more efficient network of police and social assistance, these are the bearers of a new kind of social control. (Melossi and Pavarini 1981: 6)

Therefore unlike Foucault (1991) and Ignatieff (1978) they identify a further later shift in the punishment of the offender. This coincides with the argument made in this work, that although a major shift occurred in the middle of the nineteenth century, a further significant movement occurred later.

A similar argument is made by Tobias (1972) who identifies the same period and the same causes, that is the rapid industrialization of Britain, particularly London in the early nineteenth century, leading to a new type of offender and a new set of responses to crime. He argues that as the conditions of the London working classes improved over the century so crime fell and punishment became more benign.

These changes and the discovery of previously hidden populations extended outwards beyond the adult male offender and led to the so-called reformatory principle being advocated by a handful of vociferous campaigners (Radzinowicz and Hood 1986: 173). Mary Carpenter and Matthew Davenport Hill are the names usually associated with this movement. Crucially, they and their colleagues focused on children, that is those not yet touched by prison discipline. John Stack's history of the reformatory movement argues 'in 1854 the government bowed to pressure from the reformatory movement and passed the *Youthful Offenders Act*' (Stack 1994: 62). This allowed courts to send a child to a Reformatory School instead of prison but only after the child had spent two weeks in prison. The schools were to be privately funded and run, the first such school had been set up at Redhill in 1849 and run by the Royal Philanthropic Society. Stack goes on to argue that two campaigning groups formed, one based around Carpenter and Davenport Hill which argued that any form of prison was bad for a child and another which regarded the two-week rule as a useful deterrent. Mary Carpenter and her colleagues therefore established a number of Industrial Schools where no such rule applied. After a close consideration of the available statistics, Stack concluded, 'the humanitarian camps efforts to substitute commitment to reformatory or industrial schools for commitment to prison had clearly not been a success' (Stack 1994: 67). The problem being that the schools simply recruited younger children rather than those who were on their way to prison. On the one hand Radzinowicz and Hood write:

> By the turn of the century the reformatory and industrial schools had in their grasp more than 30,000 children: one in every 230 of the juvenile population between five and fifteen years. (Radzinowicz and Hood 1986: 181)

However, they seem to support Stack's point when they note that the largest proportion of children were minor offenders, normally with one conviction and that for larceny. Stack argues that the reformatory movement's real success was that its campaigning led to fewer child prosecutions and a number of more sympathetic courts, and the first separation of child from adult offenders. Pearson

(1983: 179) too comments on the originality of the reformatory movement but cautions us that the movement also had a steely edge to it; he writes:

> When they are placed in their proper contexts, however, the ambitions of philanthropy clearly had little to do with the caricature of soft-boiled sentimentality, and began to look more like a system of discipline and regulation. (Pearson 1983: 181)

This view was shared, incidentally, by Radzinowicz and Hood (1986: 194).

The middle of the nineteenth century was therefore characterized by the arrival of the prison as the central punishment available to the courts and the belief that it should be the site for the reformation of the criminal. However, this was a particular type of prison, a panoptican based on surveillance and normalization which was to replace the old gaols and jails a number of which dated back to the Middle Ages and earlier. There is also evidence of the reformation of the juvenile criminal being seen as distinct from the reformation of the adult criminal. This move from deterrence via terror aimed at the whole of the population through the body of the criminal to an appeal to the soul of the offender (young or old) via religion or silent contemplation in prison paved the way for the application of powerful discourses such as psychology and social work to the offender.

The mission

So moving from major changes in the treatment of crime in the middle of the nineteenth century we can see that these changes had specific and practical consequences. It is against this backdrop that George Nelson was appointed the first police court missionary in 1876. The changes we have just considered focused heavily on the prisons but Nelson's appointment was indicative of changes in legal practices and the lower courts slightly later in the nineteenth century. They reflected a changing relationship between the law and the rapidly growing urban working class and poor. Nelson went to work in the Police Court in Southwark (London). Davis (1984), in her work on the nineteenth-century London Police Courts, describes them as 'centres of advice and charity for the working class, who attended the courts in large numbers' (Davis 1984: 310). She points out that a substantial proportion of the prosecutions brought to the courts were from the poor of the area, usually for offences of larceny or assault. She also detects a growing association between the courts and the, still relatively new, police as the century wore on. Emsley (1996) notes a similar trend referring to debates about the creation of a public prosecution service in the early nineteenth century; however, the police came to dominate prosecutions such that '(f)or victims it probably seemed logical and preferable to hand over prosecutions to the police who increasingly claimed to be the experts in the "war" against crime' (Emsley 1996: 192). Nonetheless the courts were more than simply concerned with crime control. There is an element of welfare, concern with the conditions of the poor but there is also a clear element of surveillance, even normalization as Foucault might call it.

Added to this mix was the rapid expansion of summary justice in the late nineteenth century, epitomized by the *Summary Jurisdiction Act 1879* which vastly increased the number of offences that could be dealt with in the lower courts. Emsley (1996) sees this as a long-term project when he writes:

> The number of offences which could be tried summarily increased during the eighteenth century and even more markedly during the nineteenth century, particularly with the passage of the *Juvenile Offenders Act 1847* and *1850* and the *Criminal Justice Acts 1855 and 1877*. (Emsley 1996: 14)

The new police constables were also making their presence felt as they expanded both in the capital, the larger cities and into the rural areas of the country. Storch (1981) argues that they were initially very unpopular and quotes a common response to them as '…a plague of blue locusts' (Storch 1981: 86). He does concede that after the initial struggles, which occasionally broke out into armed conflict, by the 1860s they were at least tolerated. He writes:

> The impression is left that once the police were successfully entrenched the open warfare of initial contact was replaced by a state one may characterize as armed truce. (Storch 1981: 106)

Thus by the end of the nineteenth century the police were relatively well established both on the streets and in the courts of many of the substantial towns and cities of the UK.

The magistrates themselves were either local worthies working voluntarily unless they worked in the larger cities and London where many would have been full time and were expected to be experienced barristers before their appointment. The picture we get is that George Nelson and his early colleagues walked into a court that would have been very busy, presided over by a magistrate of a very different social standing and background to those he passed judgement on but a court that took a paternalistic even occasionally caring approach rather than simply being simply a law enforcement agency.

Vanstone's (2007) account of the early days of the mission to the police court includes some fascinating detail about its origins. He sees connections with the Anglo Saxon legal principle of 'Benefit of Clergy' and the later mediaeval principle of recognizances. Both were means by which a court could defer or alleviate the full punishment that a crime warranted. Recognizance particularly allowed a court to call a sentenced person back to court if they reoffended or breached any conditions of that recognizance. As we moved into the nineteenth century he cites the example of Matthew Davenport Hill, a Warwickshire Magistrate in the 1820s who would release juvenile offenders to a 'confidential officer' on the promise that they would be of good behaviour. He discusses other similar examples – Edward Cox the Recorder at Portsmouth, for example (see Vanstone 2007: 5), where courts would refrain from imposing full punishment on the promise of good behaviour and to return to court.

In 1941, Timasheff produced a comparative history of probation and like Vanstone (2007) sees the origins of probation in the well-established common law practices of recognizance, good behaviour and keeping the peace all of which existed in the USA, too. He also sees evidence of similar practices in Canada and New Zealand and the reasons for these were 'humanitarian and utilitarian considerations' (Timasheff 1941: 2). The early system of probation in the UK began in Warwickshire; in the USA it began with John Augustus, a shoe maker from Boston who attended court to plead for drunkards and to ask the court to suspend sentence on the promise of recognizance and supervision of the defendants. Augustus died in 1859 and his work in Boston was continued by Rufus R. Cook who, Timasheff says, was described as a probation officer and had a group of volunteers working with him who would attend court to provide reports and suggest probation to the courts (see Timasheff 1941: 9–12). Timasheff writes, '[T]he invention of M. D. Hill was analogous to that of Mr Augustus' (Timasheff 1941: 13).

Other histories of probation (for example, Bochel 1976, King 1958) usually trace the origins of probation in Britain to a letter from Frederic Rainer to his friend Canon Ellison and co-founder of the Church of England Temperance Society. The Society had been established in 1862 as the Church of England Total Abstinence Society and had changed its name ten years later. Rainer had been moved by the plight of released prisoners he had seen and sent a donation of five shillings so that a representative of the society could attend court. Shortly afterwards the Church of England Temperance Society appointed its first police court missionaries: George Nelson went to the Southwark and Lambeth Courts and William Batchelor went to the Bow Street and Mansion Courts. Both men were ex-Coldstream Guards. As Vanstone (2007) points, the operation grew steadily such that within ten years there were seventeen missionaries working and a further six female missionaries.

Vanstone describes this as the orthodox account of the origins of probation and in his following chapter writes a 'revisionist' account where he revisits the origins of probation to 'describe the purposes of probation as a response to political, religious and social concerns' (Vanstone 2007: 19). This second chapter places the mission in its political and social context and moves away from a 'steady march to enlightenment' approach to the history of probation, of which Wiener (1987) is particularly critical.

This study will borrow somewhat from Vanstone's revisionist approach but rather than taking a linear timeline it will start from the police court missionaries themselves and look outwards. That is, it will focus on the last few yeas of the nineteenth century, before the appointment of the first probation officers. By this time the police court missionaries were expanding and establishing not just in London but across the country. Rather than focusing on the steady expansion of the mission to the police courts, this work will use contemporary material to show how the mission operated and understood its own theoretical, even moral basis.

The day-to-day work of the mission

The London Diocesan Branch of the Church of England Temperance Society was responsible for the police court missionaries who worked north of the Thames and their third Annual Report for 1895 gives a wonderful account of the assumptions on which their work was based and what the missionaries actually did. It is worth looking at in some detail. Early on the Report notes:

> Not only were indoor meetings held, but, where possible open-air campaigning was vigorously carried out, with the result that generally the Mission was successful. The number of pledges taken is a test of the effectiveness of a Mission .... (CETS 1895: 4)

This reinforces the notion of mission in the work of the organization and that this was a temperance movement. The Report states that the missionaries in the police court helped 17,494 people and then goes on to give some indication as to how the missionaries and the mission worked. For example:

> The fact is, as the magistrates have so well and so often put it, the missionary is able to intervene just at the most opportune moment in so many lives, just

when their hearts are most alive to real sympathy and friendship, hence it is that so many have taken the one more chance which has been given them, signing the pledge, or going back to their old employer, through the intercession of the missionary, or offering to go into a home, and so they are saved from the goal taint, and prevented from joining the criminal classes. (CETS 1895: 22)

The next page of the Report includes a detailed breakdown of the work done that year by the mission in this part of the capital. It includes:

Pledges taken - 1405.
Visits to and re offenders and to Police Courts and Sessions - 11,756.
Visits to prisoners and prisoners' visits to Missionaries - 4,406.
Men places in situations - 198.
Women placed in situations - 83.
Boys placed in situations - 113.
Girls placed in situations - 59.
Special cases handed by Magistrates to Missionaries - 958.
Girls and women rescued from shame and degradation - 609.
Women inebriates handed over to the Women Missionaries - 1,368.
Employers persuaded by Missionaries to re-instate at work persons charged - 118.
Clothing, blankets, food and fuel furnished to persons and families - 6,798.
Letter written by Missionaries re cases - 5,333.
Lads restored to friends, sent to sea and to homes - 493.
Persons variously helped - 17,494. (CETS 1895: 23)

The Report goes on to note, 'work food and homes are provided for starving men' and 'families are kept form the Workhouse while the husband is in prison' (both from CETS 1895: 23).

Not all the missionaries were men; in fact there was a well-established small team of women missionaries. The description of their work does seem slightly different and their client group and its needs are also seen as different. Here the Report notes:

There are six Mission Women who do a most important work visiting at their homes those women who have been charged at the police court with drunkenness. The police court missionary first talks to these offenders at the court, and the Mission Women follows up his interview by visiting and watching over these persons who are handed over to her custody and care.

1368 cases were reported by the Police Court Missionaries to the Missionary Women; 537 of these gave false addresses, 831 women inebriates were then reported, 9319 visits were made, 230 pledges were taken, 27 situations were found for women, 43 women were taken to Homes, 30 women have kept their pledges from 1 to 3 years, 66 women have done well for a few months.

Estranged husbands and wives have been reunited, young girls from 14 to 19 years of age have been reclaimed from drunkenness, others have been returned to their homes or friends. Many letters of gratitude have been received from the girls and their parents. (CETS 1895: 26)

The London Diocesan Branch of the Church of England Temperance Society spent £1,265 7s 0d in the previous year which is not an insignificant sum. There is a strong religious element to the work done but the help provided seems to be very practical. This report describes the mission's work in London but the Church of England Temperance Society existed across the country, nor was it the only temperance society in existence. We can get a flavour of the work outside the capital by scouring the regional press for the last few years of the nineteenth century.

For example, *The Liverpool Mercury* of Tuesday 17 February 1877 reports a meeting of the Ladies' Temperance Association. At a recent bazaar, funds had been raised which:

enabled the committee at the commencement of the year to engage a secretary and two more missionaries. These additions gave the society a staff of a secretary and four missionaries. One of the missionaries spent three mornings a week in the police court … The rest of her time was spent in visiting such women as came under her notice in the court and appeared to need visitation, and in conducting meetings in different parts of the town, as a means of bringing together those over whom she had gained an influence.

The same article furnishes more detail about the work of the missionary in court when it reports:

… she had been called upon to reconcile husbands who naturally felt themselves degraded by their wives appearing in the police court and had declared that they would not receive them again. She had been asked to go and see to children (one a baby in a cradle) when the mother was in the cells and the father away from home. Many such requests had been acceded to. The number of visits paid by the secretary and missionaries was 15,334 and the number of pledges taken 411. Some 3,600 tracts had been circulated, chiefly through their missionaries.

Two things particularly stand out in this article, firstly it was written just a year after the first police court missionaries were appointed in London. In fact Jarvis (1972) points out that police court missionaries were appointed in Liverpool and Rochester swiftly after Nelson's appointment in London. Secondly, the operation seems well organized and well financed and operating in and outside the court. The same paper reports on 28 February 1891 the case of Bridget Conroy, a young woman who appeared in the Liverpool Police Court charged with theft of 6s from her father. The result was that '[t]he girl was discharged and Mr Gorlder, police court missionary, volunteered to advise the father as to what was the best thing to do with his daughter'.

It was not just the large cities where the mission operated. *The Hampshire Telegraph and Sussex Chronicle* of 18 March 1893 reported that a new CETS missionary, Mr Pettifer, had just been appointed to the Fareham Court '… in order to be of use in any cases which his services might require'. The following year, *The Derby Mercury* of Wednesday 18 April reported the case of Fanny Thorpe charged with 'wandering about' with her five-year-old son. It transpired that she had no partner but did have a father in Nottingham. She was discharged and the court agreed to pay her fare to Nottingham. The report continues, 'Mr Layton, the police court missionary, said he would see the prisoner's father, and in the meantime he would put both the woman and child in a home'. Moving south a little, the *Reynold's Newspaper* of Sunday 12 August 1894 reports the case from Croydon of Emily Lewis, a young woman of twenty-three who was apparently smartly dressed and described as a dressmaker who was charged with '… misconducting herself outside West Croydon Railway Station'. In court she was '… ordered to be detained in custody until six o'clock, the police court missionary being asked to speak to her in the meantime'.

There are many similar cases reported by the local press around the country. *The Western Mail* of Friday 21 December 1900 reports on various police court cases in the Cardiff area, one of which was thirteen-year-old Francis J. Sydenham, a kitchen boy working at the Cardiff Infirmary. The lad stole a cheque of £21, but when the court heard '… evidence as to his good character' and that 'Mr Deereux (police court missionary) gave similar testimony, and promised to try to find other employment for the boy' the court decided to bind him over in the sum of £5 to be of good behaviour. On the other side of the country *The Newcastle Weekly Currant* of Friday 20 July 1888 reports the case from the local police court of Agnes Bevars, age 26, appearing for the 108th time for an offence of being drunk and disorderly. The result was that 'on promising to sign the pledge, with Mr Thomas Barker, police court missionary, she was discharged'.

We begin to get a picture of the type of offenders and type of offences that the missionaries were being asked to deal with. It is also apparent that the missionaries were not just working with those convicted of offences. There was a much more welfare type approach, even what might be termed 'social worker to the court' view of their role. This could lead to some very bizarre uses of their labours. For example, *The Illustrated Police News* of 8 December 1900 reports:

> At Folkestone, the South Coast Mutoscope Company were summoned for the exhibition of indecent photos. in mutoscopes. The police court missionary, called to corroborate the evidence, said that the pictures were so indecent that he would rather have lost five guineas than have seen them. He had never been to a theatre in his life he added proudly. After inspecting the photos. privately for half an hour the magistrates ordered 'Three Men in a Girl's Bedroom', 'Where Ignorance is Bliss' and 'Should Ladies Wear Bloomers' to be destroyed.

Curiously, notice of appeal was given.

The same local press also regularly reported on various temperance society meetings. These too reveal the nature and range of work undertaken by the police court missionaries. For example, The Lord Mayor of London addressing a meeting of the London Police Court Mission at Mansion House in 1889 said:

> The principal work of the police court missionary is to get hold of men and women, and especially young women, on their first appearing before a magistrate on charges of drunkenness, and to stop them on what too often proves a downward course. Both men and women who have fallen required sympathy and encouragement to save them from despair; and in many cases material help to retrieve their lost character. (*Daily News* 19 October 1889)

It was not just the Mayor of London. A few years later the Mayor of Derby addressed a large public meeting at which he said:

> ....the work done by Mr Harding, the police court missionary, had been excellent for he noticed that during the past three months he had attended the police court 77 times, visited 16 cases at their own homes, and induced 47 to sign the pledge, besides placing three cases with the Church Army Labour Home, and addressing 17 meetings. He also kept in touch with the Sanitary Committee, and was thereby able to find employment for men. (*Derby Mercury* 24 July 1889)

Just a few years later the Portsmouth Police Court and Prison Gate Mission held its general meeting under the auspices of the British Women's Temperance Society. The police court missionaries, Mr Chappell and Mr Dore, both spoke and the work of the lady missionary was also discussed. Her work was described so:

> During the year the missionary, Miss Strawbridge had met at the prison gate, 195; had handed over to her at the police court, 13; taken pledges, 22; sent

to their own homes, 11; into various homes, 16; into the workhouse, 5; and obtained situations, 8. In conclusion, the Committee appealed for gifts of left-off clothing which were greatly needed as many poor women were scantily clad on leaving prison.

At the Annual General Meeting of the Stockton Branch of the Church of England Temperance Society of 1895 plans were discussed to appoint a police court missionary in the town. At the meeting Councillor W. C. Langley reported:

> As an evidence of the need of such a missioner he instanced that during his year of mayoralty about 770 cases came before him personally, a very large proportion of which, he was bound to say, were attributable to intemperance. (*Northern Echo*, 20 February 1895)

Again we can see similar themes, temperance, basic welfare needs and the missionary closely linked to the court and particularly the presiding magistrate. Crucially, though, we see that they were not concentrated in London. In fact in the large cities the mission seems well organized and well funded but even in the provincial towns missionaries are known of and used by the courts. To claim any sort of national coverage of the system would be very dangerous but the geographical spread of these articles is remarkable.

Although these accounts are very useful in giving us an insight into the day-to-day work of the police court missionaries, they are rather glowing and more critical accounts are harder to come by. There is one group of people who saw the missionaries at work on a daily basis who could be seen as being more objective; that was the police. On 19 October 1907 a memo was sent to the superintendents at all divisions of the Metropolitan Police which asked them to, '[p]lease report ... *confidentially* for information of the Commissioner, upon the work done by the Police Court Missionary and your opinion of the value of it'.[1] Perhaps because of the confidentiality the responses are interesting. The Inspector at Vinnie Stret Police Station provides a beautiful account of the work of the police court missionary which illustrates, in action, ideas about 'deserving' and assessments as to whether certain cases appearing before the court were deserving. The Inspector writes:

> As a rule he is at the Court early to assist person in distress who attend for Magistrates advice and are referred to him when the case has the appearance of being a deserving one.
>
> He is in touch with various Philanthropic Institutions, Rescue Homes, and Homes for Working Lads.

Frequently in the case of prostitutes who appear penitent and express a wish to return to work or their family, they are put back by the Magistrate to see what can be done for them by the Missionary, who communicates with the various Homes or prisoners friends with a view to their being able to get away from their mode of life and make a fresh start.

Lads or girls who are charged with larceny in which a sudden temptation or bad company appears to have been the cause, and appear contrite, and hopeful for a fresh start are in many cases bound over in a recognizance and handed over to his care.

In addition to this Habitual Drunkards are often preferred to the Missionary with a view to being put with a Voluntary Home in preference to be sent away as Inebriates.

Enquiry is also made by him in cases of very poor persons requiring Surgical Appliances, Trusses etc, but are unable to pay. Such cases he refers to the Surgical Aid Society with a recommendation for instrument required.[2]

In this account we also see the missionary acting as a gatekeeper to resources, often very practical resources at that, which is a theme we have seen in other accounts. The missionary is also generally making themselves useful to the court, what might be termed 'social worker to the court'. A further theme that is repeated.

The roles performed by the missionary can be problematic and this is highlighted in some of the other responses collected. For example, the Inspector at Bow Street writes:

In many cases of drunkenness persons dealt with by the Court are seen by the Missionary and asked to sign the pledge, but apparently very little good results from pressed momentary convection formed when the mind is incapable of estimating its value.

This is perhaps not a surprising observation but other problems emerge. The Inspector goes on:

So far as the Police are concerned it is thought that the Missionary does but very little good. Prejudice and interest no doubt influence him and his enquiries cannot therefore be conducted with the same freedom as by an independent person.

This is slightly more obtuse but probably refers to the fact that the missionary is employed by a religious and abstinence based organization. It could of course refer to the fact that the missionary is, unlike a police officer, not independent.

The Inspector at G. Division makes an interesting point when he writes that ' … it would seem to be the proper duty of the clerical staff of the Court to do some of the things which the missionary has been accustomed to do'. The Inspector at Southwark which covered the Tower Bridge Court commented:

> Much depends on the personality of the Missionary and even more hangs upon the disposition manifested towards him by the Magistrate. Some Magistrates refer to the Missionary whenever cases present features which cannot be met by … the court. Others apparently ignore his presence.[3]

The latter comment has resonances and it is a problem that was encountered by both missionaries and probation officers throughout the period covered in this work.

Another outsider looking in at the work of the police court missionaries in London was Hugh Gamon who at the time he wrote had just graduated from Oxford and was resident at the Toynbee Hall Settlement. They commissioned him to produce a survey of the work of the Police Courts of London which coincidentally was published in 1907, the same year as the *Probation of Offenders Act*. Thus we get a picture of the operation of the mission to the Police Courts in London just as they are on the cusp of change. Gamon was an unabashed advocate for reform of probation and early in his book writes that 'I have endeavoured to make myself familiar with the probation system in American publications' (Gamon 1907: xvii).

Gamon paints a familiar picture, that of a missionary busy in all parts of the court and in all aspects of the court work, generally operating as a social worker to the court by making themselves useful to the magistrate and those in the cells and waiting rooms. However, he introduces some new information. For example, he writes of the missionary:

> He is not in orders, but he affects not infrequently a semi-clerical costume, and his wife, like the rector's wife, affords her husband gratuitous assistance, when some special need for a woman's help arises. (Gamon 1907: 162)

This stresses a clear religious element to the work and particularly mirrors contemporary ideas of mission. His book also hints at some difficulties for the missionary. Again, quoting directly from Gamon:

> In the London courts, at least, he holds a semi-official position, which both widens his sphere of usefulness and clothes him with greater authority. In some provincial courts he is still looked upon with suspicion as an interloper, and the magistrates are loath to consult or employ him. They as much as possible ignore him. (Gamon 1907: 167)

However, even in the capital he goes on to write that 'London magistrates are not all equally cordial to him ... But his position in the court is definitely recognised' (Gamon 1907: 167). These comments support those made by the police inspectors above regarding the attitudes of magistrates.

As noted, Gamon was an advocate of probation reform and in a number of places in his work urges change to the system of probation he witnessed. In one of these sections he writes:

> The missionary is a sort of probation officer as well. The probation system would substitute in many cases a watchful supervision and moral discipline for punishment either by fine or prison; and the probation officer is the supervisory agent. The system is openly and notoriously at work in America and Australia; a near relation of it is at work in the London courts, but without confession of the relationship. (Gamon 1907: 172)

This assumes a vision probation that is distinct from the mission to the police courts and echoes Timasheff's (1941) comments about a supervisory element being key to an effective system of probation.

We can now see some clear identifiable strands in the work that the police court missioners were doing by the close of the nineteenth century. The missionaries were court based, not just in the court but in the waiting rooms, corridors and cells. The strategy seemed to be based on making themselves useful to the court and particularly to the magistrates. However, after the court hearing the supervision of offenders was much less clear. In court, decisions were made about cases that were deserving and cases that were not deserving with the missionary working with those deemed deserving, the final decision seemed to rest with the magistrate, in consultation with the missionary. There was a heavy emphasis on the pledge and the evils of drink and the missionary acted as gatekeeper to a huge range of resources that went from artificial limbs to jobs to homes and on to clubs. The missionaries themselves were not 'of the people', they were not the same class of people as those who appear in court and were in fact closer (thought not equal) in social class to the magistrates. At the same time they were clearly well acquainted with the community they worked in. We can also see that although the mission was funded by donations and managed by a patchwork of regional committees, it does appear to have been well funded, well managed and countrywide. It operated outside London and the larger industrial cities, indeed in many of the smaller towns.

However, we have as yet only considered rather straightforward descriptions of the work of the police court missionaries at the close of the nineteenth century. The analysis needs to be moved on and some depth to that analysis introduced.

Personal accounts of the police court and the police court mission

There are also accounts of the work of police court mission in the memoirs of former missionaries or those who had worked in the courts. Care should be taken with some of these accounts as they tend to be rather idiosyncratic; they are also written with the benefit of hindsight. They do though allow us to see the reasoning, the theory behind the practice as the authors discuss not only what they did but why they did it. Arguably the most well known is Thomas Holmes and his writings are discussed by many of the histories of probation; Vanstone (2007), for example, discusses the impact of eugenics and psychology in his writing and makes some very interesting connections. Thomas Holmes (1846–1918) became a police court missionary at Lambeth in 1885 when an accident at work meant that he could no longer work as an iron-moulder. In 1889 he moved to the North London Police Court. In 1905 he gave up this work to become Secretary of the Howard Association. The *Dictionary of National Biography (1912–1921)* comments, 'Holmes became known both in England and abroad as a criminologist of imagination and judgement, and gained both profit and reputation from his writings' (see p. 263). However, Rose comments that 'Holmes had a considerable flair for writing in a popular, if rather diffuse and sentimental, style' (Rose 1961: 68), which is worth bearing in mind as we consider his work.

In his writing we see accounts of the missionaries work similar to those we have already seen. For instance, Holmes writes, 'first thing in the morning, the magistrate sits for the purpose of giving advice to any who require it – and people come to enquire about all sorts of things' (Holmes 1901: 325). We have already seen how the police court played a role in giving advice to the poor (see Davis 1984) as well as acting as a court of justice. Here Holmes shows it in action, an example of a middle-class mission to an urban poor. In a similar vein he writes, 'The Magistrate calls on him (i.e. the Missionary) to act as an arbitrator, or to go and pacify the violent husband; or to investigate the servant girls case' (Holmes 1901: 325). It is only after this work has been done that the court deals with the criminal matters of the day. Holmes describes his role in these cases as

> Finding lodgings, then; putting released prisoners on the road to honest work, communicating with parents and friends on behalf of those who have got wrong – this is the kind of work a missionary must do, as well as the work of comfort and advice in the waiting room and the cell. (Holmes 1901: 326)

His writings also reveal something of his assumptions about crime causation and how it should be responded to. In an interview he gave in 1901, Holmes states, 'The public house is a grand recruiting agency for the ranks of the sad procession passing through our courts' (Holmes 1901: 327) which echoes much that we have already seen about intemperance and crime but Holmes adds another dimension to this when he writes that '(d)rink brings the evil to the light, but there are causes behind that which lead people to drink, and which need to be remedied, as well as the drink evil. The social conditions of life are greatly at fault' (Holmes 1901: 237). When discussing younger offenders particularly Holmes sees 'social conditions' as crucial but he means something specific by that term. He writes:

'The streets are the playground of the poor, and the state has need to be thankful, in spite of the drawback in disorder and crime, for the strength and manhood developed there'. He goes on, 'Robust play even though it be rough, is an absolute condition of physical and moral health'. (Holmes 1908: 169 and 170)

However, in respect of adult offenders his explanations are more individualized and there is a clear medical tone in his analysis. Quoting from the same work:

I am persuaded, after many years close observation and many years friendship with criminals, that disease, mental or physical, is a tremendous factor in the causation of crime. (Holmes 1908: 131)

Earlier he comments:

It is the lack of grit, of continuity of purpose, of moral principles, combined with inferior physical health and a low standard of intelligence, that makes the position of many discharged prisoners so helpless. (Holmes 1908: 105)

On a similar theme he describes the burglars he has met so:

Underfed and undersized, of little intelligence., with no moral consciousness, they are a by produce of our civilisation, a direct product of our slum life. (Holmes 1908: 33)

It is a combination of urban living, individual moral and physical weakness that causes criminality. In fact Vanstone uses the term 'eugenist inventory' (Vanstone 2003: 39) to describe the list of those likely to offend. There are individual and societal factors interacting Holmes's in his analysis. At the same time he discusses intemperance and he describes his work in terms of material help to those appearing court. It is a rather strange mix of explanations but again caution should be used when generalizing about the mission from Holmes' work.

We get a slightly different view of the mission to the police court from Alfred Plowden, who originally trained as a barrister and in 1888 was appointed a Police Court Magistrate in London. In 1903 he looked back on fifteen years' experience in the court (see Plowden 1903) and made some interesting comments about his relationship with the police court missionaries he had met. When it came to their personal qualities, he noted that they were teetotal, he was not and describes them as 'that latest product of Christianity' (Plowden 1903: 235). He clearly sees the missionary as a crucial part of the court process when he writes, '(t)here is hardly a week, or a day, when a Magistrate is not glad to have recourse to the Missionary' (Plowden 1903: 235). He then goes on to make an interesting comment when it comes to deciding the fate of youngsters who appear before him. He writes:

> … all the time he is weighing these alternatives the Magistrate is conscious of being watched by the Police Court Missionary and the School Board Officer, each of whom look upon the lad as his lawful prey, to be sent either to a home or an industrial school, or perhaps a reformatory. (Plowden 1903: 233)

The comment suggests that not only were the missionaries making themselves useful in court, there was an element of the 'busy body' about them. Plowden also discusses the Poor Box and sees the missionary as playing a very important role in helping him to distribute the money it contained (see Plowden 1903: 236). The role of missionaries in distributing material help is one we have already come across.

We get another perspective on the work of the police court missionaries from Harry Ayscough who was the long serving Secretary of the Central Church of England Temperance Society and in 1923 looked back on the organization's work in the police courts (see Ayscough 1923). His book is titled 'when mercy seasons justice', which immediately suggests the discrimination between deserving and undeserving cases or what we will see later called special pleading. Clearly, Ayscough's is a partial history but his comments about the work of the mission at the end of the nineteenth century are revealing. For example, early in the work he writes, '[t]he report of Mr G. Nelson – the first missionary – on his labours during the first seven years shows how similar the duties were at that time to what they are to-day' (Ayscough 1923: 14). His book also reflects the range of work the mission undertook; for example, he describes the situation in Liverpool, where in 1884 the missionary Mr Mercer would spend Saturday morning outside the jail as up to 100 prisoners were released. His work there included:

> Several women were taken to Homes and thus rescued form a life of sin and shame, several were restored to their parents: a number of men had employment

found for them: while others were assisted to emigrate, and this had a new start in life given to them. (Ayscough 1923: 28)

By 1890, he reports that there were thirty-six police court missionaries working, twelve of whom were in London. In the same year two 'labour yards' were opened in London which offered work to youngster who had appeared in court, it seems in the form of firewood chopping (see Ayscough 1923: 50). This he refers to as rescue work but uses the same term again when describing new developments in 1891:

This year also saw the commencement of special Rescue Work in the opening of a Home for Inebriate Women at Torquay, called Temple Lodge. (Ayscough 1923: 51)

The overall picture is one of steady expansion over the last few years of the nineteenth and early years of the twentieth centuries. Labour yards opened in Birmingham, the number of cases visited rose substantially, the number of prison gate missions grew and the number of pledges signed increased. In 1900 he writes that there were 100 missionaries working, by 1907 that had grown to 124, 19 of whom were women (see Ayscough 1923: 63 and 68). There is a religious element to his account and Ayscough is clearly a man of deep religious conviction; for example, he writes:

The main endeavour is to bring each soul into contact with the Divine Saviour, and to implant in each that spirit of life and strength, who can alone make the weak ones strong. (Ayscough 1923: 62)

The quote reminds us that this was a religious movement and although Holmes's account of his work makes less of this theme it was very important to many who did the work or supported it financially. Vanstone actually refers to 'conflicting ideologies and motivations underlying the probation project' (Vanstone 2007: 30), stressing the combination of eugenics, degeneracy, deservedness and religious calling all combining in the work of the missionaries.

An overview of the mission and its methods

By considering a number of sources we begin to get a picture of how the police court mission operated. It reflected late nineteenth-century views of social work, crime causation and the correct responses to crime. However, those views are seen very much through a lens of religious faith, temperance and the role of the state. Histories of probation, including those by Le Mesurier (1935), King (1959),

Bochel (1976) through to Vanstone (2007), all spend the early part of their books looking at the work of the mission as a precursor to the system of probation officers introduced in 1907.

More general histories of nineteenth-century social work tend to focus on the Charity Organisation Society but late nineteenth-century views of social work were actually much broader than what we might today understand by the term. Casework, or what was termed 'social casework', came later. To understand the work of the missionaries we need to place it within contemporary social work and to get back to late nineteenth-century views of social work and so identify a social work discourse that moved and contained within it different, even competing, strands.

It is possible to see two strands of contemporary social work in the work of the missionaries, one based on the work of the Charity Organisation Society and one based on contemporary ideas of mission. Firstly, though, it should be pointed out that at this time the term 'social work' had a very different definition to that which it has today. This is illustrated by Haldane's (1911) *The Social Worker's Guide,* which has entries on such diverse topics as commercial morality, drainage, child labour along with the police court missionaries. This demonstrates a view of social work as 'work that was social' rather then a therapeutic or helping relationship. It is perhaps for this reason that many connected with police courts regarded the court as being more than a legal entity but as a source of help and advice to the poor. This is a view expressed by Plowden (1903) and Holmes (1908), whereas Davis (1984) offers a contemporary perspective. Plowden himself actually writes:

> … thus the custom has grown up in all courts not only to grant process for legal wrongs, but to advise generally, whenever a sympathetic answer on the application of a little common sense or knowledge of the world is likely to give relief. (Plowden 1903: 266)

At the same time of course, Plowden, like the missionaries and social workers visiting the poor, was not of those classes. Indeed, he writes, 'I am constantly being sympathised with for having to pass my days in such an atmosphere' (Plowden 1903: 313). Many of the police courts were actually situated in the working class districts, where their clients were located.

Arguably the most significant social work agency at the turn of the century was the COS (or Charity Organisation Society). It had been in existence since 1869 but by the time one of its main organizers, Helen Bosanquet,[4] wrote *Social Work in London 1869–1912,* her approach was noticeably defensive, feeling the organization to be under siege and misunderstood. The aim of the COS was no less than the eradication of poverty. Woodroofe describes the philosophy of the COS as:

> Charity given indiscriminately and thoughtlessly demoralised: it encouraged habits of thriftlessness and dependence and these, the Society considered, were a root cause of poverty and pauperism. True Charity, administered according to certain principles, could encourage independence, strengthen character, and help to preserve the family as the fundamental unit of society. (Woodroofe 1962: 28)

Poverty was therefore the responsibility of the individual, as Woodroofe writes, 'to them character, not circumstance, was the explanation of failure' (Woodroofe 1962: 34). Bosanquet puts it rather more succinctly: 'our intention was to cut off charity from the worthless and divert it to the deserving' (Bosanquet 1914/1973: 41). Decisions about who constituted a deserving case and therefore eligible for the money, clothing and other help the Society had within its power were made by the social workers of the Society.

If the COS's beliefs about poverty sound a little out of date, the structure of the organization sounds strikingly modern. The organization set up districts committees which collected all the monies donated to charity and to whom individuals or families could apply for help. The committees and those who worked for them would then go out and investigate the applications and make an assessment as to their level of deservedness and what help should be given. Help was to be given only to those who had a realistic chance of being lifted out of poverty by that help and who would therefore be self-sufficient with that help. The COS was also determined to eradicate the possibility of people cheating or getting more help than they deserved or squandering any help given. Theirs was to be a 'scientific charity' and to this aim they maintained detailed individual case records of all the work they did and all the help distributed. In effect this was the first social work case record. The other novelty the COS introduced was the training of their social workers. It began in 1890 with lectures being given to their workers and grew to become the School of Sociology and Social Economics by the turn of the century. This was in turn was incorporated into the London School of Economics (LSE) in 1912 (Yelloly 1980).

Bosanquet's account of the work of the COS has clear resonances with the work of the police court missionaries; for example, a belief in the idea of visitation accompanying any help offered. Bosanquet writes:

> From the earliest days the Society has endeavoured to enlist the services of voluntary workers in visiting the homes of those in need of assistance. That

any material assistance given should always be accompanied by such friendly visitation is one of its first principles. (Bosanquet 1914/1973: 53)

Later she discusses pensions provided by the COS and writes that ' … we continue to take up new cases, provided that the applicants come up to the standard of personal character, including evidence of having made efforts to provide for old age' (Bosanquet 1914/1973: 299). Visitation, investigation along with assessment of deservedness were also common practice for the police court missionaries. The newspaper reports considered above where the missionary was involved are of cases where the full force of the law was suspended because of the particular circumstances of the offender or of the offence. Often it was the youth of the offender, the fact that they were first offenders or perhaps simply a judgement about culpability. They were all deserving of special treatment.

Young and Ashton's history of social work also places much emphasis on the connections between the working methods of the missionaries and those of the COS. They assert, 'the methods used by the Police Court Missionaries were essentially casework' and they go on 'they were probably influenced by the teaching of the COS' (Young and Ashton 1956: 179). However, there was a difference in approach between the two organizations. Young and Ashton argue that 'all the men and women entered the work with strong Christian beliefs, and the work was pursued as God's work' (Young and Ashton 1956: 180). Unlike the COS the 'missionaries never wanted to be, and never became, relief agencies' (Young and Ashton 1956: 182), thus emphasizing that there were clear links between the organizations but at the same time clear distinctions. This religious, spreading the word of God, approach leads us to the next major influence on the mission's methods.

The ethos and guiding principles of the police court missionaries came from another late Victorian creation, namely mission. Stocking (1987) describes the Victorian notion of mission as an attempt to deal with problematic populations both at home and abroad. He sees a close link between missionaries who went to Africa, for example, and those who went to the slums of the large cities of Britain. He writes:

Although lower-class women and criminals might differ in many respects, they shared a similarity to 'savages'. The list of social categories thus equated was quite extensive: in addition to criminals, women and children, it included peasants, rustics, labourers, beggars, paupers, madmen and Irishmen – all of whom were at times likened to savages or to 'primitive' man.

What they shared, with each other and with savages, were certain mental characteristics – characteristics that placed them at a lower point on the unitary scale of intellectual and moral development: governed more by impulse, deficient

in foresight, they were in varying degrees unable to subordinate instinctual need
to human rational control. (Stocking 1987: 229)

The higher levels of intellectual and moral development were inhabited by
middle class males who were able to defer gratification and to act in their own
interests by subordinating their animal instincts. As Wiener (1990) points out,
they could do this as their character was fully formed, unlike the categories
of people highlighted by him and by Stocking Jr., between which there is a
noticeably high degree of crossover.

The 'savages' of both England and the far reaches of the Empire required
a missionary to go out amongst them to 'civilise' them by developing their
character. Stocking Jr. describes the rationale:

> Civilizing efforts on behalf of dark-skinned savages could, over time, eliminate
> their hereditary incapacity... [therefore].... it was both scientifically and
> morally respectable for civilized Europeans to take up the white mans burden.
> (Stocking 1987: 237)

It would therefore be quite understandable that the CETS would refer to their
workers sent into the police courts as missionaries. This would tie in with late
Victorian views of the criminal and how criminals should be turned from a life
of crime.

Many of those bringing civilization to the urban working class were housed
in settlements in the inner city. The Settlement movement was another late
Victorian creation that sought to address the problems of the urban working
class poor and which had connections with the mission to the police courts.
These settlements originated in a religious revival in the universities (Young
and Ashton 1956) in the middle of the nineteenth century. Like the COS the
settlements were also concerned with poverty; however, the solution they offered
was very different: 'the East End suffered from the absence of a class of well to
do people with leisure, a "resident gentry" who could help the less fortunate by
living alongside them' (Briggs and Macauley 1984: 4). The settlements sought
to overcome this by reconnecting the social classes and bringing the middle
classes back to the working class urban centres. Concerns about an increasingly
radical and politicized working class also provided an impetus (Meacham 1972,
Steadman-Jones 1971).

The first, and one of the longest standing, was (and still is) Toynbee Hall,
in the Whitechapel area of East London, opened in 1884 (just a few years after
George Nelson started work) and was run for many years by its founder Reverend
Barnett. Mainly due to the influence of Barnett, Toynbee Hall was more than
a religious institution, as Young and Ashton note: 'Barnett always viewed the

mission as an instrument of education. He thought that the social problem was at root an educational one, that those who strove to raise the standard of living were powerless without knowledge' (Young and Ashton 1956: 227). However, the education offered was not vocational, but general even higher. It was no less than training for citizenship.

The young people who went to work at the settlement were typically recently graduated from Oxford or Cambridge[5] and went there to gain experience of working class life, often prior to a career in politics. There was therefore a belief that education in Toynbee Hall was a two-way street and that the settlement offered something of a social laboratory for the middle classes to experience working class life. Residents were expected to stay for a year or two and provide their services, usually in terms of education, free. However, by the end of the century Toynbee Hall was becoming increasingly involved in local and to some extent national politics. With the reform of local government at the end of the century many working class people were able to vote and even stand for the local council. Some were encouraged to do so by members of the settlement and some members of the settlement stood in the same elections.[6] Their politics was occasionally quite radical, during the Dock Strike of 1889 Union meetings had been held at Toynbee Hall and residents were involved in supporting the strike action (Briggs and Macauley 1984: 38).

Thus, although Toynbee Hall and the settlements based their work on mission and aiding the working classes out of poverty, theirs was a much more participatory approach, working with local residents. We might today call it community work, in contrast to the COS's social casework. Both offered the urban working classes an opportunity to strengthen and develop character, one via education, one via self sufficiency.

What this discussion shows is that the police court missionary's practice was rooted in contemporary views of social work and perhaps more generally how to help the poor. The mission to the police courts was a product of the late nineteenth century. We will also see, as the story unfolds, how a changing social work discourse and changing concerns about the urban poor were reflected in the changing policy and practice of probation.

Theorizing the mission to the police court

It is clear from the above discussion that there was a moralistic element to the work of the missionaries. We have also seen the role that religion played and particularly organized religion but Pease (1999) introduces a character he calls 'Al Truism' in his discussion of probation's development. He looks for a theoretical or moral underpinning for probation and he sees the work of the missionaries as 'saving souls through the intervention of divine grace' (Pease 1999: 3) and the 'tone of the service was moral' (Pease 1999: 14). In fact Pease's article is heavily influenced by the first of McWilliams's celebrated articles on the history of probation. In this he focuses on temperance and drunkenness. He writes that 'offences of drunkenness and drunk and disorderly behaviour increased dramatically between 1860 and 1876' (McWilliams 1983: 133). At the same time the Church of England Temperance Society sought 'the promotion of habits of temperance, the reaffirmation of the intemperate, and the removal of causes which lead to intemperance' (McWilliams 1983: 134). It would therefore be logical for the mission to go into the lower courts as that is where they would be seen to be needed.

The Church of England Temperance Society were not alone in their concern about the links between alcohol and crime. Radzinowicz and Hood (1986) discuss what they term 'the lot of the common criminal inebriate' (Radzinowicz and Hood 1986: 302). They point out that the Departmental Committee on the Treatment of Inebriates was appointed in 1892 after considerable lobbying by the temperance movement. It was decided that something had to be done and finally *The Habitual Drunkards Act* and *The Inebriates Act* both of 1898 were passed. These introduced the compulsory detention and treatment of those convicted of offending under the influence of alcohol. Interestingly both Acts were regarded as failures as magistrates refused to detain criminals for long periods if the offence they committed did not warrant it (see Radzinowicz and Hood 1986: 309)

Once established in the police courts, McWilliams argues that the missionary's role expanded rapidly often with the support of the presiding magistrates, to a more general saving of the 'deserving'. McWilliams elucidates:

> Mercy is the concept which provides the key to understanding the missionaries'
> place in the courts and in particular their social enquiry practice. (McWilliams
> 1983: 137)

He uses the phrase 'special pleading' in his essay to describe the work of the missionaries in court and goes on to write that 'it is more correct to see the central aim as the saving of souls through divine grace' (McWilliams 1983: 138). This religious, moral underpinning or motivation is not incompatible with late nineteenth-century views of social work, particularly when we consider the very broad definition of social work common at the time and combined with contemporary views of 'deservedness'.

A more recent study by Rowbotham looks at the role of Hope (she writes the word with a capital letter) as a means to turn offenders away from crime in the work of the police court missionaries in the late nineteenth century. Rowbotham describes the missionaries as 'likely to be working class and men (and women) of deep religious conviction, which spurred them on in their work' (Rowbotham 2009: 117). They brought to the police courts of the late nineteenth century what she terms 'a practical support and a moral impulse'. Regarding the latter she writes:

> Hope was accepted as being rooted in moral impulse, but in practice related very strongly to the social context in which the individual offender found him/ herself. (Rowbotham 2009: 118)

Thus, to prevent reoffending the social context of the offender needed to be changed in order to provoke that morale impulse which as we have already seen, and as Rowbotham points out, 'making a fresh start away from criminality ... was thus the main objective for London Police Court Missionaries' (Rowbotham 2009: 118). Personal relationships were also very important, as Rowbotham notes, 'the emphasis on marriage as a factor in promoting a hopeful personal context, is very clear from the records. Often a first step in desistance promotion was the regularisation of a hitherto irregular relationship' (Rowbotham 2009: 121). This work has already discussed the amount of time and effort the missionaries invested in finding employment or 'positions' for those released by the court. Rowbotham makes the very interesting point that these were views shared by the magistrates in the courts where the missionaries were working; she writes:

> Magistrates were .... often sympathetic to the idea of using moral suasion to promote desistance. They were thus ready to bind over repeat violent offenders to keep the peace, ... (Rowbotham 2009: 115)

There was in effect an alliance between the magistrates and missionaries, a shared set of beliefs about how to prevent reoffending. The fact that there is no legal or legislative framework for the missionaries work only reinforces the informal or assumed nature of that alliance. It is also interesting to note that the mission did not extend to the higher courts. Those offenders were 'picked up' by the prison gate mission but only after they had served their sentence.

Many histories of probation spend at least some time discussing the mission to the police court and some of those histories identify similar themes. For example, the first guide for probation officers published in 1935 (see Le Mesurier 1935) writes that 'they proved many times over that often the policy of mercy succeeded in reclaiming an offender whom punishment would only harden' (Le Mesurier 1935: 193). Le Mesurier also writes of the missionaries' zeal and the 'informal character' (ibid) of their work. She reminds her readers that all of those working for the Church of England Temperance Society as missionaries were required to be communicant members of the Church of England.

King's (1959) survey of probation focuses on the religious element of the mission and the work the missionaries did with habitual drunken offenders appearing in court. She sees this as the key driving force in their work when she writes:

> The emphasis placed by the Mission on the evils of drunkenness and on the importance of inducing offenders to 'take the pledge' is understandable when consideration is given to the large part played by drunkenness at this period in offences of violence and cruelty, especially within families, and the extent of its effect on young people. (King 1959: 5)

This comment does have resonances with the contemporary material we have looked at earlier, though it is not the full story. Bochel (1976) explicitly sets out to write a history of probation and hers is realistically the first attempt to do so. Interestingly she makes very little reference to the mission to the police court and sees it almost exclusively as a temperance movement when she writes that '[t]heir main interest was to increase temperance and they sought out drunkards everywhere' (Bochel 1976: 21). She sees their link with probation in terms of a 'century old movement to reduce the number of imprisonments by providing alternative ways of dealing with offenders' (Bochel 1976: 1). The evidence discussed above does suggest that though the mission was a temperance movement at the outset it very quickly found itself involved in a wider range of concerns when it entered the police courts.

One study that does spend considerable time considering the work of the mission to the police court is Page's history of probation in London (see Page 1992). Page tends to focus on the organization rather than the practice of the mission in London but identifies the year 1893 as crucial in the mission's development in London. The work of the mission enjoyed quite a rapid expansion in this year so that many of the London courts had a missionary appointed to them and a number of homes, refuges and work yards were opened in this period. This mirrors some of the evidence we have seen outside of the capital where the mission seems to have expanded in many of the large towns particularly in the last few years of the nineteenth century. Page highlights some interesting facets of the work of the missionaries. As agents of a religious society and what today might be called a voluntary society it is perhaps surprising to read Page refer to them as 'semi-official'. He writes:

> … although the C. E. T. S. missionaries had no role in court defined by law and no statutory powers they were official in the sense that they were authorized representatives of the still powerful State Church, working in court on a regular basis with the public blessing and sanction of the magistrates. (Page 1992: 47)

He describes them as almost devoid of theory pointing out that new ideas about crime causation being discussed at the very end of the nineteenth century (discussed in more detail later) rather passed them by. They were, he argues, 'sustained by their religious faith and strong sense of vocation, with the pledge card as their principal tool and a ready recourse to prayer and the bible' (page 1992: 52). At one point he uses the term 'muscular Christianity' (see Page 1992: 53) which is an indication of the stamina, faith and strength of purpose required of the missionaries.

A much more recent attempt to write a history of probation was made by Mair and Burke (2012) who focus very much on probation and discusses the mission to the police court rather briefly early in their work. They do make the interesting point that:

> Probation emerges from a number of disparate ideas, developments and initiatives that can be found in the nineteenth century; a variety of factors that were not necessarily related to each other in any clear way at the time, although it is now possible to discern linkages. (Mair and Burke 2012: 7)

They then go and list these initiatives and developments many of which have been discussed above. For example, a link between penal reform and evangelism was a product of the nineteenth century. That in turn linked to the growth of philanthropy which was not new but became linked with religion and penal reform at this point of time. Crime statistics were also collected far more widely in the late nineteenth century. Crucially though Mair and Burke (2012) highlight a growing disenchantment with prison combined with a search for exceptional cases – that is, groups which should not face the full impact of prison discipline; for example, a belief that children should not experience the full rigors of prison. They write:

> During the preceding centuries, children had been simply treated as small adults but as the nineteenth century began there were increasing significant developments in dealing with juveniles who were either criminals or who seemed to be on the verge of becoming so. (Mair and Burke 2012: 12)

Other groups were selected, the inebriate for example, who came to be seen as in need of help or treatment rather than prison.

Thus, as we draw this chapter to a close we return to Vanstone's two-pronged attack at a history of the police court mission. The second, or what he terms his 'revisionist account', discusses the mission in terms of being 'actively involved in assisting that process of separation' (Vanstone 2007: 27). Those decisions were made in court where the deserving were selected from the undeserving and the saveable separated from the unsaveable. He sees an implied if not actual, psychological assessment of the offender being undertaken by the police court missionary in cahoots with the magistrate. That psychology was grounded in a contemporary concern about the physical and moral degeneracy of the urban working class. These are concerns that were more prominent in the early part of the twentieth century and we will return to them in Chapter 2 of this work. Vanstone (2007) places less emphasis on religion, temperance, philanthropy and social work. He sees less of a moral dimension, a 'saving souls' approach to the missionaries work. It is a point well made; the missionaries were in court to save those that were deserving and saveable. The assumptions they made and the methods they employed were a product of late Victorian society.

By the time we move into the twentieth century the police court missionaries were well established, well organized and well funded. They had a relatively clear working method and an ethos. Most of the country knew what a missionary was, no matter which social class they belonged to and would have had an understanding of what a police court missionary might do. At this stage though the state was not involved, unlike other agencies such as the police and the prisons where both central and local government had the key role. There was no statutory framework nor legal backing for any kind of supervision, unlike the system being developed in parts of the USA (see Timasheff 1941 and below). However, overlapping the expanding work of the police court mission changes were taking place that precipitated the arrival of probation officers. They were products of the early twentieth century and initially at least needed to be seen as distinct from the mission. The appointment of the first probation officers is the focus of the next chapter and the early stages of that story run parallel to much of the above.

2

The First Probation Officers:
Probation 1907–1914

Having looked at the mission to the police court in the later part of the nineteenth century, this work will now turn to focus on the arrival of the first probation officers and the introduction of a system of probation in England and Wales. It will focus attention on how the system was envisaged, lobbied for and an account of the system that was finally introduced. The chapter will follow the legislation that introduced probation and look at how the system fared in its first few years. Clearly there is an overlap with the time period we have just covered but this history will argue that the mission to the police court was seen as largely unconnected with the system of probation introduced by the legislation. Tradition histories of probation tend to see a somewhat linear progression from police court missionaries to probation officers, whereas this work seeks to separate them out and give them their own histories. Those histories do cross and meet and we'll see that as this chapter progresses.

In the meantime we need to stay in the late nineteenth century but shift our focus onto other developments in that period.

Crime and the criminal in the late nineteenth century

Histories of crime and its treatment that focus on the very late part of the nineteenth century are somewhat sparse. This is unfortunate as it is precisely this period that saw the first appearance of the term 'probation' in English Law. However, there is a detailed history of the penal system in England over this period provided by Radzinowicz and Hood (1986) who identify the year 1895 as particularly significant. In this year the Gladstone Committee reported on its review of the prison system (Home Office 1895) which had been precipitated by a great deal of criticism and debate around how prisons should operate. The Gladstone Report is a lengthy and well-considered document that argues:

> The responsible authorities of the prison should have sufficient at their command to observe prisoners individually, and sufficient discretionary power to give or obtain for an individual prisoner that guidance, advice, or help which at such a crisis in his life which may make a priceless change in his intentions or disposition. (Home Office 1895: col. 27)

The Report contained a number of novel ideas. For instance it gave special consideration to the young criminal, commenting 'lads grow up predisposed to crime, and eventually fall into it' (Home Office 1895: col. 38) and that 'with few exceptions, no prisoners are absolutely irreclaimable' (Home Office 1895: col. 84). The Report was not prepared to say no children should be in prison but that 'children should be subject to special treatment, and in every way kept absolutely apart from other prisoners' (Home Office 1895: col. 82). The Report also advocated separate regimes for habitual criminals and that mentally ill prisoners should be treated as patients. Thus a number of groups were singled out for special attention and deserving of release from the full rigours of the prison routine. This is a position we have seen already but now we see it being discussed in official circles and in respect of the prisons.

Martin Wiener (1990), in his book *Reconstructing the Criminal*, also pays particular attention to the last few years of the nineteenth century. Wiener describes his work as a cultural history and attempts to put into a political and social context changes in the treatment of the criminal. Like Foucault (1991) and Ignatieff (1978) he argues that the 1830s saw major changes in the treatment of the criminal. However, Wiener also notes a further change taking place right at the end of the nineteenth century and this was a view that certain people should no longer suffer the full of consequences of the penal law. These groups included children, juveniles, the mentally ill, drunkards, habitual criminals and women. What these groups had in common was that they could not be seen as fully responsible for their own actions as they had yet to achieve full rational maturity. They were therefore unable to restrain their own primitive and natural urges. For this reason prison discipline (segregation, isolation, etc.) was doomed to failure as what these categories of criminals needed was help to curb their natural, uncontrolled more primitive instincts. Wiener goes on to describe how this problem was to be addressed; he writes, 'almost all participants in mid-Victorian political discussion accepted that character – the constantly reinforcing disposition to restrain one's animal instincts – was the prerequisite for responsible independent behaviours' (Wiener 1990: 144). This late Victorian notion of character and character building will be returned to in this work as a crucial component of probation practice; for the moment it is worth bearing in mind Wiener's definition of it.

Responses to crime at the turn of the century is Garland's (1985) particular focus. Like Wiener, Garland sees certain deviant and 'less developed' groups amongst the population as being singled out for special attention (Garland uses the phrase 'dangerous classes'). He writes, 'At the end of the nineteenth century then, there was a period of crisis and transformation produced by a complex series of intersecting events and developments' (Garland 1985: 65). The cause of this crisis he sees as including a general loss of faith in the 'laissez faire' system of economic organization, the discovery of poverty thanks to the surveys of Booth and Rowntree, the failure of the prisons, the spread of socialism, concerns for a degenerating working class all of which created major concerns about the condition and expansion of the 'dangerous classes'. Part of the solution to this crisis was a new role for the state, which was to be much larger than before and with the election of a reforming Liberal Government in 1906 saw its expression in the creation of what Garland (1985) calls the Penal Welfare Complex. This included the creation of three new major institutions: probation via the *Probation of Offenders Act 1907*, the Children's Court via the *Children Act 1908* and the Borstal via the *Prevention of Crime Act 1908*. Within these new institutions, a group of competing discourses sought to address the problem of the dangerous classes. The four discourses Garland identified were based on criminology, eugenics, social work and social security and they each enjoyed varied success. Each of these discourses was applied in varying degrees but this work will focus on the social work and criminological discourses as they were considered particularly appropriate for the offender and became closely linked with probation.

It is very much open to debate whether the changes in policy we are about to consider, and which Garland (1985) and Wiener (1990) identify, were precipitated by concerns about levels of crime. The work of Gattrell et al (1980) suggests that this was not the case. Their study focuses on crime figures for the period just discussed (second half of the nineteenth century) and they conclude that crimes of theft and personal violence, the most common ones, actually fell over this period (see Gattrell et al 1980: 286, 293 and 304). Taylor (1998) also found no change in the level of crime in this period.

In fact there was a lively debate on just this topic between two of the leading experts of this time contained in *The Nineteenth Century*, a popular journal. The Rev. W. D. Morrison was Chaplain at Holloway Prison and wrote that 'serious crime has unmistakably increased with the last decade' (Morrison 1892: 953). He goes on to assert:

> In short, police statistics are a striking confirmation of prison statistics, and the statistics of trials; and all of them point with singular unanimity to the conclusion that crime during the last thirty years for which we possess official returns, has not decreased in gravity and has been steadily developing in magnitude. (Morrison 1892: 956)

However, no less an individual than Edward DuCane, Chair of the Prison Commissioners and thus probably the most important person in criminal justice at the time, disagreed. He argued that the prison population had actually fallen since 1887 and the numbers subject to penal servitude had also fallen. The increase in numbers of those actually appearing in court he attributed to ' … the efficiency of the preventive measures and preventive institutions, and the means of bringing offenders to justice; [which] have produced the effect expected of them' (DuCane 1893: 484).

Morrison attended a lecture given in 1900 at the Royal Statistical Society when, along with many others interested in penal reform, he heard a paper given by Rosa Barrett titled *The treatment of juvenile offenders: together with statistics of their numbers* (see Barrett 1900). Those in attendance heard that the number of offenders convicted in court under sixteen years of age had decreased, particularly those convicted of serious offences but the numbers of those between 16 and 21 convicted in court was rising. Barrett does go on to comment that ' … the fact that juvenile prisoners were only one sixth as numerous as they were thirty years ago, this did not mean that offenders had decreased, but only that methods of dealing with them had changed' (Barrett 1900: 270). The evidence suggests that at the time there was not a commonly held consensus about crime levels. The reality seems to be quite complex but it is hard to avoid the conclusion that the reforms we are about to consider were not prompted by major concerns about levels of crime.

Armed with this knowledge of major changes in approach to the criminal over the closing years of the nineteenth century this work will now move on to look at how and why a system of probation officers was created in the early years of the twentieth century.

Probation's roots

We have already seen how the mission to the police court was not a product of any legislative change though its expansion coincided with, and was therefore very much helped by, changes in the law. As we have also seen, the legal framework for the mission came from much earlier ideas about recognizance and more modern legal reforms expanding the role of summary jurisdiction. We have also seen the same practices emerging in the USA and one or two of the British Colonies. At this stage though the state, or indeed the government, showed very little interest in the mission to the police court. As we moved into the tail end of the nineteenth century things began to change.

The previous chapter has shown how mission to the police court had benefited from the move to summary justice of the late nineteenth century and one important piece of legislation. This was the *Summary Jurisdiction Act of 1879*, section 9 of which allowed a magistrate's court to release a defendant on their own recognizance so long as they agreed to come back to court if called upon to do so. Section 25 of the same Act allowed a court to imprison anyone who failed to comply with conditions imposed on their recognizance. This was the first appearance in English Law of a sentencing option that resembled probation, though without any provision for supervision.

A second piece of legislation which was also used by courts wanting to hand over defendants to the care of the police court missionaries was the slightly later *Probation of First Offenders Act of 1887*, which is the first time the term 'probation' was mentioned in law. This Bill was sponsored by Howard Vincent, Tory MP for Sheffield Central. Sir Howard Vincent (1849–1908) was the second son of a minor aristocrat and after a public school education became an army officer, he then trained to be a Barrister shortly after which he was appointed Head of the CID, in 1878. In this role he was responsible for the prisoners released on 'ticket-of-leave' for which purpose he set up a separate branch of the Metropolitan Police, with eight officers responsible for as many as 1,500 newly released prisoners (Vincent 1883). These officers required a particular personality, Vincent writes:

> ... a person taking part in such work among discharged prisoners must throw all the sympathy in his nature into his intercourse with them. He must listen to their several histories – strongly infused though many of them may be with falsehood – and must be a man to whom they will open their hearts and who will study the peculiarities of each case. (Vincent 1883: 329)

When it came to the causes of crime, he is quoted at a speech in 1881 as saying:

> No man was born a criminal. Defective education, evil influences, drink, bad companionship, and very likely real want, led you into crime. Then you joined the criminal class by your own action. It is free to each one of you to leave in a like manner. (Jeyes and How 1912: 97)

When he married in 1884 Vincent and his new wife made the 'usual' world tour of a recently married Victorian lady and gentlemen. They began in the USA where Vincent:

> at Boston he made a systematic study of the Massachusetts Probation of Offenders System, which had been instituted two years before by a former superintendent of police. The plan was to defer operation of a sentence (for minor offences) until a period of probation should have elapsed. Vincent was so well pleased with the results attained in America (reformation of about 85 per cent of the persons thus treated) that on his journey he recommended this experiment to the various Colonial Governments, and in the House of Commons made it the basis of this First Offenders Act (1887), to be followed twenty years later by a larger Government measure. (Jeyes and How 1912: 153)[1]

Timasheff (1941) gives an account of the system that Howard encountered in the USA. He focuses particularly on Massachusetts where an Act had been passed in 1878 creating a system of probation based on investigation, recommendation and the supervision of offenders released. The Act specifically referred to probation and the role of a probation officer (see Timasheff 1941: 17). Other states like Michigan, New York and Vermont followed suit but in their legislation; there was no mention of supervision. It's the element of supervision that Timasheff highlights in Massachusetts; he writes that by 1897 '[O]nly seven states had enacted statutes on probation and most of them were of a quite rudimentary nature' (Timasheff 1941: 24). From his point of view the more advanced systems of probation included this element of supervision.

Interestingly, Timasheff discusses the arrival of probation in New Zealand and Australia and in both places he refers to a visit from Vincent being the catalyst for the introduction of a simple system of probation. It seems that Vincent was something of an evangelist for the proposal and spread of the word as he continued around the globe on his extended honeymoon. As Mair and Burke (2012) comment, 'policy transfer would certainly seem to have taken place with regard to probation in the later nineteenth century' (Mair and Burke 2012: 19).

On his return to the UK and his election to Parliament he began to lobby for a system of probation and, crucially, probation supervision in the UK. The initial fruit of this was legislation. In fact, the *Probation of First Offenders Act of 1887* was a very short piece of legislation which allowed the court to release defendants on their own recognizance's, to reappear in court when called to do so. In particular, with 'regard being had to the youth, character, and antecedents of the offender, and to any extenuating circumstances under which the offence was committed, it is expedient that the offender be released on probation of good conduct' (*Probation of First Offenders Act 1887*, section 1). Here again we see the view that certain groups within the population should not, in this case by virtue of their lack of a fully formed character, be subject to the full rigours of the prison or legal regime. The Act though says nothing about supervising the offender after release from court unlike the system Vincent had seen in Massachusetts.

Vincent's Act is usually seen as the precursor of the system of probation officers introduced almost exactly twenty years later. In fact the Act had a very chequered history and the original Bill drawn up by Vincent was quite specific. Probation was to be used in cases where an offender had been convicted of a 'first offence for which he might be sentenced to imprisonment' and it was to run 'for any period not exceeding the longest term of imprisonment to which he might have been sentenced'. Furthermore, and crucially, the court could 'direct that he shall be subject to police supervision'.[2] It seems reasonable that Vincent would suggest the police as supervisors of those on probation as that was the system he operated with released convicts and it was the system he had seen on his travels in Massachusetts. The Bill went through the Commons but received short shrift from the Law Lords who threw it out when it reached the upper house. It was debated in the House of Lords on 22 June 1886, where Lord Sudley commented, '[t]here could be no doubt that if the measure was passed it would be absolutely necessary to have a very large increase of the Police Force'.[3] He argued that 'it involved very considerable alteration in working the Criminal Law'. Others in the House called it unworkable, The Lord Chancellor objected to its vagueness and Lord Halsbury said that 'it contained no machinery by which it could be carried out'.

Timascheff describes Howard's original Bill as 'an attempt to adopt the American pattern to English institutions' (Timasheff 1941: 27) and it only passed through the Commons on the basis of a misunderstanding which was that the MPs had not realized just how difficult and expensive the introduction of system of supervision would be. He describes Vincent's Bill as being 'mutilated'

(Timasheff 1941: 27) because of the proposed system of supervision it included. The result was that the Bill was finally passed 'in such a way that nothing was left of the American pattern' (Timasheff 1941: 30). Clearly, it was the element of supervision after court that was the great stumbling block.

Unsurprisingly, Vincent was not impressed and so began what was to become a fairly regular series of letters to the editor of *The Times*. A month after the Bill fell he reproduced there his correspondence with Hugh Childers, the current Home Secretary, in which the Home Secretary refused to discuss the reasons for his objections to the Bill. Howard seems to have put it down to 'the strange Parliamentary attitude of the Gladstonian Administration'.[4] Fortunately for Vincent the Liberal Government left office a month or so later to be replaced by the Conservatives and a new Home Secretary, Henry Matthews, was appointed. Vincent tried again but this new Bill also attracted opposition in the Lords who insisted on the removal of any reference to police supervision. The Act finally passed simply made no reference to supervision and in the House of Lords debate the Earl of Kimberly commented that:

> He was glad that the error had been avoided of trusting to the police the supervision of liberated offenders; but had some doubt whether the supervision that would be provided would command the confidence of the public.[5]

In effect the legislation as passed added very little to existing court powers and the debates reveal some very powerful opposition to the supervision of offenders in the community. Vincent was very disappointed as one of the key principles of his proposal was rejected; he wrote some years later, 'I had such a narrow escape of defeat in the House of Commons that it was wise not to attempt its reinstatemente'.[6] He persevered and seems to have regarded the 1887 Act as a job only part done.

In the meantime the American system of probation had attracted other supporters in Britain. In a report published in 1881 the Howard Association advocated a system of probation officers similar to that in Massachusetts. Unlike Vincent though, their view was that probation would be specifically used for the juvenile offenders who would be spared prison whilst ensuring that their parents did not evade their responsibilities by allowing their children to be fed and educated at the expense of the state in Reformatory and Industrial Schools.[7] The proposal of the Howard Association had been prompted by a Home Office Circular written by the Home Secretary William Harcourt which asked all magistrates 'to consider in what way the law ought to be amended especially with a view to the prevention of imprisonment of young children'.[8] Many histories including Mair and Burke (2012) note the important role the Howard Association played in the introduction of probation. Vanstone notes that '[s]upport from the Howard Association was pivotal to the eventual introduction of probation into the British system, and it contributed to ideologies that were to be prominent in the fledgling organization' (Vanstone 2007: 35).

Like Vincent's original proposal The Howard League clearly envisaged an element of supervision. In an addendum to their Report they write:

> And it is here that the Massachusetts plan appears to be suggestive. For it makes a definite provision for the individual visitation of the parents, or friends, of children who are either offenders or in danger of becoming such. This visitation is by means of state-appointed officers, whose object is, in the first place to endeavour to secure the exercise of parental responsibility in these cases, by means of voluntary effort, after persuasion, or other similar assistance. (Howard Association 1881: 4)

In these discussions it is clear that the government were generally supportive of proposals that would reduce the child prison population and were keen to see first offenders and young offenders avoid the full penalty of the law. It is also equally clear that they were not prepared to see the introduction of a system of probation officers and supervision then already operating in parts of the USA nor were they prepared to consider using the only organization already existing that might have been able to cope with the task, namely the police. Yet a mere twenty years later the Home Office introduced a system of probation officers, what's more, one that they were prepared to appoint and fund. Things were clearly changing.

Incidentally, in none of these debates was there any reference to the police court missionaries. Their voluntary and religious based efforts in the police courts, as we have seen, gradually expanded as these debates took place. This does seem to add weight to the position that the two systems, one proposed and one already existing, were seen as quite distinct.

A deteriorating population

As Vanstone (2007) notes, and this study would very much support him, events outside probation and indeed criminal justice generally have had a major impact on the development of the probation system. In his revisionist chapter on probation's early history he advocates consideration of the social and political context in which it emerged. As we move into the very early years of the twentieth century that context was about to intrude on the system of probation then operating.

In the very early years of the twentieth-century political debate in Britain was dominated by concerns that the population was deteriorating and that the British Empire was thus on the point of collapse (Hynes 1968, Masterman 1901, Pick 1989, Searle 1971, Semmel 1960). Hynes's (1968) detailed and very readable work, though perhaps a little out of date now, is a survey of the politics of this very particular period and he argues that concerns about a deteriorating population had a number of sources. Firstly, there were the surveys of Booth and Rowntree: 'the effect of such studies was to make poverty in England actual, a matter of facts and figures that demanded public attention' (Hynes 1968: 55). However, not only was the population poor, other surveys of the time found that 'between the mid-seventies and 1910 the birth rate in the United Kingdom dropped by nearly thirty percent. Most Englishmen regarded this decline as a clear and present threat to the country' (Hynes 1968: 197). However, what Hynes does not make explicit and Davin (1978) does, is that concerns about a falling birth rate and a more general decline in human stock was actually a decline in working class stock and a falling birth rate amongst the middle classes. She describes attempts to encourage working class mothers to feed their families better (not an easy matter on very low wages) and middle class women to have more children.

As many historians have noted, including Garland (1985), Pick (1989) and Semmel (1960), the late nineteenth century was a period when the science of eugenics was particularly popular. The eugenic argument served to heighten contemporary anxieties. Sir Francis Galton's seminal work *Inquires into human faculty and its development* (1883) was republished in 1907, after a renewal of interest in his Social Darwinian explanations for inherited ability. Galton[9] had also funded the Eugenic Laboratory at London University where Professor Karl Pearson[10] was working. He in turn was later to encourage and assist in Goring's mammoth work *The English Convict* (1919). We have already seen its influence on Thomas Holmes's thinking.

Daniel Pick (1989) looks at concerns about deterioration across Europe but in the UK argues that Galton's work was very much influenced by that of his uncle, Charles Darwin. Ironically though, as Pick points out, 'when Galton first proposed his stark hereditary ideas in the late 1860s they were still poorly received or even ignored, in the last three decades of the century there was growing enthusiasm for his work' (Pick 1989: 198). Put crudely, the eugenic argument stated that the working class urban population was deteriorating but perhaps the most concerning thing was, as Pick points out:

> Evolutionary scientists, criminal anthropologists and medical psychiatrists confronted themselves with the apparent paradox that civilisation, science and economic progress might be the catalyst of, as much as the defence against, physical and social pathology. (Pick 1989: 11)

In other words it was the scientific, economic and social advances of the late nineteenth century that were the cause of the problem. It created a particular urban, modern 'city type'. Pick goes on to make links between concerns about the moral degeneration of the poor, particularly in the cities with contemporary concerns about an increasingly political and radical working class politics of the time. Quoting Pick again:

> The language of 'demoralisation' gave way to urban degeneration. Drink, early marriage, improvidence, irreligion, idleness were increasingly seen as symptoms rather then simple causes in a process of physical and moral degeneration fostered and reproduced by the city itself. (Pick 1989: 202)

Thus demoralization, physical decline and modern urban living became linked and of real concern for many.

As Hynes (1968) also points out, not only were the working classes deteriorating but the moral influences upon them were becoming less beneficial. He argues that there was much writing published that was critical of the existing social order. In fact Steadman Jones (1971) and Meacham (1972), in their work covering this period, both describe an increasingly radicalized and even revolutionary working class. Hynes (1968) also points out how new mass entertainments such as the music halls and cheap press were felt at the time to be an unwholesome influence on the working classes. He writes:

> Through the years before the war, organisations dedicated to the improvement of other people's morals so proliferated that by 1910 there were enough of them in London alone to be collectively organised as the Conference of Representatives of London Societies interested in Public Morality. These groups were voluntary and unofficial, but they were never-the-less extremely powerful. (Hynes 1968: 279)

One of the most formidable of these groups was the National Council of Public Morals. Hynes writes of them, 'the manifesto is a clear example of the way conservative fears interconnected and supported each other; fear of national decline; fear of the fall in the birth rate, fear of the spreading knowledge of birth control; fear of the corrupting power "pernicious literature"; fear of the growth of a degenerate lower class' (Hynes 1968: 287).

Concerns about a national decline, or a degenerating population were not confined to the cultural or social level described by Hynes but national politics were also dominated by similar concerns. Searle (1971) argues that British self-confidence was beginning to falter by the end of the nineteenth century, particularly as both the Germany and US economies were more productive than the British (Hobsbawm 1969). The Boer War (1899–1902) became something of a catalyst and brought these nagging doubts about British supremacy abruptly into everyday debate. The war was seen as a military and administrative disaster and led to, what Searle terms a 'quest for national efficiency'. In the early years of the century this term was to become a political mantra, Searle describes it like this:

> 'National efficiency' was not a homogeneous political ideology. It served as a convenient label under which a complex of beliefs, assumptions and demands could be grouped. At its periphery, the agitation for Efficiency shaded off into programmes and ideologies, like Tariff Reform, Compulsory Military Service and Eugenics, which had the support of some members but were emphatically rejected by others. (Searle 1971: 54)

The Boer War heightened concerns in another respect. In the latter stages of the war it was widely reported in the press that as many as 60 per cent of working class city dwellers were not considered to be in good enough physical condition to join the British Army (Hynes 1968: 22). Fears already noted about the poor condition of the working classes seemed to be more than justified, and the result was that 'journalists and politicians continued to discuss the problem of "physical deterioration" in a language which often bordered on panic' (Searle 1971: 61).

These concerns along with the immediate revelations about the British army led to the appointment of the *Inter Departmental Committee on Physical Deterioration*, which reported in 1904. According to Hynes the Report did little to allay concerns; he writes:

> The terms of reference, frame in careful circumlocution, the true nature of the problem. 'Certain classes of the population' meant in fact the urban poor, and the committee properly directed most of its attentions to conditions of life in city slums ... If the intention of this report was to ally apprehensions, it was a failure. The very fact that a report on 'Physical Deterioration' existed was enough to make the idea current; and deterioration quickly became interchangeable with degeneracy or decadence, thus adding an implication of

moral decline to the idea of physical worsening which the report was in fact
intended to refute. (Hynes 1968: 23)

Despite the controversy of the time, the Report is actually a measured, well-
researched consideration of the conditions of the working classes in Britain
in the very early years of the twentieth century. It was quite categorical that
witnesses did 'not support the belief that there is any general progressive physical
deterioration'.[11] In fact the Report argues that the conditions of the working
classes had improved of late as wages had risen and the cost of food and coal
had fallen. The poor condition of the working classes was due to such things as
overcrowding, the evils of drink and 'the fact of ignorance and neglect on the
part of parents is undisputed, and is testified to by a crowd of witnesses'.[12]

Concerns about a physically and even morally degenerate urban working
class which needed addressing were key factors when 'the Liberals won a
landslide victory at a general election from which extreme radicals were returned
to the Commons in droves' (Searle 1971: 163). Dangerfield's *Strange Death of
Liberal England* is a fascinating though rather partial account of the new Liberal
Government but his work does illustrate how novel the new government was,
the enthusiasm with which it was greeted and the new breed of politicians
it swept into Parliament. One of the younger, radical, newly elected Liberals
was Charles Masterman, described by Hynes as 'one of those young Liberals
who carried the Victorian radical tradition into the twentieth century' (Hynes
1968: 57).[13] We get an impression of his and his colleagues' views when in 1901
Masterman contributed to and edited *The Heart of the Empire* in which he and a
number of friends who had been at Cambridge together produced what Gilbert
(in Masterman 1901/1973), in a recent introduction to the work, terms a 'call to
arms' for the Liberal Party following its election defeat in 1900. The book sold
out in a matter of weeks, and was to become a very significant work for many
in the political field. Of the contributors Bentley notes that 'without exception
each of them earned substantial success within his chosen field'.[14] This was the
work of the rising stars of the Liberal Party early in the twentieth century.

Masterman's work combines many of the concerns we have just noted about
a degenerating working class and it caught the mood and concerns of the time.
He describes the creation of a modern 'city type':

> The result is the production of a characteristic physical type of town dweller;
> stunted, narrow-chested, easily wearied; yet voluble, excitable, with little
> ballast, stamina or endurance – seeking stimulus in drink, in betting, in any
> unaccustomed conflicts at home or abroad. (Masterman 1901/1973: 8)

He singles out a number of groups of people deserving of particular concern; these include the unskilled workers, criminal, those living in overcrowded conditions and the inebriate. He goes on to bemoan the lack of religion in these peoples' lives noting the fact that 'the population have now abandoned church-going' (Masterman 1901/1973: 31). These problems were most developed in London but they were a product of urban life generally, he argues, and their solution lay in a material improvement in the living conditions of the poor and in their spiritual improvement via a revitalized Church.

Another contributor to the same work was Reginald Bray who was a colleague of Masterman's at the university settlement in Camberwell, which is where Masterman was living when he wrote the book.[15] Bray's contribution was a chapter titled 'The Children of the Town', where he shares many of the same views as Masterman on the impact of modern urban living. However, his analysis of the problem is slightly different; he writes:

> Experience tells us that a definite environment tends to create a definite type of human being. If, therefore, we know the circumstances under which the child's life will be passed, it is possible to say in advance that, when he grows to be a man, he will have stamped on him certain distinguishing characteristics. (Bray in Masterman 1901/1973: 111)

Thus the determining factor in respect of character was environment, rather than any hereditary capacity as the eugenicists of the period argued (Galton 1907). It was urban life that damaged children. Bray elucidates, 'children possessing as they do a surplus of energy, are naturally easily excited; but town children are marked by this characteristic to a far greater extent than those who have their homes in the country' (Bray in Masterman 1901/1973: 122).

Bray's solution included the urban child being reconnected with the countryside, to the healthy environment available there, hence his supporting holidays in the country for urban children. The schools also had an important role in developing the physique and character of the urban child; Bray argues:

> The physical conditions to be found in the homes and in the streets all work together to rear an unhealthy race, so that the schools must not be slow to counter balance this effect. Drill and physical exercise will be everywhere encouraged, and, with a view to making them as effective as can be, a hall containing a piano will be provided. (Bray in Masterman 1901/1973: 159)

As Pearson (1989) notes Bray and his colleagues saw physical exercise in the form of organized sport, including football, as another solution. They advocated the provision of sports fields for the young men from the working classes to play football on. This was an idea borrowed almost directly from the public schools where sport taught pupils physical and mental discipline. As Pearson writes:

> And so it was that the respectable England set about the business of teaching the young men that there was more to football than just kicking a ball about and that it was to be regarded as a training for life. (Pearson 1989: 25)

By bringing football off the streets and into organized clubs on land set aside for the purpose the damaging physical and moral impact of life (and games) on the city streets could be counterbalanced by the beneficial affects of organized physical exercise and games.

Considering the character forming potential of the great outdoes, organized sport and discipline, it is unsurprising that a popular solution to a degenerating working class youth favoured at the time was the Boys Clubs movement which enjoyed phenomenal popularity. A number of contemporary writers besides Bray extolled the virtues of these groups (Morgan 1939, Paterson 1911, Russell 1906, 1932) and there are recent histories of the field (Pearson 1989, Springhall 1972, 1977, Wilkinson 1969) that confirm this. What all these show is that groups such as the Boys Brigade and the Church Lads Brigade were well established at the turn of the century, and if not popular amongst the sons of the lower working classes were bringing drill, exercise and religion to some of the sons of the working classes. As Vanstone (2003) points out, this approach to group work was advocated by police court missionaries and the early probation officers and he sees there the origins of group work in contemporary probation.

The turn of the century saw the almost explosive arrival of the most popular youth organization in the world, namely the Boy Scouts. Its founder, Baden-Powell, first proposed the idea in a series of pamphlets in 1908. Its growth was meteoric: by 1910 there were 107,986 boys in 3,898 groups, by 1918 the membership had risen to close on 200,000 boys and the highpoint was reached in 1933 when the Boy Scout movement claimed a membership of 461,740 (Springhall 1977: 138–139). The established Boys Clubs were left trailing in its wake.

This phenomenal growth suggests that the Scouts struck a very important chord. Baden-Powell himself provided a charismatic leadership and seemed to embody many contemporary virtues; he was something of a national and military hero at the time. In these early days the Scout movement emphasized a love of nature, outdoor life, self-reliance and devotion to Church, all ideas that were popular with the new bread of Liberals we have just discussed. Baden-Powell also added a high degree of patriotism and imperialism into this heady mix. The motivation behind the formation of the Scouts was concerns that we have already come across; Springhall writes, 'Imperialism, social Darwinism, the cult of national efficiency and certain fashionable attitudes towards social reform are among the intellectual currents which all found their way into the influential Scouting ideology of the pre-1914 phase' (Springhall 1977: 59). As regards Baden-Powell himself, 'his new career resulted from a fear of the degeneration of the young and for the survival of the British Empire which they would have to maintain' (Springhall 1977: 56).[16]

The only fly in the ointment was that although Baden-Powell set out to recruit the boys from the slums of the major industrial cities these were not the youngsters that joined the Scouts. Instead most of the recruits came from the middle and lower middle class areas of London and the cities (Springhall 1972: 138). Thus the degenerate working class youth, who concerned Bray and his colleagues, remained untouched.

To recap, what we have seen is that concerns about a degenerating and dangerous working class population were a major political issue in the early years of the twentieth century and were a significant factor in the election of a reforming Liberal Government in 1906.[17] There was a major strand within that newly elected Liberal Government that held distinct views about how this problem should be viewed and approached. It was a view that avoided the more radical socialist ideas of the time in favour of a belief in the character forming possibilities of mission, the great outdoors and sports, of which the Scout movement (very much a product of concerns of the time) was perhaps the most vivid manifestation.

The first probation officers

It was against this social and political backdrop that the newly elected Liberal Government introduced probation officers to Britain in 1907. The new Liberal Home Secretary was the veteran William Gladstone and his Junior Minister was Herbert Samuel.[18] It was the latter who took responsibility for the changes we are about to discuss and the Home Office files of the period suggest that it was Samuel who took much of the lead in this area within the department.

For a number of years prior to the 1907 Act there had been considerable lobbying for changes to the system of probation as it then existed. The Howard Association continued to push for changes for the system to be extended. A Report of 1898,[19] based on a survey of members, magistrates and senior police officers, advocated the extension of the *First Offenders Act* and, significantly, advocated the appointment of probation officers based on the scheme in operation in Massachusetts. A similar view was held by Sir Edward Ruggles-Brise, Chair of the Prison Commissioners who wrote to the Home Office in 1903 following a trip to the USA, advocating a system of probation officers similar to the one he had seen over there. At the same time the Home Office also collected information on a system of probation officers operating in New Zealand.[20] Ruggles-Brise also reported a speech from a visiting American Judge about the probation scheme in the USA and sent a copy of the newspaper article about it to the Home Office with a letter proposing 'probation rather than punishment for drunkards'.[21] Crucially, all parties advocated the appointment of probation officers to supervise offenders as operated in the USA and many of those working in criminal justice at the time had seen for themselves or had read reports of the scheme in Massachusetts.

The Home Office was also receiving correspondence from around the country about the operation of Vincent's original Act. It was becoming apparent that the *Probation of First Offenders Act* was not being used to its full potential. As early as 1890 the Home Office were made aware of the varied use being made of probation as defined under this Act; they noted:

> The return obtained under the *Probation of First Offenders Act* show that up to the 8th August 1888 the County Stipendiary at Manchester had used the Act 6 times, the City Stipendiary had used it 68 times.
>
> At Salford the Act had not been made use of at all – a large number of first offenders however having been dealt with under section 16 of the *Summary Jurisdictions Act 1879*.[22]

This issue of 'justice by geography' is one that concerns of probation today, thus we see here that it is far from novel. Clearly though the Home Office were beginning to show an interest in Vincent's Act.

As for Vincent himself he had always regarded his original Act as a job only half done and he continued to press the Home Office. Following his Act the Home Office had begun in 1888 to collect figures as to the use made of his *Probation of First Offenders Act* (Home Office 1891, 1900, 1903, 1906). These figures demonstrated again to the Home Office that probation was being used very unevenly around the country.[23] The later reports also provided figures for the use made of probation nationally and showed that the *First Offenders Act* use rose from 3,040 in 1897 to 7,087 in 1905. The Summary Jurisdictions Act of 1878 section 16, or release on recognizances, was used a great deal more and climbed to 43,691 in 1905.

On his arrival at the Home Office in 1906 Herbert Samuel was given this information. He, his colleagues and senior civil servants were being lobbied to introduce some changes, if not introduce a whole new system of probation officers along the lines of the system used in parts of the USA. Considering that many in his party shared the views of Masterman and his colleagues (see above) it is perhaps not surprising that things now began to move quickly.

Clearly sensing some potential for change, in 1906 Howard Vincent introduced yet another Private Members Bill to the Commons, called *The Probation of First Offenders Bill*. This Bill authorized the appointment of probation officers, something that his early Act had not done. He remained loyal to his idea originally proposed about twenty years before and the Bill stated that 'a Police Authority may appoint one or more probation officers, either male or female, to assist in the reformation of persons'.[24] The proposal that probation officers should be employed by the police may sound novel to modern readers but Vincent, as we shall see, was not the only one to make the assumption. The Home Office watched the progress of Vincent's Bill carefully and Samuel commented in early 1907 that 'it has probably no chance of progress, and anyhow could not be allowed to proceed, as it is proposed to introduce a Government Bill on the subject'.[25]

Sensing that reform of probation was under discussion, the Temperance Societies also began to lobby the new government to have probation linked with the signing of the pledge for offenders convicted of drunkenness. The response of the Home Office to these calls was:

> It is hoped that the Bill when it becomes law will be largely applied to cases of drunkenness, but it seems neither necessary nor desirable to make special provision for them.[26]

This lobbying, the discussions and the Home Office response to them suggest that the Home Office was refining a view of probation that was wider than that envisaged by the Temperance Societies and different to that proposed by Vincent. It is also evidence of a government and Home Office willingness to get involved. This illustrates a clear shift in government thinking, one precipitated by social and political concerns of this specific period.

As part of his planned reform Samuel also instigated some research around the country as to how a system of probation officers might be viewed by magistrates (Home Office 1907c). The specifics of the document deserve a close look, it is headed:

> Return showing, for each petty sessional court in England and Wales, the number and disposal of Children and Young Persons under 16 who were charged

with offences during the last three months of 1906, and showing whether the defendants would probably have been released on probation under supervision, if such a system had been available; and also what steps, if any, are taken to separate Children and Young Persons in court from adult prisoners. (Home Office 1907c: 1)

It is noticeable that the Home Office's concern was the young offender and this is a concern that was mirrored in the USA. Timasheff (1941) identifies a 'juvenile court movement' (Timasheff 1941: 44) spreading across the USA at this time. It was based on a belief that children needed protection and guidance and should not be considered criminal. He goes on to write, '(I)n this way a new field was opened for probation in so far as there was yet no general adult probation' (Timasheff 1941: 47). This is another example of the similarities between the systems of probation in Great Britain and the United States at this time.

In the UK reform of probation was being considered alongside a more general reform the treatment of the juvenile offender and the Home Office were particularly interested in the application of probation to the juvenile offender. The language used by the Home Office takes us straight back to Garland (1985) and Wiener's (1990) identification of certain groups who should be sparred the full rigours of the penal process – in this case it is children and young persons. The Return allowed each court the opportunity to offer a short comment on a proposed system of probation officers for children. The responses were varied and revealing, and can be grouped. There were those like magistrates in Aberaven who wrote, 'the appointment of probation officers is not recommended' (Home Office 1907c: 43) or those in Blackburn who wrote 'official supervision is not deemed desirable' (Home Office 1907c: 16). This raises the spectre of state involvement in the scheme being considered a bad thing. This is a view that we will come across later. Other magistrates commented on the existing system. In Bristol the court noted that 'at present the justices utilise the services of the Court Missionary and others as probation officers, with good results' (Home Office 1907c: 12). A similar view was offered in Newcastle where 'the Court enlists the police, the court missionary and other agencies in supervising children, and rarely convicts except after repeated cautions' (Home Office 1907c: 24). They were not the only court to use the police to supervise young offenders released from court. Some of the rural courts objected because the numbers would be too small and in Melford the court commented 'supervision by probation officers would be prejudicial in country districts, as it casts a stigma. Cases are rare and justices avoid convicting when possible' (Home Office 1907c: 32).

What emerges is that there was no real pattern to the answers except that courts already using a missionary tended to be sympathetic and that large urban areas tended to have some sort of arrangement already in place. However, beyond that very different responses were offered by neighbouring courts. For instance in Stockton the court felt that probation would be best for 'trifling cases', in Sunderland for 'indictable offences', in Durham they commented that 'the same can effect can be obtained under section 16 of the *Summary Jurisdiction Act, 1879*'[27] and in Darlington they (like others) wrote 'extended powers to order corporal punishment [were] desirable' (all from Home Office 1907c: 10).

Despite these widely varied responses the government decided that reform was desirable and that the existing system of missionaries could not be adapted so the *Probation of Offenders No. 2 Bill 1907* was put before Parliament. The No. 1 Bill was proposed by Vincent and was very close to his original 1886 Bill. This second, government sponsored Bill, stated that a person could be released 'on probation' with or without sureties after the court had had regard to his 'character, antecedents, age, health or mental condition'. In fact all are groups that Wiener (1990) had classified as deserving particular exemption from the full rigours of prison and penal discipline. The first Home Office pre-printed Probation Orders actually asked the court to specify on which of these grounds the court were making an order.[28] This same Bill also referred to a court being able to consider 'the trivial nature of the offence, or to the extenuating circumstances under which the offence was committed'. Crucially, the Bill introduced probation officers into the criminal justice process. The Bill also gave some detail as to how the newly appointed probation officers might work. Officers were to be appointed by a petty sessional division in the same way a court clerk would be. The Bill stated: 'a probation officer when acting under a probation order shall be subject to the control of petty sessional courts for that division for which he is also appointed'. This is a clear departure from Vincent's proposal and it places probation officers very firmly in the courts.

The Bill became law towards the end of 1907 and was actually implemented early in 1908. The final Act included a provision of the appointment 'where circumstances permit' (*Probation of Offenders Act 1907*) of special probation officers called children's probation officers. The Act also gave the Secretary of State power to make rules for the operation of the probation system. The role of the probation officer was to visit offenders, make sure they observed any conditions the court had set, to report to the court on their progress and famously to 'advise, assist and befriend'. This phrase was to remain with the service for nearly 100 years. It was essentially an enabling piece of legislation allowing courts to appoint probation officers which at the time was a novel idea and a distinctly new profession. The Act included no reference to police nor to the Temperance Societies.

It was therefore a significant step forward, it widened the existing arrangements to include many new groups, it focused largely on juvenile offenders and, crucially, it introduced probation officers to the courts. It was a radical departure from that which had gone before. Many histories of probation (Bochel 1976, King 1958, McWilliams 1983) usually stress the role of the police court mission as a foundation on which the 1907 Act was built.[29] As we have seen, that is misleading; the 1907 Act originated in concerns that were contemporary; it set out specifically to deal with juvenile crime and juvenile offenders and saw a central role for the state. Herbert Samuel himself suggests such when he wrote his memoirs nearly forty years later. In these he discusses the probation system operating in the USA as a key influence and goes on to write, 'we had nothing of the kind in this country; except that in London and a few other places, a voluntary organisation maintained Police Court Missionaries' (Samuel 1945: 54). Samuel's assertion is quite reasonable, the government's inspiration regarding supervision by probation officers came from the Massachusetts system of probation and concern about child offenders was contemporary and mirrored in the USA. The police court missionaries operated under very different legislation, with a different client group and used different methods.

Some of the controversy that preceded the Bill does not appear to have been reflected in the Parliamentary debates as the Bill went through Parliament. The Earl of Meath addressed the Lords saying of the Bill 'it is not one which creates a great deal of excitement or … is heralded by the shouts of politicians and the clash of Parliamentary steel'.[30] At the second reading in the Commons the Under Secretary at the Home Office said, 'the Government had not heard a whisper of opposition to it from any quarter in the House'.[31] This is something of a simplification as at the Second Reading concerns were raised including whether policemen could act as probation officers, the details of what a probation officer would actually do and whether there should be a separation of children's and adult's probation.[32] Incidentally, at the Third Reading of the Bill one MP commented, 'the probation officer might be the friend, and the welcome friend, of the children'.[33]

Vincent was not impressed by the new Bill, perhaps not surprisingly as the Home Office had 'hijacked' his Bill. In another of his letters to the editor of *The Times* he referred to two particular criticism of the government's Bill. The first that it was far too general as 'such a wide extension cannot fail to minimise that certainty of punishment which, after all, must remain the principal deterrence from crime'. He also took issue with the operation of the new system and asks, 'would it not be better to make the Chief Officer of Police the probation authority and enable him to act through representatives ... ' (both from *The Times* 27 May 1907).

In its new role as coordinator of the probation system the Home Office, in the following year, published guidance on the running of the probation system in the form of a Home Office memorandum. It stated that the Secretary of State was 'satisfied that in a considerable number of cases, especially cases of juvenile delinquents and of adults of respectable antecedents who have been exposed to special temptation, the punishment can safely and properly be suspended for a time' (Home Office 1908: 4). This reinforces the Home Office's view that the new system of probation was considered particularly suitable for juvenile offenders. The memorandum went on to say that 'the success of the Act will largely depend on the character and qualifications of the persons appointed probation officers' (Home Office 1908: 4). They continued, 'in all cases the officers should be persons of good education, and having some knowledge of the industrial and social conditions of the locality' (Home Office 1908: 5). They were also specific that police were not suitable to be appointed as probation officers and probation officers should not wear uniforms. The memorandum also specified that the Home Office would pay the salary of the newly appointed children's probation officers in London. Meanwhile the CETS and other societies would receive a grant to cover half of the salary of their missionaries working in the London courts. Outside of London local authorities and the societies operated a number of varied and locally agreed practices when it came to funding. At this stage the Home Office had very little to do with the organization or funding of probation outside of the capital which was a reflection of the perceived role of central government generally (see Taylor 1975) at the turn of the century. Nonetheless, the state, in the shape of the Home Office, was now firmly involved in the running of the probation scheme, particularly in the capital, and this signalled another crucial change.

The temperance societies were delighted with the new legislation. The London Diocesan Police Court Mission of CETS held their Annual Meeting at the end of 1907 which was reported in *The Times*. At that meeting the secretary announced that:

> the society's missionaries had been appointed probation officers under the new Probation of Offenders Act at Tottenham, Edmonton, Wood-green, Highgate, Brentford, Middlesex sessions, and the Central Criminal Court. The probation

work had been done to a large extent hitherto through the Police-court Mission. (*The Times* 2 November 1907)

The St Giles Christian Mission were also delighted to report in their Annual Meeting that 'under the Probation of Offenders Act many a juvenile offender had been handed over to the mission with lasting beneficial results' (*The Times* 29 November 1907). This was before any Home Office probation officer had ever been appointed.

The Home Office clearly expected the new probation officers to work with juvenile offenders. The connection with juvenile offenders would have been even stronger at the time as the following year the same government, and the same Home Office officials and ministers wrote and guided through Parliament the *Children Act of 1908* and *the Prevention of Crime Act 1908*. The first of these created the Children's Court to deal with all defendants under the age of 16, the so-called 'Children's Charter' whilst the latter introduced the Borstal system for juvenile offenders sent to custody. Detailed histories of both pieces of legislation are included in Elkin (1938), Rose (1961), Radzinowicz and Hood (1986), Garland (1985) and Bailey (1987). All three pieces of legislation dealt with the juvenile offender and they reflected a particular issue that concerned many, including legislators; this was the general danger of urban life to working class youth. This is the same concern that prompted the arrival and meteoric success of the Scout movement. What all three pieces of legislation have in common is that they provided for good influences to be brought to bear on working class young people to counter the unwholesome influence of urban life, *before* they became hardened criminals. In the case of probation, that influence was to be provided by probation officers.

The reality of probation

Following the passage of the Act the Home Office appointed two probation officers to work in the newly created children's courts of London. These officers were referred to as children's probation officers and were direct employees of the Home Office, receiving their salary from the Receiver of Metropolitan Police. This meant that two systems of probation now existed, one CETS dominated and based in the adult courts and one Home Office funded and based in the children's courts in London. Outside of the capital a patchwork of arrangements existed with various societies part funding officers. Matters were further confused by the fact that two pieces of legislation operated. The older legislation allowed the court to release an offender without statutory supervision beyond recognizance's, whereas the new system made specific reference to supervision by a probation officer. For the moment though we will focus on the arrangements for probation in the capital as they reveal the emergence of a new system of probation officers working alongside the existing missionaries.

The first two Home Office probation officers appointed were Miss Ivimy and Miss Croker King;[34] their role was to work with children placed on probation by the newly created children's courts of London, which meant that each was responsible for a number of courts. Both women had worked for the COS in one of their District Committees and had experience of working in playgroups.[35] Miss Croker King lived in Bethnal Green; she had also worked in a college settlement and had been involved with Poor Law Committees and a range of clubs, guilds and other youth organizations. The following year she was joined by Miss E. D. Cheshire and they became lifelong friends. Her retirement was noted in *Probation* in 1934 (Vol. 1, No. 18, p. 284) and she died just over ten years later. Miss Ivimy had also done club work and resided in a college settlement but she had been superintendent of a rescue home for two years and been secretary of a Women's Holiday Fund before her appointment as a probation officer. By 1913 there were seven children's probation offices in post (see Home Office 1913 and below). Nonetheless, the Home Office operation in the children's courts was still dwarfed by the CETS operation in the adult courts. It is interesting to note that neither of the new children's probation officers had a temperance background nor were they expected to be practising Anglicans. Their's was a social work background.

Almost immediately the new system of probation encountered problems. Rose confirms as much when he writes, 'it was soon, however, abundantly clear that the Act was not being worked successfully' (Rose 1961: 83). A number of problems emerged; firstly, the Home Office realized that they had little control over who was working as probation officers in the adult courts as although they were paying part of their salaries the Societies were appointing the staff. They were also rather in the dark as to who was doing what; they note, 'it is therefore quite impossible for the Secretary of State to know how often the officers whom they have named will be employed'.[36]

It also soon emerged that the two children's probation officers were encountering difficulties. In relation to the existing missionaries it was noted that 'the Police Court Missionaries are getting the bulk of the cases'.[37] The same Home Office file also includes correspondence between the Home Office and various magistrates in London where the latter asked if it would not be possible to use the police court missionaries in the children's courts. The reply from the Home Secretary was not sympathetic; Home Secretary Gladstone replied saying that Miss Ivimy had been appointed children's probation officer on a Home Office salary and that she should be used if at all possible.[38] In August of 1908 the London Magistrates Association wrote to the Home Office saying that 'the Magistrates are of the opinion that there are plenty of probation officers appointed'[39] and in October 1908 Jack Myers (a missionary probation officer) complained to the Home Office. He wrote that his salary was far too low, that many probation officers appointed were doing far too little work and magistrates were taking little notice of the Act or were unwilling to act on the advice of probation officers.[40] The following month the Receiver of the Metropolitan Police (who paid the officers salaries) noted, 'there has been little occasion to make use of the services of the children's probation officers during the quarter in question'.[41]

Despite this distinctly unpromising start, the Home Office persisted with the children's probation officers and by 1910 two more had been appointed. The children's officers had been awarded a pay increase and Miss Ivimy was now paid 200 pounds per annum. The Metropolitan Police Receiver was not impressed and wrote, 'the salaries suggested seem to me too high' as 'it is true that at least two of them come from the artisan class but one of them is a doctors wife'.[42] He also commented that the women officers should be paid less.

Moving outside the capital arrangements changed very little and the usual varied set of practices continued. Here of course there were no children's probation officers and though some towns and cities had police court missionaries who were now acting as probation officers others made their own very peculiar arrangements. For instance in Saffron Walden, when Mary Dorothy Reed (under 14 at the time) was convicted of theft of a pair of shoes no one could be found to act as a probation officer. As she came from the 'rough' part of town, the local policeman was appointed. The Chief Constable objected as this contravened the advice sent out by the Home Office following the Act (see Home Office 1908). The Court Clerk wrote to the Home Office for advice, who replied,

> It is undesirable to encourage the appointment of officers of Police as probation officers – still more undesirable to appoint them as probation officers for girls or children – but in this particular case it would not be unreasonable to put her under the supervision of a PC. Saffron Walden probably does not offer much in the matter of probation officers.[43]

By way of a contrast magistrates in Birmingham wrote to the Home Office in October of 1910 to inform them of developments there. They had appointed three probation officers, one in the adult court and two in the Children's Court. They were also planning to appoint another and to create a third court to deal with the 17–21-year-old age group. The Permanent Under Secretary noted curtly, 'they may try it if they like, but I do not think the Home Office should be involved'.[44] The magistrates even included a copy of their annual report which noted that courts often asked probation officers to furnish the court with a report on a defendant which commented on an 'offender's character, surroundings and mode of life' before sentencing. The same report also stated that police officers were used as probation officers which 'has worked satisfactorily', and that magistrates had been in touch with colleagues in Leeds to discuss how they worked the probation system there.[45]

Those early years following the Act were clearly difficult and particularly so in London where the new arrangements had the greatest impact. The Home Office–appointed children's probation officers were sparse on the ground and struggling to find work. The CETS and other religious societies dominated the work in courts, although many were now called missionary probation officers and part funded by the Home Office. Despite the financial support and the new rules for probation from the Home Office, the missionaries continued to be appointed and supervised by the religious societies to whom they may well have felt far more closely tied. Outside the capital a varied picture of ad hoc practices continued to exist and which varied greatly between courts in the large industrial cities and small market towns. Indeed the evidence suggests that the Act had very little impact in those early years.

Two reviews of probation

The most radical change that the 1907 Act introduced was (arguably) not the system of probation officers it introduced but the central role it gave to the Home Office in the management of a new court sentence. So before going on to consider how the Home Office reacted to those early difficulties, it would be as well to consider the Home Office, its operation and its personnel. This is particularly significant as the senior civil servants at the Home Office will be shown to play a crucial role in the development of probation as our story unfolds. Those officials had a quite clear vision for probation but this was not a static vision. As we will see, the Home Office's views changed and those changes sometimes coincided with the retirement or promotion of senior civil servants. Many of these same senior civil servants had long and illustrious careers, often in sharp contrast to their political masters at the Home Office some of whom were only in post a matter of months. The relationships between senior civil servants and government ministers at the Home Office is fascinating and we'll see it in action as we follow probation's development over the next fifty years or so.

As the *Probation of Offenders Act 1907* was being drafted and implemented the impact of the wide ranging reforms began by the Northcote Trevellyan Report of 1854 had begun to impact on the very highest reaches of the civil service. This Report had advocated an open competitive examination as a means of recruiting the higher civil service. These recruits were to form a professional and intellectually gifted administration who were to be the leaders of a new administrative apparatus both at home and across the colonies. The lower clerical ranks were to be kept separate and perform the more mundane administrative tasks. As Chapman and Greenaway (1980) write change was slow with the Home Office being one of the last departments to adapt. Pellew's (1982) history of the Home Office describes a department of 33 full-time officials in 1870 which grew to 176 by 1914. Not only had the work of the Home Office expanded greatly in these years but the top-ranking officials had changed enormously. As Chapman and Greenaway note:

> The first and most important [shift] was the replacement of the rather heterogeneous group of leading mid-Victorian administrators with an exclusively academic elite, drawn largely from Oxford, Cambridge and the Scottish Universities, as a result of the reforms in recruitment after 1855 and 1870. Such an elite, trained predominantly in the liberal humanities, began to dominate the higher civil service from about 1890. The intellectual calibre of such recruits was higher than that of their predecessors, and it may not be coincidental that about the time when such recruits reached the very top positions the pace and character of most government departments began to change, with the official contributing more to policy-making. Moreover, the ideals of public service, preached by Jowett at Baliol, and the enthusiasm of the Oxford Idealists[46] percolated through the civil service. (Chapman and Greenaway 1980: 199)

In fact Pellew (1982) takes the analysis one step further arguing that the new senior civil servants saw themselves as a self-conscious intellectual elite embarking on a career of public service. The fact that they often had the same social background and education as their political masters meant that they saw their work as equally significant in the pursuit of the countries well being. Significantly they saw themselves as the equal of their political masters, perhaps not surprising as they had much in common with them. The 'flip side' of this story is included in Cannadine's (1990) *The Decline and Fall of the British Aristocracy*, which describes an older amateur civil service seen as a safe career for the younger sons of the aristocracy being replaced by a professional, educated and middle class higher civil service.

In the case of the Home Office the first open competition recruit to arrive at the top job was Edward Troup who was appointed Permanent Under Secretary in 1908. He was born in Scotland and educated at Aberdeen and Oxford Universities. Troup joined the Home Office as a junior clerk in 1880, became Assistant Under Secretary in 1903 and Permanent Under Secretary in 1908, before retiring in 1922. A close colleague of his was H. B. Simpson who was educated at Winchester and Oxford. He, like Troup, joined the Home Office shortly after his graduation in 1884. Simpson rose to become Assistant Secretary and retired in 1925. Neither had aristocratic connections though both had solid middle class upbringings and a very good education. They were the first of a particular type of men who were to dominate the higher civil service at the Home Office.

What Troup, Simpson and many that followed had in common was a public school education which is important as it was here that many of the attitudes they displayed in their professional lives were formed. As Mangan, in his history of the English public school system, writes, 'what the public school boy did was to take his school world and its symbolic actions and trappings with him into the outside world' (Mangan 1986: 145). In the late nineteenth century these beliefs would have been characterized by what Mangan calls a 'Christian manliness', which implied an anti intellectual attitude to education and crucially a high commitment to games. Mangan writes, 'as much as masters they (the pupils) subscribed to the ethical value of games as the source of good sense, noble traits, manly feelings, generous disposition, gentlemanly deportment, comradely loyalty' (Mangan 1986: 132). Earlier in the same work Mangan makes the point about games that 'it was a genuinely and extensively held belief that they inspired virtue; they developed manliness; they formed character' (Mangan 1986: 9).

As we have already seen, Edwardians understood something quite specific when they discussed character. We have already come across it in the descriptions of social work practice at the turn of the century and in discussions about the work of the police court mission and their attempts to build character. Bray (1907 and 1908) and Masterman (1901) remind us how important outdoor activity and games were seen to be for the healthy physical and moral development of children. Additionally, we have seen these attitudes given their most practical example in the Boys Clubs of the period and the new Boy Scout movement.

It is worth keeping this context in mind as we follow the early years of probation and particularly the newly appointed probation officers in the newly created children's courts. The probation system was only two years old when the Home Office first reviewed it. The main inspiration for this review was the problems already highlighted, particularly the lack of use being made of the Act and the children's probation officers, the problems the Home Office were experiencing in supervising the work of the police court missionaries (despite part funding it) and the varied arrangements being established outside of London. Edward Troup, by then the highest civil servant at the Home Office, was forced to conclude, 'the Act is not being worked as it should'.[47] The Committee was appointed in March 1909 and reported in December that year; it was chaired by Herbert Samuel and included amongst its members the London Magistrate John Dickinson and Troup himself (Home Office 1910a). As Mair and Burke noted, 'at least three of the five Committee members were strong supporters of the probation system' (Mair and Burke 2012: 32) which may explain the approach the Report took.

The Report concluded, 'the Act has already proved to be of great value in a large number of cases' (Home Office 1910a: col. 8); however, it also noted 'that the courts have availed themselves of the Act to a very unequal extent, … there were considerable differences in the extent to which probation orders were made in areas of similar characteristics' (Home Office 1910a: col. 9). The Report also noted the confusion that appeared to have developed in courts where the new Act of 1907 was used largely with juvenile offenders only and older offenders were released under the older version of probation or on recognizance's. Additionally, the Report noted that some magistrates made objections to probation because they 'regard the visits of a probation officer to an offender as an intrusion' (Home Office 1910a: col. 118). Generally, the Report was happy with those appointed to work as probation officers but did note that some courts were using police officers to work as probation officers and wrote, 'in no circumstances should the same man be engaged both on probation work and on ordinary police duties' (Home Office 1910a: col. 135).

The Minutes of Evidence (Home Office 1910b) reveal a little more detail about the concerns expressed to the committee. They show a belief that the 1907 Act introduced little that was new. A London Magistrate commented, 'the conclusion to be drawn is that the magistrates were doing what is practically probation work on a large scale previous to the passing of the Act in 1907' (Home

Office 1910b: 2). A view echoed by the Secretary of the CETS said, 'it seems to me that the actual cases which are handed over to the missionaries are the same cases exactly as were handed over in the old days' (Home Office 1910b: 12).

The Minutes also reveal a possible explanation for the lack of use made of the 1907 Act with adult offenders. The following exchange between the committee and a magistrate giving oral evidence was typical,

> … dealing with adults, you prefer to discharge an offender without the supervision of an officer?
>
> Yes.
>
> On the grounds that some of these adult offenders would resent being coaxed and soothed?
>
> Yes.
>
> (Home Office 1910b: 7)

The same witness regarded a probation officer as useful primarily with the young because they were open to good influences in a way that older offenders were not. Regarding the issue of the varied use of probation, the Secretary of the CETS in London commented, 'when you consider the enormous number of cases that come into the police courts, I was astonished, and I think many other people have been astonished that it (the 1907 Act) has not been put into operation more than it has'. His explanation for this varied use of probation centred on the idiosyncrasies of the Magistrates (Home Office 1910b: 13).

The Minutes also reveal a criticism of probation that was alluded to in the debates in Parliament when the Act was passed but which was not mentioned in the Report itself. It was voiced by Sir William Grantham, a Kings Bench Judge, when he said, 'I would never give a man a sentence and so much police supervision, which is practically your probation officer'. He continued, 'they become like a body of policemen, only of course of a different class' (Home Office 1910b: col. 2856). Perhaps the Home Office sensitivity to this type of criticism might explain why they were against the appointment of police as probation officers, though the usual comment was that juvenile offenders were unlikely to confide in a policeman who had perhaps arrested them earlier.

Overall though the committee seemed pleased with the new probation system and little radical change was proposed. The Report recommended that a Home Office memo be circulated to all magistrates encouraging them to make more use of the Act, that the Home Office should appoint an official to look after probation work, that officers should be paid a salary and not per case, that there should be an officer for every court and that the distinction between the two types of officer should not be rigid (Home Office 1910a: col. 78). A Home Office memo was circulated to all the magistrates around the country referring to the committee's report and advocating use of the new system. As Mair and Burke point out, beyond that the committee were not prepared to go and allude to the fact that no central oversight was deemed necessary which leads them to describe probation as a 'cottage industry … based on personal relationships' (Mair and Burtke 2012: 38).

The committee had also suggested the formation of an association for probation officers and in 1912 Sidney Edridge, clerk to the justices at Croydon Magistrates, took up the challenge. He convened the first meeting on 22 May 1912 at Croydon Town Hall at which about forty probation officers from London and the surrounding areas attended (see Bochel 1962a). The organization was named the National Association of Probation Officers and it thrives today. Those early days were difficult, money was always tight and recruitment difficult. The organization was very much dominated by Edridge who ran it until his resignation on the grounds of ill health in 1928.

Shortly after its formation, Edridge wrote to the Home Office seeking their approval and as Bochel notes, '(t)his was readily, if not enthusiastically, extended' (Bochel 1962a: 33). Relations though were good and by 1918 the Home Office regularly sent speakers to the annual conferences and NAPO were invited to give evidence to all subsequent Home Office committees considering anything that might impact on probation.

The organization struggled to recruit amongst the missionary probation officers and Bochel puts this down to the association's new journal. She points out that 'the journal continually carried articles which called for the abolition of dual control, a sentiment unlikely to have been viewed with favourably by the Missions' (Bochel 1962a: 35). This referred to the arrangement where missionary probation officers were funded by the Home Office but employed by the societies. The missionaries though may also have felt a much closer allegiance to the societies who actually employed them than an organization exclusively for probation officers. That was not the only difference; Bochel also refers to the appointment of two of the new children's probation officers to the executive committee, namely Miss Ivimy and Miss Lance, and comments that they were:

> Better educated than most of their colleagues, probably less dependant upon this particular job than others and more confident in their relations with their employers, these women were able to make a worthwhile contribution to the service in its early years. (Bochel 1962a: 35)

Even in these early days NAPO clearly took a particular view on the operation of probation and was given access to the Home Office and so the opportunity to advocate that view to key decision makers.

Despite the recent review, the Home Office memo and what followed problems with the new system of probation persisted, particularly so in London. In 1913 the Home Office received complaints about the probation system from two significant sources. In March of that year C. E. B. Russell wrote pointing out 'what seems in the view of our correspondents and ourselves to be faulty administration of the *Probation Act of 1907*'.[48] Russell had, for many years, been heavily involved in social work and the Boys Clubs movement in Manchester but at the time of this letter was serving on the Home Office–appointed committee which had begun in 1911 to review the work of the Industrial and Reformatory Schools.[49] The committee reported in 1913, shortly after which Russssell was appointed Chief Inspector of Industrial and Reformatory Schools by the Home Office. Russell's letter went on to specify particular criticisms including 'the failure on the part of most Magisterial Benches in the country to appoint whole-time probation officers, and to rest content with appointing as probation officers person of both sexes already attending the courts on behalf of Police Court Missions and other philanthropic societies'.[50] Russell listed other criticisms including the low pay of officers, the lack of prior enquiries before placing on probation and the lack of organization of officers' work. The Home Office were not impressed; their response was that 'the information in possession of the Home office does not suggest that much importance need be attached to the criticisms of Mr Russell, which reach us unsupported by evidence and are of extremely vague application'. The same minute went on to comment that:

> Most of the points which they make concern difficulties which are inherent in the nature of the Probation of Offenders Act an could not be removed by any action the Home Office could take, but these same points have been largely foreseen and dealt with … Probation is essentially a subject in which local authorities must work out there own solutions, and there is good reason to think that in most places they are doing so satisfactorily.[51]

But the Home Office received notification of other problems with the new system.

There were problems 'on the ground' faced by the new children's probation officers and in the same year Miss Croker-King, one of those officers, wrote to Sir William Byrne (Assistant Under Secretary at the Home Office) stating:

> Miss Cheshire and I are in despair, we hear nothing about getting paid as full time workers, and we are really tired of working as we do and not even being

able to live on our salaries, ... It is impossible to do the work alone even working 12 hours a day .... We feel that we are more then badly treated.[52]

As a result of this their salaries were increased from 120 to 130 pounds per annum. In the meantime the Home Office continued to monitor articles in the press and be lobbied by the Penal Reform League for the extension of probation.[53]

Clearly these criticism struck a chord, particularly concerns about the financial arrangements, such that the Home Office appointed a committee to look at the new system of probation just a few years after the whole system had been reviewed. The committee's original 'brief' was very specific; it was appointed in January 1913 to look at 'the remuneration of Probation Officers in the Metropolitan Police Court District' (Home Office 1913: 2). However, it took a slightly wider view and looked at probation in the capital generally. The committee was made up of Sir William Byrne, Assistant Under Secretary at the Home Office, John Dickinson, a London Magistrate, and George Tripp, Receiver for the Metropolitan Police District, responsible for paying probation officers. It met seventeen times, took oral evidence from twenty witnesses and written evidence from others. Those witnesses included secretaries of both Church of England Temperance Societies in London, a number of police court missionaries now acting as probation officers, witnesses nominated by the newly formed National Association of Probation Officers, five of the seven 'Lady Children's Probation Officers' (Home Office 1913: 3) along with a number of magistrates. Their report was produced in December 1913 and though it does not have a Command Number it is in the usual format of a departmental committee except that it is marked 'confidential' and 'for official use only'. No other history of probation discusses this Report[54] though Page's (1992) work does refer to its existence when he writes that 'no copies of this pre-War report have come to light' (Page 1992: 105).

The early part of the Report looks in some detail at the salaries and grants paid to the various organizations and probation officers. The committee discovered that the methods of paying police court missionaries varied from salaries to payment by case to a combination of both salaries and fees. It was also apparent that the Home Office grant did not cover the cost of the probation officers provided by the various societies. Salaries were not very high and one CETS sponsored officer claimed that his salary was not high enough for a married man to live on. The two CETS that covered London (the London Diocesan Branch north of the river and the Southwark Diocesan Branch south of the river) paid different salaries and via different methods. The newly appointed children's probation officers were the better paid and the women missionaries were extremely poorly paid. Both CETS secretaries resisted any suggestion that the Home Office should pay their missionary probation offices directly and insisted that the Home Office grant be paid to the central organization.

Regarding the cost of probation officers to the state, the committee noted:

> … there can be no doubt of the substantial success of the system of probation in diminishing the number of cases of relapse into crime; and every person who is saved by this means from imprisonment represents a saving to public funds, a saving which in cases of frequently repeated terms of imprisonment would be of appreciable amount. Moreover, in fixing the sums to be recommended we had regard to the large increase in the number of cases on probation that is practically certain to rise in the triennial period. (Home Office 1913: 10)

When it came to the salaries of the children's probation officers specifically (which the Home Office paid), the Report noted:

> As regards the expense entailed by the appointment of special Children's Probation Officers with liberal salaries at the several Juvenile Courts, we would point out that there can no doubt that the system of Probation has diverted a considerable number of cases from certified Reformatory and Industrial Schools. (Home Office 1913: 15)

Bearing in mind that the Home Office paid all the costs of prisons and Industrial and Reformatory Schools it becomes a little clearer as to why they might be desirous that probation succeeds.

However, the committee went beyond simple finances and took evidence from the newly appointed children's probation officers. In fact in many places in the Report they are referred to as 'special Lady Children's Probation Officers' (Home Office 1913: 4) stressing the fact that the original Home Office–appointed probation officers were all women. By 1913 there were seven children's probation officers working in eight newly created juvenile courts in London. They included Miss Ivimy at Bow Street and Westminster, Miss Dalglish in Greenwich, Miss Huddleston and Miss Lance at Tower Bridge, Miss Croker-King and Miss Cheshire at Old Street and Clerkenwell, and the newly appointed Miss Rosalie Reade at South Western Police Court. In her evidence to the committee Miss Croker-King gave an account of her work. They summarized it so:

> In the course of the evidence it was accepted that the duties of the Children's Probation Officer might be epitomized thus, viz., the Probation Officer should –
>
>   1. Keep an eye on the child and its doing, and report to the Magistrates thereon.
>
>   2. Improve the character and outlook of the child and the parents by visitation, advice and encouragement.

3. Direct at the child all available beneficial influences, school, employment, boys clubs etc.

The Lady Probation Officers thought of these that the most important factor was the influence brought to bear on the child and the parents. (Home Office 1913: 12)

Thus monitoring, advice and, crucially, developing character were seen as the role of the probation officer working with children. This was slightly different to the work reported in the CETS Annual Reports noted earlier. Children were seen to have a character that was pliable and open to the good influences of kindly 'upright' adults.

The committee also spent a good deal of time discussing the qualities and qualifications of the various probation officers employed and therefore the remuneration they could expect. In this respect clear differences emerged between the new children's probation officers and the missionary officers and there was also some disagreement on the topic. The Report states:

One section of opinion attached great importance to the appointment of ladies of superior education, experience, and position, such as those hitherto appointed to act in that capacity, on the ground that they exercise greater influence than a woman of humbler rank over the child placed on probation, its parents, home and surroundings, and, in addition, command more attention and assistance from employers of labour, schoolmasters, clergy, the authorities of benevolent institutions and other persons in a position to promote the probationers' chance of doing well.

The other view put before us is, that women of the social grade and acquirements of the female Police Court Missionaries are quite capable of doing everything possible in the child's interest, and are likely to possess a more intimate and useful knowledge of the home life of the poorer classes of the community, and the conditions in which they live. (Home Office 1913: 10)

The confidential nature of the Report might be explained by the fact that the committee then asked a number of the police court magistrates to express their views, in confidence, as to what they thought was the preferable option. They were evenly divided.

The committee then took evidence from the children's probation officers on the same question and these answers reveal much about working methods. In her evidence Miss Ivimy stated:

The witness said that influencing of homes was a very important part of her work and regarded character building as the corner-stone of Probation.

She went on:

> The innate experience of working-class women was valuable with regard to
> conditions of life, purchasing power of money etc. They might do the framework
> of Probation equally well but were apt to be too easily content. (Home Office
> 1913: 12)

Miss Huddleston, in her evidence, argues that 'a visitor of the educated class
brought out more. Working class women ... were too near in class to the people
dealt with to command the necessary respect and authority' (Home Office
1913: 13). The committee concluded:

> We are of the opinion, after going very fully into the question, that the ladies
> hitherto appointed to the post of special Children's Probation Officer possess
> qualifications of a higher order and have performed the work extremely well.
> (Home Office 1913: 14)

However, in the recommendations the Report suggested that 'it is undesirable to
restrict to one class of person the appointments to the post of special Children's
Probation Officer, and that a trial should be made of the capacities of some of the
female Missionaries as occasion offers' (Home Office 1913: 20).

Not only were the children's probation officers and missionary probation
officers from different social strata, they also had quite distinct training and
professional experience. Curiously, very little is said about the training of
the women missionary probation officers but the Secretary of the Southwark
Diocesan Branch of the CETS commented:

> The standard of the education of the men is similar to that of an elementary
> school teacher. Most of them have a year's training at the Society for the
> Promotion of Christian Knowledge College at Stepney. (Home Office 1913: 6)

The children's probation officers on the other hand tended to have experience of
clubs, settlement work or teaching. On this mater the Report comments:

> The training afforded by the Charity Organisation Society was in particular very
> highly spoken of by these witnesses, and one witness pointed out the importance
> of keeping up to date in the matter of reading and lectures, as well as on the
> practical side, which would include some knowledge of the parents' trades and
> conditions of life. (Home Office 1913: 12)

After reading the Report it is hard to escape the conclusion that working
methods, social and educational background of officers working in the children's
courts and wholly paid for by the Home Office were different to those employed

by the societies. More than that, their methods of payment were different, their organization and management were also different. In a number of places the Report refers to the relative cheapness of the missionary probation officers and particularly the women missionary probation officers. The new children's officers were noticeably more expensive but the potential cost saving of keeping children out of Reformatory and Industrial Schools was seen to more than counterbalance that expense. It is interesting to note that all the specialist probation officers appointed were women (see Annison 2009) and that they tended to be better qualified and better paid than the missionary probation officers.

After the report was completed, a Home Office circular was drafted which included many of these findings whilst copies of the Report were sent to the various societies employing officers with a note written by Troup that said 'the report should not be communicated to probation officers',[55] though he is not clear as to why. We are rather left to speculate on this issue.

Thus by 1914 a well-established system of police court missionaries, many of whom were now called missionary probation officers, worked in the adult courts and continued to base their work on mission and temperance. Their methods and organization had altered little since their foundation in the 1880s, though it had expanded. In many respects they reflected what Foucault (1991) calls the initial move 'from the body to the soul of the offender', and the rapid expansion of summary jurisdiction described by Hay (1975).

In addition to this were a handful of children's probation officers working in the newly formed children's courts of London. Their origins and working methods were influenced by contemporary concerns about a degenerating urban working class youth and a belief in the power of 'character' and 'influence' of an interested and educated middle class to divert from a life of crime. Although they shared earlier concerns about the body of the offender, it was now the young offender, and it was to be nurtured and strengthened either on the 'playing fields of Eton' or the Lads Clubs of Manchester[56] as a prerequisite for character development. The new probation officers were creatures of the Home Office who had lately entered the field and whose support was based at least partially on their cost-cutting potential. Their roots lay in experiments began in Massachusetts and were part of an international trend identified by Timasheff who writes:

> The later history of probation in the English speaking world was largely that of raising the level of probation in England, and in those parts of the English speaking world which had closely imitated the English pattern, to the level already reached in the most progressive parts of America. (Timasheff 1941: 83)

By this he means the arrival of probation officers and supervision of offender in the community. Incidentally it is a trend he sees spreading across the rest of Europe in the early years of the twentieth century (see Timasheff 1943: 21).

Looking at the UK we can say that six years into its introduction the new system of probation's impact was marginal, its survival unsure, but its symbolic importance great. Those early officers were some of the first state funded social workers operating in the community and they marked a further significant expansion by the state into the lives of the working class.

The Home Office Takes Control as Treatment Arrives: Probation 1914–1928

Our story now moves on to the Great War and deals with probation from its outbreak to the publication, fourteen years later, of the *Fourth Report of the work of the Children's Branch* at the Home Office (1928). Like the previous chapter one key piece of legislation and its consequences looms large, in this case the *Criminal Justice Act of 1925*. The previous chapter of this study has shown that the introduction of a system of probation officers in 1907 was met with indifference from the Courts. This chapter will focus on the response of the Home Office and others involved in criminal justice to probation's inauspicious start. It has also already been shown that there was a high degree of concern for the new system of probation officers as witnessed by the appointment of two committees before the war (Home Office 1910a, 1913), the latter working in secret. A further committee was to be appointed in the period covered by this chapter (Home Office 1922).

The relationship between the set of policies slowly emerging from the Home Office and probation practices will be crucial to this chapter and we'll see just how closely interlinked they were to become. The years covered by this chapter also coincide with the arrival of notions of the 'treatability' of various 'conditions' via the relatively new disciplines of psychology and very tentatively psychoanalysis. The application of these to the field of the criminal, and in particular the juvenile delinquent, begins in earnest in the time period covered by this chapter. A new discourse arrived in probation practice to work alongside and on occasions compete with the discourses we have already identified and seen in operation in probation practice.

Social work also underwent major changes in the period to be covered; particularly it began to make claims for a professional status (Yelloly 1980). As both probation officers and police court missionaries regarded themselves social workers changes in the social work profession were to have an impact on the probation system.

The central piece of legislation covered in this chapter is The *Criminal Justice Act of 1925* which was to prove extremely important for probation. Arguably, the major lasting effect of the Act was the central role it gave the state in setting probation policy the consequences of which are still being felt today. Many of the other changes about to be described in relation to the practice of probation arrived by other means. The Act created a different and significantly larger space for probation to operate in. It is worth stressing that this legislative change resulted in a recognizable shift in the trajectory of probation.

Crime, probation and the Great War

A history of the impact of the Great War on those left at home is not the topic of this work. However, it is possible to detect a distinct shift in approach by policy makers to working class youth in these few years. Most significant was a move from general concerns about the condition of working class youth described in the previous chapter to one that focused on juvenile crime specifically. This is illustrated in two key studies from this period; one was Leeson's (1917) *The Child and the War*. At the time of publication of the book he was Secretary of the Howard Association and had already written about the probation system (Leeson 1914). He asserts very early on in his work, 'Juvenile lawlessness has spread through the country like a plague' (Leeson 1917: 9). He argues that this was a dire problem that needed to be addressed, but his reasoning is interesting. He writes:

> The blunt truth is that the State cannot afford juvenile offenders. With a population decimated by war, it is the concern of everyone to prevent waste of human material. Towards the spending of life, of child life, and especially male child life, our attitude henceforth must be one of extreme parsimony. In the reconstructive work after the War, the country will require to make each human unit go further than ever before; and whether or no the next generation proves equal to the demands made upon it very largely depends upon the wisdom and foresight displayed in our actions now. (Leeson 1917: 10)

Ideas of reconstruction and the role of the state in that reconstruction permeated much of society by 1917 and were perhaps expressed best in the phrase: 'A land fit for heroes'. Here we see it in terms of the role of the state in safeguarding the next generation.

The Commissioner of Police for the Metropolis seems to, in some respects, support Leeson's assertion. In his report for 1915[1] he writes:

The total number of persons apprehended for all offences during the year 1915 was 114,259 as compared with 131,841 in 1914, showing a decrease of 1,555 in indictable offences, and 16,027 in minor offences, making a total decrease of 17,582. (*Mepol 2/1267*: 7)

This shows that crime was actually falling quite substantially during the war. On the other hand, the situation was very different when considering youth crime. Again quoting from the same report:

4,744 children and young persons under the age of 16 were taken into custody for various offences as compared with 3,346 in 1914, and 3,464 in 1913. The increase arises from a number of causes brought about by the war. With so many of the fathers serving in the Field and mothers in temporary employment, it is not surprising that the children suffer from lack of control. The darkness of the streets gives children opportunities for pilfering which they do not have in peace time. (*Mepol 2/1267*: 8)

The Report for the following year showed that the number of children taken into custody in 1916 had risen to 6,023.[2] However, again the Report comments on the reduction in serious crime and notes that the increases were primarily in offences of larceny or such things as, 'larcenies by servants and stealing growing fruit' (*Mepol 2/1267* 1907: 8). A picture emerges of falling adult crime and even serious crime but substantial increases in relatively petty juvenile crime.

Leeson's explanations for the increase in juvenile crime show how concerns and solutions offered before the war were heightened by war conditions. For instance he writes:

The causes of the present increase in juvenile delinquency are chiefly to be found in the withdrawal from child-life of adult personal influence, and in the curtailment of those social and educational agencies that hitherto have occupied so large a part of the child's life, and on which those responsible for him had come to rely. (Leeson 1917: 22)

Many fathers were away in the armed forces, and many mothers also worked during the war, often in the munitions factories. On the subject of working mothers Leeson writes:

The absence of mothers at work outside their homes was well known before the war as a predisposing factor of juvenile delinquency, but where mothers, normally at home, have for the first time undertaken work outside of their homes, the results to the children are much worse. (Leeson 1917: 25)

With many mothers being left responsible for the child's discipline and if they too were out at work then discipline became very lax within the home, argues

Leeson. Thus the assumption that a mother's place is in the home has a strongly crime preventative connotation.

The other key site for a lack of male influence over the child was the school, and here again Leeson points to the fact that many of the men were away in the forces leaving the teachers behind predominantly female and so not nearly so well equipped, in his view, as male teachers to influence the children. Leeson also notes that many children were excused school to go to work, or via various bye-laws allowed to attend at school part time. This was exacerbated by the type of jobs the children were doing. Leeson writes:

> Most of the factory work that they do is 'blind alley' work, fitting them for nothing afterwards; and to do it, lads are sacrificing physique, efficiency, and in many cases – character. (Leeson 1917: 36)

These are the exact words that we have already seen to describe a problematic, urban working class youth, but to Leeson the war simply made a bad situation worse. The one ingredient that Leeson does add is his concern over the newly invented cinema. This new media encourages stealing, by over stimulating the children and encouraging the children to remain within the unhealthy environment of the cinema (Leeson 1917: 41). He concludes:

> Had we set out with deliberate intention of manufacturing juvenile delinquents, could we have done so in any more certain way. (Leeson 1917: 46)

The solution he offers draws from a number of ideas we have already encountered:

> Build the juvenile court with its back to a common and its front to a church, a gymnasium on one flank and a rifle range on the other – and a fine clubroom the Juvenile Court will make! (Leeson 1917: 63)

Thus juvenile criminals were not separated from working class youth generally to any great extent; it was simply a matter of degree; they all, Leeson argued, suffered the same background and conditions and were therefore exposed to the same risk. Leeson writes:

> It is not the comparatively few delinquent children, but the greater number who live in the unwholesome conditions from which delinquents come, that are the more important problem. (Leeson 1917: 68)

A second and equally influential work that deals with juvenile delinquency during the Great War was William Clarke-Hall's *The State and the Child*[3] which was published in the same year as Leeson's work. Clarke-Hall spends considerable time discussing probation and describes a system where the probation officers, in his Court at least, worked with those put on probation by the children's courts and the police court missionary supervised the adults. What he adds to the debate is an increased emphasis on the role of the state to prevent this 'waste of human material'. He asks, 'does it not become incumbent, at the present time above all times, both upon the State and all individual members of it, to see that this waste shall, as far as possible, cease?' (Clarke-Hall 1917: xiv). The long-term cost-saving benefits are not lost upon Clarke-Hall and he points out the relative cheapness of probation. This leads him to conclude that probation needs far more support from the state. He argues:

> It is none the less obvious that ultimately it will be necessary to place the whole matter upon a more systematic basis and under one direct control. (Clarke-Hall 1917: 108)

He goes on, 'it is incumbent on the state to make larger and better provision' (Clarke-Hall 1917: 119). Like Leeson he writes with one eye on the situation after the war when he envisaged the state would take a far greater role in the running of probation. This was not an unreasonable assumption bearing in mind the increased role the state had assumed in peoples' lives during the war (Crowther 1988, Taylor 1975).

The analysis of the situation offered, as the end of the First World War approached, by both Leeson and the police in London seems to have been one shared by the Home Office. Their records show that the Department was also concerned about the increase in juvenile crime, sufficient for them to write to various Police Districts seeking explanations. The replies focused largely on the lack of parental control with fathers away in the forces and mothers out at work. Other concerns such as the cinema were also mentioned, as were such things as gaming machines and air rifles.[4] Many of the solutions offered by the police entailed the extension of the availability of corporal punishment. William Clarke-Hall offered a slightly different solution in his correspondence with the Home Office; he wrote, 'I find that probation is of little use if the boys are allowed to remain in the same neighbourhood, as they quickly succumb again to temptation by their former companions.'[5] The solution he suggested was that boys should be boarded out to the provinces to work in munitions factories and so get away from the bad influences in London.

Much of the analysis offered by Leeson and Clarke-Hall seems to have been accepted at the Home Office. At a speech to the Congregation Union in Birmingham on 3 October 1916, G. A. Aitken, who was an Assistant Secretary (and head of the Children's Branch) at the Home Office, argued that the increase in juvenile crime was a product of wartime conditions. He advocated more use of probation and short terms at Industrial or Reformatory Schools. He also suggested more use could be made of corporal punishment.[6] Traditional solutions of good influences, the character forming potential of corporal punishment and the removing of the offender from bad influences were the solutions to juvenile crime.

Perhaps because of this, the use of corporal punishment during the war years increased dramatically (Home Office 1938a). In contrast, the use of probation during the war remained remarkably constant. Home Office figures for the number of offenders placed on probation immediately before and after the war are shown below[7]:

1908	–	8,023
1909	–	8,962
1910	–	10,223
1911	–	9,521
1912	–	11,219
1913	–	11,071
1919	–	9,655
1920	–	10,735
1921	–	10,293

The London Diocesan Branch of CETS also notes a similar consistency throughout the war in their work with adult offenders. Fortunately, their figures go right through the war years and show 1,294 cases in 1913, 1,332 in 1914, 837 in 1915, 1,328 in 1916, 1,472 in 1917, 1,780 in 1918 and 1,757 in 1919. Unlike the Home Office their figures show a rise immediately after the war.[8] In the Juvenile Courts in Britain 3,568 were placed on probation in 1910; this rose to 6,781 in 1916 but fell to 5,812 in 1924.[9] Although the figures fluctuate quite noticeably, there is no discernable pattern, certainly not one of a steadily increasing use being made of probation by the Courts.

In his analysis of crime in the Great War, Mannheim (1941) pointed out that the number of police officers fell by 10 per cent and those left had to give a great deal of consideration to civil defence measures, suggesting that the detection of petty crime may not have been their major consideration (Mannheim 1941: 97). He also argued that there was a subtle shift in the types of crime committed over the war period with crimes that were a product of war conditions, such as pilfering, handling stolen goods and offences connected with prostitution, becoming more significant after 1916. As regards the increase in juvenile crime noted in the Police Reports, Mannheim speculates that this increase may have not been that great. He writes:

> To some extent this increase may have been more statistical than real. Owing to the absence of their husbands, many mothers, unable or unwilling to deal with naughty children, are said to have brought them before the juvenile courts instead of trying to exercise proper discipline at home. (Mannheim 1941: 121)

He continues by pointing out that 4–5 million men had gone into the forces leaving fewer people at home to offend (Mannheim 1941: 98). He argues that in wartime conditions many prosecutions of juveniles were a result of concern about the youngster's home circumstances. The consequences of which were:

> For the choice between making a Probation Order and committal to an Approved School the home conditions of the offender will in most cases be decisive, and it has already been indicated that the absence of fathers and elder brothers, the war work of mothers, and similar factors frequently force the Juvenile Courts to prefer Committal to a Probation Order. (Mannheim 1941: 144)

This would imply that after the war the use of probation might be expected to increase as home conditions improved and probation officers were released from the Forces. As we have seen from the statistics, that did not happen.

Although the numbers placed on probation remained fairly consistent throughout the war, there is some evidence to suggest that probation itself did not have a 'good war'. In 1916, for example, the Home Office received a number of deputations from the State Children's Association. They met with the Home Secretary in February 1916 and again in July 1917 and following the latter meeting they sent a memo outlining the problems:

> Reports of children's courts procedures and the evidence of experts show that the probation system – admittedly so valuable where it is well administered – is neither being used fully nor as suitably as should be the case.
>
> 1. Too often the probation officer is an elderly police court missionary, fully occupied with other work, uninstructed in child psychology and with little if any knowledge of modern reformative methods and efforts, and is, therefore, unwilling to accept suggestion.
>
> 2. He is often the paid officer of some religious or philanthropic body, receiving in addition from children's courts a capitation fee for each juvenile probationer places in his charge. This naturally makes him wishful to take as

many cases as possible, and makes him in desirous of using the help of voluntary workers, whose attendance at the court is discouraged.

    3. Not only so but educated voluntary helpers would be reluctant to work under the direction of persons whose outlook is narrow and of a past generation.[10]

In fact one of the members of the deputation, Henry Bentnick, a colleague of C. E. B. Russell (see above), is recorded as stating that 'the probation system … had never been satisfactory and had now utterly broken down'.[11] The response of the Home Office to these deputations was interesting; the minute notes:

> I think there is some grounds for the criticism of the present workings of the probation system. The Secretary of the C.E.T.S. and the P.C. Mission told me recently that they are not satisfied that their missionaries who act as probation officers in various places are always fit for the work, and they are appointing more women. The figures show that in some of the larger towns probation officers have more cases than they can supervise properly.[12]

Although probation was probably not the only organization to suffer a huge reduction in staff during the war, we have already seen some of these criticisms before. They were in evidence during the two earlier reviews of probation (see above) and appear to have remained pertinent.

    However, Mair and Burke see the potential for growth after the war. Although as they note, '(i)t is all too clear that the Home Office did not wish to get heavily involved in the new probation system' (Mair and Burke 2012: 42), they see probation attracting influential support from the likes of Cecil Leeson and William Clarke-Hall. The creation of NAPO also helped so the basis was there for growth once peace was restored.

The *Juvenile* Organizations Committee Report of 1920

We have already seen how concerns about the level of juvenile crime were sufficient for the Home Office to send a circular to various groups including the police to illicit their views as to the reasons.[13] The Metropolitan Police reply included:

> I may point out that when the war is over and the parents return to their normal sphere of influence, the general conditions obtaining in the community will be less favourable to the development of juvenile crime and it may reasonably be hoped that the increase now observed is merely a passing phase which is definitely attributable to the conditions now obtaining.[14]

It would appear that this was not an analysis the Home Office shared. The problem was more significant so they looked to the various youth organizations for a solution. For instance, the national Executive Committee of the Boys Brigade wrote to the Home Office telling them of a resolution passed at their meeting offering to help juvenile offenders whereby, 'by taking a personal interest in their improvement and welfare, and, where found suitable by admitting them as members of the Boys Brigade'.[15] The Home Office were impressed and wrote to a number of Justices' Clerks in the large cities asking them to bring the offer to the attention of probation officers and magistrates. A similar offer was made by Baden Powell when he wrote to the Home Office in 1916 saying that the scouts would adopt an 'urchin' as an honorary member.[16]

One of the country's most celebrated youth leaders was C. E. B. Russell,[17] and as Chief Inspector of Industrial and Reformatory Schools he was one of the most influential experts on juvenile crime within the Home Office. He set out his views on the matter at a lecture at Oxford University the following year (see Russell 1917). His analysis of the problem differs in a number of subtle ways to that offered by Leeson and Clarke-Hall. For instance Russell said:

> There is really no indication that the boyhood of the nation is forming definitely anti-social and criminal habits. But the truth is that for many reasons opportunities for misapplied energy on the part of young people are much greater than before the war. (Russell 1917: 4)

Here Russell contradicts comments made in the years leading up to the war about the physical deterioration of the urban working class (Bray 1908, Holmes 1908, Masterman 1901). He goes on, ' "crimes" of the less fortunate,...., are in the main expressions of animal vigour, of exuberance of spirits, of energy misapplied for want of legitimate outlet' (Russell 1917: 5). Russell does not regard crime as being a result of fathers being away in the forces or mothers working in munitions factories. Instead he argues that young criminals 'come from homes where both parents, whether at home or not, are weak, irresponsible, slack, idle, and unsteady, teaching their offspring no moral standard and possibly paying occasional visits to prison' (Russell 1917: 7). His stress is on relationships within the family and particularly the importance of parental example.

The solutions to juvenile crime he proposed reflected his own experience as a Boys Club leader in his earlier life (Russell 1906, 1910). He writes:

> If boyish delinquency is to be checked, it must be recognized by all concerned that for our adolescent population healthy physical exercise and games, both in and out of doors, are not a luxury, but an absolute necessity. (Russell 1917: 11)

For every boy over the age of 12 or 13, he advocated that they 'should be made a member of some organization which will provide for him healthy exercise, harmless amusement, fresh interest, discipline, and, most important of all, a religious motive' (Russell 1917: 11). Although his analysis of the problem is slightly different, his solution of providing good influences helping to build character are echoed in much of the analysis we have already seen.

The Home Office decided to address the problem and convened a conference in the hope of bringing the disparate groups together to come up with some proposals.[18] The Junior Minister at the Home Office, Herbert Samuel, was to attend, as was C. E. B. Russell. The Conference took place in October of 1916 and proposed the establishment of a national group called the Juvenile Organisations Committee to be appointed by the Home Secretary to consider and report on:

> in view of the officially reported increase in juvenile delinquency, what steps could be taken to strengthen and extend the work of voluntary agencies concerned with the welfare of boys and girls. The Committee have been and are mainly occupied in developing schemes for increasing the provision of facilities for the healthy recreation of young people, which they consider to be of prime importance in relation to the prevention of juvenile delinquency. They have, however, made enquiries from time to time into the procedure in juvenile courts and as to the administration of the *Probation of Offenders Act 1907*. (Board of Education 1920: 5)

Although originally appointed by the Home Office, the Committee was transferred to the Board of Education in 1919 and it was under their auspices that it finally reported in 1920. The remit of the Committee, as quoted above and its membership reveal just how much the approaches of people like Leeson and Russell had permeated the officials and politicians at both the Home Office and Board of Education. The committee was chaired by J. Herbert Lewis who was a Minister at the Board of Education and of the other twenty-six members, thirteen are described as representatives from various youth organizations. These ranged from Baden-Powell of the Boy Scouts, to representatives of the Church Lads Brigade, the Boys Brigade and the Liverpool Union of Boys Clubs. Also on the Committee was a representative of the Church of England Temperance Society, representatives of the London County Council and the Home Office. The Committee appointed a Sub-Committee to look at the work of the Juvenile Courts whose membership included William Clarke-Hall; it was chaired by the Home Office representative. The fact that the Committee was also regarded as falling within the remit of the Board of Education was something of a portent for the future and indicated where some regarded the solutions to the problems of juvenile crime were properly to be found.

The Report focused heavily on poverty as a cause of juvenile crime, in particular overcrowding. The Committee concluded, 'The evil effects upon the child's nature of overcrowding, both in the home and in congested districts, must be included among indirect causes of law-breaking'. The Report went on to argue that the figures show that poverty does not cause crime but 'they do show definitely that, while there is more theft than any other form of law breaking, this is markedly so among those from very poor homes' (Board of Education 1920: 11). The Report also looked at physical or mental defect and noted how:

> Many of the children brought before the courts are physically and mentally defective, sometimes both. However; frequently defects are only discovered in the case of children sentenced to a punishment which demands a medical examination, e.g., birching or committal to a reformatory or industrial school. (Board of Education 1920: 12)

The Committee, accordingly, recommended a broadening of the use of medical and psychological examinations for young people appearing before the court:

> Without doubt, many children who appear before the magistrates would, if examined by an expert, show some degree of mental retardation; a doctor would often give evidence that the child was suffering from some disease which tended to make the offender irritable, passionate, and at times, perhaps, hysterical or even temporarily insane he would point out how peculiarly liable are boys and girls in early puberty to commit acts which suggest they for the time lost all sense of responsibility and control. A psychological study of the child would in many cases diagnose the reason for so many of the acts which lead to court proceedings, and would certainly assist the magistrate in deciding the effective method of treating the child. (Board of Education 1920: 12)

The suggestion that a psychological 'study' was needed to assist the court in sentencing was novel, as was the idea that puberty in itself may be a cause of criminal behaviour.

The Report also retained much that was traditional and perhaps not surprisingly it considered the membership of clubs as particularly appropriate for juvenile offenders as was the role of religious organizations. Probation officers were seen as having a very useful role here, the Report comments:

> The undisciplined lad is often unwelcome in the Sunday School as in the club, but his needs claim attention there. Probation officers and others who deal

with the difficult boy might well help him to get into closer touch with his own religious organisations. (Board of Education 1920: 15)

The power of the influence of character as a solution to juvenile offending was also covered in the Report, and again the probation officer was seen as crucial. It commented:

The value of probation depends not only upon the suitability of the case to which it is applied, but also in a very large measure upon the personality of the probation officer and the opportunities he has of exercising a positive influence for good in the lives of the boys committed to his charge. (Board of Education 1920: 31)

However, the Report added a new dimension to the probation officer's role when it commented:

Here, as elsewhere, there is need for individual case treatment and a wider outlook over the whole history of the boy and the prospects for his future. (Board of Education 1920: 25)

A phrase like 'case treatment' is likely to suggest a number of things to the modern reader that would not have been understood by those who wrote the sentence, but the phrase does suggest a move to a more individualized, scientific notion of 'treatment'. This is particularly relevant when it is remembered that the Report also made reference to a psychological 'study' to assist the court.

The Home Office records for the time also show a good deal of negotiation going on between the Home Office and the Board of Education over the transfer of the Committee to the Board of Education. The clinching factor in this was the *Education Act of 1918* (the so-called Fisher Act), which meant that it was the responsibility of the Local Education Authority to provide sports and outdoor activities for children.[19] Indeed it seems that Fisher himself had lobbied the Home Office to move the Committee to his Department. When the Report was sent to the Home Office for approval, they were 'interested' in the recommendations but commented, 'the Committee was hardly constituted in such a way that its recommendations can be taken as basis for legislation'.[20]

Although the Report recommended legislative change to vary and extend the *Children Act of 1908* and the *Probation of Offenders Act of 1907*, the Home Office were very reluctant and instead wanted to deal with the shortcomings of the existing system via Circulars. The chief civil servant at the Home Office, Edward Troup, also noted the Committee's recommendation that courts should be able to use the services of a psychologist and was not at all impressed with the suggestion. His handwritten notes on his copy of the Report include, 'surely something might be done to convince them to omit the "expert psychologist" from the (illegible) recommendations on page 31. Do they mean a psychologist or a real scientific man who (illegible) experiments on monkeys and pigeons?'.[21]

In the aftermath of the Great War the Home Office was under pressure from a number of sources to instigate change in the treatment of juvenile offenders. In 1921 the Howard League drew up the *Probation, Certified Schools and Borstal Institutions Bill* which was put before Parliament as a Private Members Bill. This Bill included a number of the recommendations of the JOC, such as the ability to fine and place on probation without recording a conviction and the creation of local probation authorities. It also recommended that probation officers should be trained. The Home Office officials commented, 'this Bill must certainly not be allowed to make progress',[22] though no explanation is offered as to why. These proposals were shortly to be taken up by the Home Office but at this particular point in time they seem to have been given very short shrift. As Burke and Mair write, The Howard League were 'a consistent and formidable supporter of Probation' (Mair and Burke 2012: 20) and by this point had been lobbying for the expansion of probation for forty years or so.

Those same Home Office files of the period include a number of articles collected from the press, which were critical of the probation system. Amongst those was one in *The Times* which commented:

> Although the *Children Act, 1908*, has been in operation for more than a decade, the reforms of which it was thought to be the prelude have only partially materialized.[23]

The pressure for legislative change was resisted at the Home Office, and no proposals were forthcoming. However, they did share some of the views expressed in the Report and lobbied the War Office to release men from military duties who could work in the Boys Clubs. In a letter to the War Office dated 22 March 1919 they wrote requesting the release of fifty men from military duty, 'who have had experience of work among boys in connection with Boys Clubs, Boys Brigades and similar organisations … [as this] … .is one of the most effective methods of checking juvenile delinquency, in view of the change in industrial conditions, the dislocation of employment, and the present unrest amongst young people, it is especially important to maintain the work of these organisations'.[24]

Probation reviewed

In her survey of probation's history Bochel (1976) also notes the criticism probation began to attract after the war. She notes how the *Criminal Justice Administration Act of 1914* had empowered the Home Office to make grants to various organizations to be used towards the payment of probation officers. The result of this was:

> The latter (i.e. the local Benches) appear to have been only too glad to be able to appoint a probation officer with little effort and without incurring much expense for their local authority. (Bochel 1976: 72)

The appointment of probation officers was still only spreading slowly and, as the figures quoted earlier show, the use of probation remained stubbornly low and consistent.

Probation was also attracting some powerful critics, one of whom was Sir Evelyn Ruggles-Brise who, as chair of the Prison Commissioners, had overseen the prison system since 1895. He was also president of the Central Committee of Discharged Prisoners' Aid Societies and it was in this capacity that he wrote to the Home Office in 1919. The society had passed a resolution calling for a conference to consider the whole future of probation, 'which, in the opinion of the Committee, requires "drastic reorganisation"'.[25] The reasons he gives for probation's failure are interesting. He writes:

> There is, however, as I understand, a strong movement in progress for the constitution of a Society of probation officers, and for bringing the whole system of Probation directly under the control of the state. Probation as an arm of the penal law, is far too grave and important a thing to be left to the discretion of individual magistrates, or to the enterprise of private individuals, good, bad, or indifferent. It is, in my opinion, primarily and essentially a concern of the State to just the same extent as the control of the Magistracy and of the Prison administration. If, as I hope, this duty on the part of the State is recognized and Probation officers are bound together into one body under Sate control, there would be no difficulty in securing their representation on the National body.[26]

Not only does he argue that the state should control the work of probation officers, he also goes on to argue that the state should have much more control over the appointment of probation officers. It is a view which resonates with that offered by Clarke-Hall (1917) but for the time being at least the independent role of the societies and their missionaries seems to have been widely accepted, particularly at the Home Office. It has to be said that at this point the Home

Office were reluctant to become responsible for the management and funding of the system of probation officers operating at the time.

Although the Home Office remained committed to the societies and their missionaries, they were regularly being lobbied by those societies for an increase in the grant they paid towards the cost of the police court missionaries. In 1919 the Southwark Branch of the Church of England Temperance Society wrote to the Home Office asking for an increase in the grant as they were finding that their missionaries were spending far more time working in the Police Courts and so had no time for the other work of the society. A little while later the individual police court missionaries of the same CETS Branch wrote to the Home Office saying that they were not able to live on the salaries being paid by the CETS. The missionaries also asked for the establishment of a system of superannuation. The Home Office responded by writing to the London Branch of the CETS telling them to pay their officers more than the £200 per annum they were currently being paid. In the following year the Home Office was lobbied again, this time by both of the London Branches of the CETS asking for an increase in the grant to pay their missionaries as the cost of living had risen so much. On this occasion the Home Office agreed to pay.[27] When it came to finances, the CETS were increasingly in something of a bind. For instance, at their Committee meeting in December 1920 they debated asking the Home Office for their court missionaries to be included in the Civil Service Bonus Scheme, but chose not to do so as

> if this step became a necessity, the Home Office would probably prefer to appoint their own probation officers and there would be no undertaking that the missionaries of the Society would be taken over and appointed.[28]

They were thus in a position where probation work was becoming a much larger part of their work but insisted on their religious and independent working basis despite being increasingly reliant on the Home Office grant to continue with that work. On the other hand, if the Home Office did become more involved and decided to take over more of the operation of probation, as was being mooted by some, a substantial proportion of their work would disappear.

In the meantime a new group entered the fray. This was the National Association of Probation Officers, which had been set up in 1912 on the recommendation of the Home Office following the 1910 review of probation. King (1958) argues that much of the impetus for the Home Office's actions were due to the activities of NAPO when she writes:

> The Association gathered information from its members and presented the results to the Home Office to show a lack of organisation, uniformity or apparent

purpose in many Branches of the Service. The outcome of this effort was the Departmental Committee on the Training, Appointment and Payment of probation officers. (King 1958: 213)

Although NAPO was not alone in criticizing the probation system by the early 1920s, it took a particular view on the future of probation and advocated that view to the Home Office. It is also worth keeping in mind that King's work was published under the auspices of NAPO so she might have been tempted to over emphasize its influence at this time; for example, Jarvis describes it at this time as 'a sickly child' (Jarvis 1972: 31). Jarvis also argues that NAPO did not enjoy the full support of the missionaries 'since it seemed to them self-seeking and in any case connected with the secular state' (Jarvis 1972: 25).

On a more day-to-day basis the Home Office were becoming aware of other problems with the probation system. Two of their own London based children's probation officers, Miss Croker-King and Miss Cheshire, who worked in the Old Street Juvenile Court presided over by William Clarke-Hall, became engaged in a battle with the Magistrate where the Home Office were forced to mediate.[29] Clarke-Hall had initiated a scheme of volunteer probation officers as the two full-time officers could not cope with the level of work generated by his Court. The full-time officers objected but the Home Office were more sympathetic to Clarke-Hall, particularly when he pointed out that 'if the voluntary principle is abandoned, an enormously increased number of paid officials will be necessary throughout the country to carry on probation work amongst children efficiently'.[30] Clarke-Hall went on in the same letter to request the transfer from his court of Miss Croker-King and Miss Cheshire. On the other hand, the Home Office were not at all sympathetic to Clarke-Hall when they learnt from the officers that he had placed a catholic child on probation with a catholic officer rather than with one of the children's officers. This running battle continued until 1922 when the full-time officers were transferred. Again, in this example there is evidence of the Home Office's reluctance to get involved particularly if it was likely that extra funds would be required.

Nonetheless, these difficulties and criticism showed that the probation system was in difficulty and it was sufficient for the Home Office to appoint the committee King (1958) refers to. The Home Office seemed determined that the focus of the Committee should be confined to considering the 'training, appointment and payment of probation officers' only (Home Office 1922) rather than look at some of the wider concerns which had been raised. The Committee was appointed in 1920 and was chaired by Sir John Baird. Its membership included Sidney Harris, who was by then Head of the Children's Branch at the Home Office; Miss N. Ivimy, one of the original Children's Probation Officers appointed by the Home Office in 1907; and Mr T. Fry, a magistrate. The Committee stuck closely to the 'brief' given it by the Home Office which suggests that as far as the Home Office were concerned the system did not need radical overhaul as some had suggested but simply to be placed 'on a better footing'.[31] Jarvis refers to it as a 'small scale domestic committee set up to assess the current situation of the probation system and see how it might be developed' (Jarvis 1972: 34). It reported in 1922.

As far as the Committee was concerned, court's failure to use probation was due simply to magistrates being unaware of its benefits rather than any inherent structural problems with probation. The suggestion made by Clarke-Hall and Ruggles-Brise that probation officers should be paid for directly out of central funds was rejected on the grounds that 'the relationship he (the probation officer that is, even though most of the children's probation officers were women) has been able to establish with the probationer, who looks upon him as a friend, not as an official' (Home Office 1922: 7). This then led to a debate about the continued role of the Temperance Societies in the provision of officers and again the Committee came out in favour of the status quo. The Report also considered the qualities and training required to be a probation officer and stated:

> Some of these witnesses urged the need for higher educational attainments and more specialised training. (Home Office 1922: 13)

This suggestion was rejected as, 'it is doubtful whether a probation service organised on the lines we consider desirable would provide opportunities or prospects which would usually attract candidates of university training' (Home Office 1922: 14). The Report held to the attitudes which we have already come across; that it was personal character and influence that turned offenders away from crime rather than anything that could be taught. For instance the Report comments, '... while we attach importance to educational qualifications, we consider that personal qualities are paramount' (*HO45/10346/142801 1906*).

Some more minor changes were proposed in the Report such as the payment of probation officers via fees or by the case should stop. Increases in officers' salaries were also recommended, though, it cautioned that setting the salaries too high might mean that officers did not join purely for the love of the work. The cheapness of the system was not lost on the Committee when they commented that, 'the cost of the system to public funds, amounting to about £27,000 a year is remarkably small' (Home Office 1922: 21). In effect the Report simply mirrored the stance the Home Office had taken in the previous discussions about the funding and management of probation.

When the Report arrived at the Home Office for consideration Troup's responded so:

> It will not satisfy the Societies which desire to have a statutorily organised and state funded Probation System for the whole country, but I think that was a bad proposal on the merits, and in any case quite impractical in present circumstances. In the report no immediate additional charge on the Treasury is proposed except perhaps a small annual sum for the salary of the Secretary to the Advisory Committee.[32]

Clearly the Home Office were trying hard to resist pressure to create a national system of probation which they would be responsible for organizing and the state responsible for funding. The dire economic state of the country would also have been a consideration here as many government departments were enduring considerable cutbacks, if not being completely dismantled (Taylor 1975: 183). The fact that probation was spared these cutbacks is significant and perhaps a reflection on its perceived ability to save money in the long term.

Once in the public domain, the Report attracted criticism largely on the grounds of its timidity. For instance, the Howard League had been lobbying throughout this period for a national system of probation with qualifications for probation officers. Their Annual Report for 1921–1922 notes the 'narrow terms of reference' of the Committee and that: 'The Report contains not a single recommendation concerning the training of probation officers.'[33] However, they also went on to note approvingly 'the appointment of a permanent Voluntary Committee, having a paid secretary, to advise the Home Secretary on the development of probation and its general administration'.[34] In its annual report for the following year the Howard League noted with disgust that the Committee had met only twice in the previous eight months.[35] On the other hand, the CETS were very pleased with the report. The London Diocesan Branch noted:

> The Committee deprecated turning Probation Officers into a class of civil servants…..Thus the religious principles for which the C.E.T.S. stands are really vindicated, and the Committee put on record how much they have been impressed by the valuable work being done by our Society and the high character of many our Missionaries.[36]

It perhaps bears repeating that by this time the mission to the police court was about fifty years old with its roots firmly in the nineteenth century.

Although government and Home Office policy for probation remained true to its roots, probation practice was being subject to some very powerful influences for change at this time. Nineteenth-century views of social work as defined by the COS were giving way to a new approach (Timms 1964, Woodroofe 1962, Yelloly 1980). Psychologists particularly in the USA were writing specifically about the treatment of criminals (Bennett 1981, Platt 1969, Rose 1985). We have already seen Troup's scepticism about expert psychologists in his reaction to the JOC Report (Board of Education 1920) but that was increasingly being seen as old fashioned as was the idea that religion and character turned criminals away from crime.

Rose notes comments made by Margery Fry, Secretary of the Howard League at the time:

> In 1924, she said, of about 250 full-time officers over 60 percent were agents of voluntary societies appointed on their recommendation and partially controlled and paid by them. Two-thirds of these were Police Court Mission appointments, and in the London adult courts they were all employed by this society. The results of this were that, in practice, there was a religious test of entry and Church of England communicants were favoured. (Rose 1961: 147)

As Rose suggests magistrates tended to accept police court missionary applicants as there was no other qualification for the job, and of course they were cheaper as the societies paid at least a third of the salaries.

To find out why these established practices were being seen by some as out of date, it is necessary to move outside of probation to consider contemporary writing on social work and psychology. Both discourses moved on a great deal in the period immediately after the Great War, and the mid-1920s saw the publication of key texts in both fields that were to have a major impact on probation.

Social work's claim to be a profession

Even the Settlement movement, a close relative of the police court missionaries, moved on in the new century (Briggs and Macartney 1984). It also became, for some, an almost overtly political call to arms and a means to lift the working class out of poverty. Yelloly writes of Toynbee Hall that by 1914, 'the early belief in personal influence had begun to wane, and there was a growing interest in social investigation leading to social reform rather than a practical philanthropy' (Yelloly 1980: 42). In 1920 the future prime minister Clement Attlee wrote *The Social Worker* whilst residing at Toynbee Hall. In this book he links together social work, social service and a quest for social justice. Social service he defines so:

It is not as a movement concerned alone with the material, with housing and drains, clinics and feeding centres, gas and water, but is the expression of the desire for social justice, for freedom and beauty, and for the better apportionment of all the things that make up a good life.[37]

This was a vision for social work quite distinct to that of the COS, of whose philosophy he was critical. He writes:

The strict division of cases into deserving and undeserving, or into Poor Law and non – Poor Law, was unacceptable to many who were inclined to doubt the validity of these categories and the scale of values upon which such discrimination was based. (Attlee 1920: 63)

On the other hand, Attlee seems to have had no qualms with the methods of the COS, even if he opposed their underlying philosophy, for instance he advocates the case record and their ideas of investigation.

In his book Attlee describes probation officers as social workers but so too were teachers, sanitary inspectors, health visitors, housing inspectors, etc. The basic quality required by all was not character but, 'The first qualification for anyone who wishes to engage in social work is sympathy' (Attlee 1920: 126). On its own this was also insufficient, social work also required training, as those practising it need an understanding of the circumstances in which they are working. He argues, 'A strong personality will work wonders, but the more forcefulness is combined with thought and knowledge the better' (Attlee 1920: 152). He envisaged a system of training that included practical and first hand experience of social conditions. Combined with this he recommended classes in such things as social and industrial history, social philosophy, social psychology, politics, etc.

Woodroofe (1962), in her history of social work, sees Mary Richmond's book *Social Diagnosis* (1917) as crucial in the development of social work as a skilled profession. Indeed it is Richmond, she argues, who is usually credited with first writing about social work in a way that would be understood by a modern social worker. Although *Social Diagnosis* was published in the USA Woodroofe describes Richmond as 'a figure to whom modern caseworkers – and in fact all social workers – acknowledge a profound debt' (Woodroofe 1962: 101).

Mary Richmond was not a social worker herself; she was an administrator for one of the large New York charities but based her work on her observations of the social workers that she supervised. The problem was, as Woodroofe acknowledges, Richmond's work was rather thin on what the actual treatment should be.

With the publication of *Social Diagnosis*, casework not only emerged as a social technique, but the title of the book suggested a new kind of professional relationship between caseworker and client. This was rather misleading, because, critically examined, the relationship as envisaged by Miss Richmond was still on a friendly, naïve, unanalysed basis. (Woodroofe 1962: 113)

In fact Richmond's (1917) work focuses on social work as a process, and in contrast to Attlee, for example, sees it as a highly individualized one. She does not regard the role of social work as improving the lot of the working class generally. She writes of social workers:

A majority of them are engaged in case work – in work, that is, which has for its immediate aim the betterment of individuals in families, one by one, as distinguished from their betterment in the mass. (Richmond 1917: 25)

Richmond is closer to the COS where social work is based on individuals in their families. It also attempts to be almost scientific, something the COS tried to be; again she writes:

Social diagnosis is the attempt to arrive at as exact a definition as possible of the social situation and personality of a given client. The gathering of evidence, on investigation, begins the process, the critical examination and comparison of evidence follows, and last comes its interpretation and the definition of the social difficulty. Where one word must describe the whole process, diagnosis is a better word than investigation, though in strict use the former belongs to the end of the process. (Richmond 1917: 62)

In fact much of her book is a detailed survey of how a social worker should go about this process; there are thirteen chapters describing the four-staged process. It is evident that Richmond's work builds on the tradition of the COS and indeed she makes reference to the work of the COS (Richmond 1917: 34). Like the COS she describes the social worker role as being the allocation and coordination of material help to families. She lays at least equal emphasis on family relationships, both within the immediate and the extended family (Richmond 1917: 134). She sees a much wider role for the social worker in healing dysfunctional families, in fact there is clearly a therapeutic element in the relationship between the social worker and her client. Richmond was therefore adamant that a social worker needed more than just personality and that training was essential, although she was a little vague about what form that would take.

Although Attlee's work has largely been ignored and Richmond's, as noted by Woodroofe (1962), has become something of a classic, what both these schools of social work had in common was the belief that the social worker possessed a number of key skills that could be taught and that were transferable from one social worker to another – in other words, the belief that social work was a set of practices that could be taught to another person. These publications and debates also reached those working as probation officers. Rose writes:

> It would be wrong to suggest that anything like a profession of social work had developed by 1921, but there was a growing recognition that it was a job which required training, and to which a professional attitude could be taken. (Rose 1961: 95)

The key to this was, 'Prior investigation, individualisation, and prolonged contact' (Rose 1961: 95). It is likely that many working as probation officers in the early 1920s may not have shared this vision of their role. The police court missionaries, who were soaked in the missionary spirit, still dominated probation and as we have seen they would have seen faith, temperance, mercy, character and crucially personal relationships as their key methods. We therefore have to be aware that probation practice can contain different and even contradictory views of that practice.

The missionaries may instead have been far more sympathetic to the version of their work described by H. H. Ayscough who was Secretary of the Central Church of England Temperance Society and published a short history of the work of that organization in 1923 (Ayscough 1923). He writes that 'the Church of England is daily tackling the lowest strata of our civilisation and seeking to redeem them' (Ayscough 1923). The nearest he gets to a method for that transformation is his description of the missionaries appointed as probation officers following the 1907 Act. He writes of their methods, 'doubtless they were the instruments in the hands of God to bring back to Him many of those to whom they continually ministered' (Ayscough 1923: 69). He regards the Home Office officials as supportive of his approach. He writes:

> At a Mansion House meeting on October 31st 1922, Mr S. W. Harris, of the Home Office, stated that it was his personal opinion that the work was more efficiently carried out by a religious society like the Church of England Temperance Society than by the Government or local authorities, and that much of the work, if not done by the Mission, would not be done at all. (Ayscough 1923: 89)

Thus religious zeal was alive and well at the same time that 'social casework' arrived in Britain from the United States.

In the meantime social work training was increasingly being offered at a number of universities and one of its earliest proponents was Elizabeth

Macadam, who published a major work on the subject in 1925.[38] Like Attlee (1920) and Richmond (1917) she makes a number of arguments in favour of training which were linked to claims that social work was a 'profession'. She writes that 'the complexity of modern conditions has produced a new type of services which for want of a better title we call social work or social administration'. She goes on to argue that 'the number of professional openings which have been created justifies the assertion that social work is a profession in the making' (both Macadam 1925: 22). However, she takes a very broad view of social work training and who would benefit form such a training. She includes in her list:

> The medical student, the future landowner or farmer, the potential businessman or manufacturer, the teacher, will all gain much in the short time at their disposal if they find their way to the school of social study. (Macadam 1925: 198)

Her definition of social work seems therefore to be closer to that of 'work that is social' rather than a definition based on a therapeutic relationship.

As she is less interested in relationships Macadam's view of social work training actually seems closer to what might be termed a 'good liberal education'. In her description of social work training she writes that would-be social workers should spend some of the training getting experience of working class life as, 'the majority of social students belong to a class without personal familiarity with working class conditions'.[39] The course content she describes is wide-ranging and along with practical experience, included formal instruction on: social history, economic history, political economy, social and industrial psychology, political philosophy and social ethics, central and local government, hygiene, and others. Macadam's experience of social work was in the university settlements and perhaps because of this she believed that social work training should be university based and that the practical elements of the training should be arranged via the university.[40] The connection with the university has a number of benefits as

> The association with the university gives the safest guarantee that the training will produce in the future worker that wide, liberal, and philosophic outlook which we regard as essential to every branch of social service. (Macadam 1925: 74)

The university's connection with the settlement offered an ideal opportunity for the practical element of the training. The aim of the practical part of the training being, 'firstly to enable students to gain a thorough and sympathetic understanding of social conditions, and secondly, to give them practice in the various forms of social administration' (Macadam 1925: 81).

As Macadam notes, social work training had been in existence for a number of years. The training of social workers began in the university settlements in the late nineteenth century, whilst the COS also provided some training for their workers. The first institution specifically set up for training was the School of Social Science (1904), which in 1912 became part of the London School of Economics. Progress was slow and Macadam writes that 'for the most part the number of students attracted was very small, and consisted mainly of women attracted to voluntary social work, or of those who were willing and able to risk the chance of not securing suitable salaried posts' (Macadam 1925: 35). The reason being that 'only very partially did social training become recognized as desirable, still less necessary' (Macadam 1925: 35). By 1918 Macadam estimates that about 269 students had diplomas or certificates in social work or social administration, of which thirty-one were men. At the time she was writing social work training was concentrated in six universities, though some courses were not formally part of a university department. The qualifications offered varied, some were designed as training for social work and others were closer to social administration. Macadam also acknowledged that few graduates were attracted to the courses, some applicants had matriculated and others had already had a good deal of experience of social work but few had academic qualifications. She accounts for this so: '… it must be admitted that few social study schools offer courses of such a quality and scope as to attract the first class graduate' (Macadam 1925: 69).

Her book contains outline training courses for a number of social work branches including probation. In this section she is rather scathing of the recent review of probation and writes, 'The question of training is dealt with somewhat meagerly in the Report of the Departmental Committee' (Macadam 1925: 139). She argues that training for probation officers is vital:

> Personality, religious conviction, the missionary spirit, are surely not less efficacious when supplemented by scientific education for a service which requires infinitely more than those much be-lauded qualities, 'kindness, firmness and tact'. (Macadam 1925: 140)

She proposed a two-year training course for probation officers which included many of the areas of study already referred but also included education, problems of adolescence, administration of justice and moral and social hygiene. The course would also involve a practical element, but she goes on to comment that 'care should be taken to introduce the future probation officer to healthy normal life before he is confronted with the abnormal atmosphere of the police court' (Macadam 1925: 142).

What this 'snapshot' of social work practice and training has shown is that in many respects the social work discourse had shifted by the early 1920s from its position in the late nineteenth century. Many of the works we have considered regarded the COS as outdated though their methods still continued even in the more advanced, as it was considered at the time, American social work scene. What had changed was the belief that although social work's claim to professional status was tentative at best, it was certainly an occupation that was believed to require thorough training as a preparation for the work. This would have been difficult for people like Ayscough and other police court missionaries soaked in missionary zeal and the influence of character. The recently completed review of probation (Home Office 1922) shows the Home Office still committed to force of character, the Boys Club movement and religious influences as the means to turn offenders away from crime. Combined with the reaction of CETS it appears that probation was lagging behind contemporary debates about social work practice. In many respects probation practice remained wedded to late nineteenth-century versions of social work.

Psychology and the delinquent

Not only were views of social work changing in the 1920s, psychology was revolutionized during this period as well. This led to a new view of crime and the methods for its treatment that were to have a substantial impact on probation. Nik Rose's (1985) work is a detailed account of the emergence of a psychological discourse. He argues that 'something significant occurred in a period from about 1875 to about 1925' which led to, 'the formation of psychology as a coherent and individuated scientific discourse' (Rose 1985: 3). More than this, the new psychological discourse had a particular end in mind. Rose argues:

> Thus psychology sought to establish itself by claiming its ability to deal with the problems posed for social apparatuses by dysfunctional conduct. (Rose 1985: 5)

This is a view that Vanstone may well have much sympathy with. His history of probation places great importance on a psychological discourse in probation theory and practice and indeed the whole probation operation. He writes early in his book that 'it is an argument of this history that probation theory and practice are an integral part of the story of psychology's dominance in the process of social control' (Vanstone 2007: 45).

The year 1925 is significant as this was when Cyril Burt[41] published his famous study, *The Juvenile Delinquent*.[42] It is tempting to see Burt's work as a 'blinding flash of light' that came out of nowhere to address the problem of juvenile delinquency. It would be more accurate to see him as one of a group of psychologists who were increasingly addressing the treatment of crime generally. There was a real blooming in the 1920s of the application of psychology to the delinquent and as Vanstone (2007) notes it was to have a major impact on probation.

The psychology discipline had received a great deal of attention during and immediately after the Great War. Thousands of former soldiers were still suffering the impact of shell shock after the war and so for the first time many ordinary and even well-to-do people saw first hand the impact of a psychological problem. In particular one that would respond to psychological treatment. As Rose comments, 'in 1921 some 65,000 ex-servicemen were still receiving disability pensions for "shell shock"' (Rose 1985: 182). The war had also seen the extensive use of intelligence testing by the US Army thus bringing masses of data and opportunities for the 'new' psychologists. It was intelligence testing and the measurement of intelligence that formed the basis for much of this 'new psychology' that was to become increasingly significant, particularly through the work of Cyril Burt (1925, and later in this work).

Psychology's influence did not stop there. Psychoanalytical approaches to the discipline were also attracting attention at this time. Freud's work had been translated into English and was beginning to attract an audience. Unlike Burt his work did not attract masses of interest in the criminal justice sector but one of the earliest to propose this approach with offenders was right at the heart of the criminal justice process. Maurice Hamblin Smith's work *The Psychology of the Criminal* was published in 1922 when he was Medical Officer at Birmingham Prison. He claimed twenty-three years' experience in the prisons and came from a long tradition of (occasionally idiosyncratic) prison doctors, which was Europe-wide, writing on the subject of crime causation.[43] As Garland (1988) points out Hamblin Smith's work 'met with much official opposition' but 'there were others, outside the establishment, who were more enthusiastic about the role of psycho-analysis' (Garland 1988: 8). These were heard more and more in the following decade and will be discussed later in this work, but for the moment, Hamblin Smith was ploughing a rather lonely furrow.

Hamblin Smith's work introduces to the criminal field some concepts and practices that were later to be very influential. For instance, he writes early in the book:

A considerable part of the book is devoted to that new development of psychology which is known as psychoanalysis, and to the possible application thereof to the investigation and treatment of offenders.[44]

Interestingly he also comments that 'He (i.e. the author) trusts the book may be of interest to all who are engaged in social work' (Hamblin Smith 1922: 16). He assumes that though social workers should be aware of his work they are not destined to be the ones delivering the treatment that he goes on to describe. For instance Hamblin Smith writes that:

> He believes that no real progress will be made, or is possible, until the system of examination of offenders is greatly extended. Until a court is in the possession of the fullest possible information respecting each case brought before it the work is really being done in the dark. And it is only by skilled examination that the absolutely essential information as to the offenders mental constitution can be obtained. (Hamblin Smith 1922: 17)

These twin concepts of the need for an initial detailed assessment prior to sentence and that that assessment is only available from an expert psychologist are both ideas that psychologists brought to the criminal justice process although, as we have seen, the *Juvenile Offenders Committee Report* (1920) had mooted similar a little earlier.

Hamblin Smith's work is littered with references to Freudian concepts being applied to criminals. For example, 'The theory of the unconscious mind introduces us to a new realm of thought as regards man's conduct, and it profoundly modifies our concept of delinquency' (Hamblin Smith 1922: 95). Not only is the unconscious a vital factor in the causation of crime, so is the 'sex urge', as Hamblin Smith writes:

> There is little doubt in the authors mind that in the majority of cases a repressed complex will be found to have a sex basis. And the resulting conflict may give rise to all kinds of offences. (Hamblin Smith 1922: 101)

Thus we see the psychological discourse, which Rose argues had arrived by 1925 beginning to embrace Freud even in the traditional prison medical apparatus.

However, it was Burt's version of psychology and his book which attracted most attention at the time (see Garland 1988). Like Hamblin Smith, Burt uses the term 'delinquent' in preference to the term 'offender' to denote that he sought to work with more than just legally defined offenders. Like Hamblin Smith, Burt also described himself as a psychologist but their approaches differed in a number of key ways. Cyril Burt was a psychologist employed by the London County Council Education Department when he wrote *The Delinquent*; he was also Professor of Education at London University and was therefore already a well established academic and practitioner when it was published. Early on in his book he sets out the parameters of his work. He writes:

> Delinquency I regard as nothing but an outstanding sample – dangerous perhaps and extreme, but none the less typical – of common childish naughtiness. (Burt 1925: preface)

This resonates with the views of people like Russell who were writing nearly twenty years earlier. However, he goes on in a mode which has more in common with Hamblin Smith; for instance:

> A crime is not a detached or separable fact, self contained and self subsisting. It is only a symptom. It is a mental symptom with a mental origin. And there is now a definite body of ascertained knowledge, tracing mental symptoms to their causes, just as medical knowledge tracks down the sources of bodily disorders, and so can prescribe for each its proper treatment or appropriate care. (Burt 1925: 4)

Burt bases his work on his study of 200 juvenile delinquent cases referred to him at the Education Department. He also used a control of 400 non-delinquent children. He describes his methods as a combination of detailed case studies and intelligence testing. His book is full of case studies. Earlier writers such as Russell and Rigby (1906), Russell (1910) had used detailed accounts of the individual stories told him by youngsters. The difference is that Burt's approach was now called a case study and was far more than a simple recounting of a life story. It is interesting to note that Richmond's (1917) individualized approach to social work also included many case studies.

There are two key conclusions made by Burt that were to become almost truisms in probation practice for many years. Firstly, that delinquency is a product of a number of factors working together; the environment, the home and the individual. Secondly that the most important influence on a child is its environment, but here Burt means the family environment. He writes:

> Crime is assigned to no single universal cause, not yet to two or three: it springs from a wide variety, and usually from a multiplicity, of alternative and converging influences. (Burt 1925: 599)

These factors combine together to create the delinquent, Burt writes:

> Heredity appears to operate, not directly through the transmission of a criminal disposition as such, but rather indirectly, through such constitutional conditions such as dull or defective intelligence, an excitable or unbalanced temperament,

or an over-development of single primitive instinct. Of environmental conditions, those obtaining outside the home are far less important than those obtaining within it; and within it, material conditions, such as poverty, are far less important than moral conditions, such as ill discipline, vice, and, most of all, the child's relations with his parents. Physical defects have barely half the weight of psychological and environmental. Psychological factors, whether due to hereditary or to environment, are supreme both in number and in strength over all the rest. (Burt 1925: 607)

Traditional physical causes of delinquency are not abandoned (Burt 1925: 248) and he also asserts that low intelligence is a factor in causing delinquency. Both have a long tradition in criminological writing that go back to the late nineteenth century (Pick 1989, Radzinowicz and Hood 1986). At the same Burt brings in new causes such as the family, particularly relationships within the family between parents and children as in his explanations for delinquency. Burt selects for particular attention the way children are disciplined within the home. He writes, 'Home discipline may be too strict, too lenient, or virtually non-existent'. He goes on to qualify that even further when he writes that:

Most frequently of all, and most disastrous, is the union of license and severity within the same home, in the person of the same capricious parent.[45]

Burt's work makes very little reference to Freud or any of his school in his work. He sees psychoanalysis as suitable only for the gravely psychotic of which there was only one in his survey (Burt 1925: 594). Later editions though discuss it more (Burt 1944: 619) and seem to imply a slightly wider role for psychoanalysis.

Burt envisages a clear role for the probation officer in his scheme for the treatment of juvenile delinquents and had quite definite views about their role and training. Burt writes:

As a rule, the probation officer for children is a woman picked for strength of character, experience of charitable work, and an acquaintance with delinquent children and their home surroundings. But her duties are in their essence professional: they need a specialist knowledge and a specialist skill. Hence, it is eminently desirable that such an officer should have received, wherever possible, an intense training in the psychology of delinquency and child life. (Burt 1925: 194)

He was therefore in favour of probation officer training but the training that he advocated was both different and narrower to that advocated by Macadam (1925). His claims for a professional status for probation officers must also have appealed to many probation officers and suggests an opportunity for something of an alliance between his version of psychology and probation.

Interestingly the above quote would not exclude a missionary approach to probation practice. However, the relationship between the trained probation officer and psychologist that he envisaged was not an equal partnership; again Burt writes:

> One hopeful sign is the readiness of probation officers to consult the psychologist, not merely about the causes of delinquency in any case, but also for scientific assistance in deciding what kind of occupation is best fitted to the child's peculiar bent. (Burt 1925: 202)

The psychologist had two special areas of expertise where she or he would lead the work of the probation officer. These were all things connected with the family dynamic and suitability for a particular occupation,[46] both of which were areas probation officers and even police court missionaries had been working at for some time. Hamblin Smith did not share this co-working approach in his Freudian based psychology.

In his account of 'new psychology' that emerged in the 1920s Nik Rose also discusses the Tavistock Square Clinic which he claims had 'struck up an intimate relationship with the probation service' (Rose 1985: 199). The Tavistock was one of the earliest Child Guidance Clinics that had recently been opened. These were based on an American model where psychologists, psychiatrists and social workers worked together to provide treatment and assessment. The first in Britain was opened in 1927 and led to the psychological expert having an 'increasing scope provided by links with schools, courts, social work and other specialised agencies, which made it possible to regard the clinic as the fulcrum of a comprehensive programme of mental welfare' (Rose 1985: 203).

What these psychologies did have in common was an explicit interest in, even a reaching out to, probation officers. Thus, the 'new psychology' proposed by people like Burt and those working in the newly opened clinics began to work closely with various social workers and probation officers. As Rose points out:

> Thus psychology entered into an alliance with welfare workers, providing the rationale for a new theory and practice of social work.[47]

By claiming an 'expert role' the psychologist required that the probation officer or social worker working with her should also be qualified so as to support that 'expert role' which has resonances with what Vanstone terms the 'semi professionalization of the probation service' (Vanstone 2007: 67) at this time. This naturally suited those who advocated a training scheme for probation officers, hence a formidable alliance began to form based on the need for probation officer training.

At the time of the publication of Burt's study probation was no more important and popular in the courts than it had been in 1907. The numbers placed on probation remained constant and the criticisms it had attracted after, and even before, the Great War had not been addressed. We have seen that the Home Office officials were not sympathetic to any of the new approaches offered by psychologists (or social work trainers). The links between probation and psychology were, for the moment, very much at a grass roots level and largely based in London where a number of the new Child Guidance Clinics were located. That is how matters would have remained had there not been a shift at the Home Office and a major piece of legislation introduced resulting in space being created for the new discourses to move into.

The Criminal Justice Act of 1925 and the revolutionizing of probation

The latest review of probation (Home Office 1922) had produced nothing that was particularly new despite this being the third such review in just twelve years. Accusations of timidity (see, for example, Rose 1961) and the Report's poor reception may have been a little unfair considering the financial state of the country at the time which would preclude very much extra money being found. Things moved on following the publication of the Report when the Children's Branch at the Home Office began to produce occasional reports which dealt with, among other things, probation.

The first of these Children's Branch Reports was published in 1923 (Home Office 1923) and included the rather surprising fact that the number of probation orders made had, as we have already seen, remained almost constant between 1907 and 1923. The Report was written by Sidney Harris who was head of the Children's Branch and by Arthur Norris who had replaced C. E. B. Russell as Chief Inspector of Industrial and Reformatory Schools. The Report reveals where the Home Office stood in respect of probation and more generally the correct responses to crime. These, as we have see were beginning to change after the Great War. For example, the Report states, 'all those who have given special attention to the question of juvenile delinquency are agreed that the right method of approach to the subject is to consider not the punishment of the offence, but the treatment of the young offender' (Home Office 1923: 7). It continues, 'Poverty, overwork, and lack of opportunity for normal modes of expression, are all potent factors in the production of juvenile delinquency'. And again, '[i]n nearly every case the root cause of the trouble is the fact that the child is living under such home conditions as have not led to a right upbringing' (Home Office 1923: 8). In essence, therefore, family and family environment cause delinquency rather than hereditary and degenerative forces which had preoccupied an earlier generation.

In respect of probation the Report noted that it was 'no longer at the experimental stage' and as for the debate about the need to train probation officers which Macadam (1925) was to advocate a few years later, the report seemed to imply that this was not regarded seriously when it stated, 'the secret of successful probation work lies in the strength of the personal influence which the probation officer can exert over the probationer' (Home Office 1923: 56). The Report goes on to comment that there were 215 courts around the country who had yet to appoint a probation officer and concludes that a '…strong inference may be drawn that in many courts too little attention is given to the value of the system' (Home Office 1923: 58). The analysis of crime causation does seem to be moving to a Burtian type of influence but the Report's view of probation seems more traditional.

A second report followed only a year later and there is a discernable shift in the language used and the attitudes to crime causation; this is a shift also noted by Mair and Burke (2012). In particular the next report comments:

> Probably the most difficult task that the Magistrates of a Children's Court have to face is that of diagnosis, because without knowing something about the causes which led to the delinquency it is not easy to prescribe successful treatment. (Home Office 1924: 9)

Words like 'diagnosis', 'prescribe' and 'treatment' were new in the vocabulary of the Home Office and may be seen as evidence of the influence of the new psychological discourse referred to above. The Report refers to the need for courts to consider a report from a probation officer on the home circumstances of the offender. Some form of report provided by the probation officer or even missionary already had a long tradition but now there was a change, 'in the case of the more serious offences the magistrates should know, if possible, something of the character of the child, his physical condition and mental "make up"' (Home Office 1924: 9). The language used to describe the probation report and the contents of that report seem close to that envisaged by Burt (1925). On the other hand, the solutions to juvenile delinquency expressed in the Report are better housing conditions, better open air recreation facilities and more boys and girls clubs which all seem a direct throwback through Russell (1917) to the work of Bray (1908) and others (Holmes 1908, Paterson 1911) before the war.

The second Report also revealed that there were 189 Petty Sessional Divisions without a probation officer and that towns of similar size and characteristics were not making similar use of probation in their courts. The Report commented that probation was used in 18.92 per cent of juvenile cases but the bind over without supervision was used in 8 per cent of cases. The Report suggests that this latter disposal was not appropriate,[48] as it involved no form of supervision. In this same year there were sixty-one probation officers in London working in the adult courts and funded at least partially by the missionary societies. There were also twelve specialist children's probation officers paid a salary directly by the Home Office (Home Office 1927: 17 and 18). As the report points out, the London Police Court Missions via the CETS were paying as much as the state towards the cost of probation officers. The picture was very similar outside the capital where the CETS were paying a substantial proportion of the costs of providing probation officers.

The uneven use of probation around the country, the stubborn refusal of numbers placed on probation to rise and the failure of many petty seasonal divisions to appoint officers despite money from central government being available clearly concerned the Home Office. Their response was the *Criminal Justice Bill 1924*, of which there were four drafts, where a radical overhaul of the organization of probation was proposed. This piece of legislation tends to be seen as a simple administrative reform and it is quite easy to overlook. Bochel for instance, sees it as simply allowing the Home Secretary to set salary levels, prescribe qualifications and arrange superannuation for officers (Bochel 1976: 99). Vanstone (2007) says very little about it and Mair and Burke regard it as consolidating probation (see Mair and Burke 2012: 53). In fact, its consequences were wide reaching and it provided a quite distinct lurch in probation's trajectory a point picked up on by Jarvis who wrote that 'it undoubtedly represented a big step forward for the Probation Service' (Jarvis 1972: 40).

The first *Criminal Justice Bill* produced in February of 1924 was a radical departure and included an unabashed attempt by central government, presumably at the instigation of the Home Office, to expand the probation system. It opened with a memo which stated:

> The main object of the amendment is to increase the development of the probation system in the light of experience especially by providing for the appointment of probation officers in each petty sessional division, by promoting the combination of petty sessional divisions for the purpose, and by improving the methods of supervising and paying probation officers.[49]

The Bill itself stated, 'There shall be a probation committee for every probation area', and that 'The probation committee of every probation area shall pay to the probation officers appointed for the area'.[50] The emphasis is on the word 'shall'. Crucially, the original *1907 Probation of Offenders Act* had been an enabling piece of legislation allowing courts to appoint probation officers, now it was to be compulsory at the behest of the state in the form of the Home Office. This marked a very distinct increase in the central government's control of probation.

The original Bill was produced by the first Labour Government elected in January 1924 which in turn was superseded by a Conservative Government elected in November of 1924, soon after which the Bill recommenced its journey through Parliament. At this point William Joynson Hicks became Home Secretary. Much of Parliament's debate of the Bill took place after the Conservatives had been elected. During the second reading of the Bill in Parliament, in mid-1925, MPs made a number of objections. For instance, Sir George Hohler stated, 'The setting up of these salaried officials will increase the charge upon the rates, which already press so severely upon the people'.[51] He went on to say, 'I object to setting up this professional paid system, a sort of civil service of paid officials under the Bill'.[52] Other MPs made similar objections focusing on the increased expenditure implied by the new system. Sir J. Nall commented, 'I venture to suggest that there is absolutely no need for this new expenditure from the public exchequer'.[53] We have already come across accusations of 'officialism' levelled at probation and the relationship between it and the Home Office.

There were other controversies, for example, some objected to the demise of the missionaries' approach which, by virtue of the creation of many more probation officers, the Bill implied. The missionary societies enjoyed much support in Parliament, and during the debates the Home Secretary agreed to go away and review the part of the Bill which said that courts must appoint their own probation officers. The original had also said that the Secretary of State would set salaries and qualifications of probation officers. This was strongly objected to on the grounds that many of the smaller rural local authorities would not be able to fund their proportion of the costs of the newly appointed probation officers and in any event 'the work has been done effectively by the church or chapel'.[54] The pressure on the local rates was also quoted as a reason for this objection.

The Bill was redrawn in the face of these criticisms in March of 1925 by which time a number of changes had been made. Significantly, it was proposed that the agents of voluntary societies could be paid to act as probation officers and their salaries paid direct to the societies. The Bill actually went on to define a voluntary society; it stated:

In this section the expression 'voluntary society' means a society carrying on mission work in connection with the police courts or other work in connection with the supervision and care of offenders.[55]

This was a remarkably vague definition of a voluntary society leaving local magistrates with a good deal of scope. The final debate on the Bill in Parliament took place at the end of 1925 when much of the debate focused on the power that the Bill gave to central government in relation to the appointment and payment of probation officers. Financial concerns of local government 'to safeguard the interests of the rate payers'[56] dominated and it was agreed that salaries should to be set locally.

It is worth remembering that as the Act was progressing through Parliament the very relationship between central and local government, particularly the financing of local government, was deeply controversial. In their history of local government Keith-Lucas and Richards (1978) give an impression of the scale:

> Neville Chamberlain, Minister of Health between 1924 and 1929, was determined to rationalise the legislation which controlled the work of his department. The reform of local rates was but one item in a comprehensive programme, concerning local government finance, Poor Law, public health, housing and health insurance, which he prepared on taking office in 1924. (Keith-Lucas and Richards 1978: 136)

They also point out that following the *Representation of the People Act of 1918* most of the adult population had the vote in local elections. In many of the larger urban and industrial towns the Labour Party now dominated, whereas many shires continued to be run by the local landed aristocracy (Cannadine 1990). A Royal Commission on Local Government had been appointed in 1923, and it produced reports in 1925, 1928 and 1929. Even after this substantial review Keith-Lucas and Richards note:

> The survival of so many small authorities became increasingly difficult to justify as transport and other technical changes made the market towns and villages less islands in themselves and more part of a wider community. (Keith-Lucas and Richards 1978: 202)

This does rather put into perspective some of the debates about probation and its funding but it is interesting to note the Home Office's continued enthusiasm for probation at such a difficult time.

This relationship between central and local government impacted on probation in other ways. The missionaries and their commitment to missionary zeal and character as a means to reform offenders were strongly identified with an anti officialdom or anti-centralism. Probation officers and particularly children's probation officers therefore became increasingly identified with central government and the Home Office in particular. Thus the probation officers may well have been seen as part of a growing trend of increased central government control and the limiting of the freedom of local authorities to make their own local arrangements.

Probation after the 1925 Act

Despite its being a compromised piece of legislation the Act had an immediate impact as by 1927 there were only sixteen petty sessional divisions with no probation officer. This is a little misleading as 255 probation officers were full time compared to 456 who were part time.[57] The problem of local authority funding for probation officers was that local probation committees appointed part-time officers. The number of probation orders made also increased; by 1925 they had risen to 13,838 (Home Office 1925). Two years later the Home Office stated that 15,094 were placed on probation of which 6,357 were juveniles (Home Office 1927). Prior to this the number of orders made had remained stubbornly consistent up until this point and it was not until 1925 and after the Act that there was evidence of any sustained and significant increase in the use made of probation by the courts.

Although care should be taken in focusing on a few key personalities in a history of probation, it is interesting to note that Edward Troup had retired as Permanent Secretary at the Home Office just a few years before the Act. He had presided over the civil servants at the Home Office through a long list of Home Secretaries, some like Churchill only lasting a matter of months in post. Troup had been there right from the start in 1907 and held a particular view of how he saw probation operating and though the original idea for probation did not come from the Home Office civil service it is questionable that without their support it would have been persevered with. Troup was one of the few constant personalities throughout this period at the Home Office.

In the same year *The Criminal Justice Act 1925* was passed Troup wrote an account of the work of the Home Office. In it he repeats a number of themes relating to probation. For instance he writes:

> More than 15,000 persons are sent every year to prison for terms of a fortnight or less: and in the opinion of the Prison Commissioners many of these could with advantage have been placed on probation. (Troup 1925: 140)

Later in the same work he comments on another theme often referred to by the Home Office which was varied use made of probation by various Justices, and with a note of exasperation he writes:

> The Home Office has in successive circulars called the attention of the Justices to this matter and endeavoured to guide them in what is admittedly a difficult exercise of discretion, and some pertinent remarks on the subject are contained in the *Second Report of the Children's Branch of the Home Office*. (Troup 1925: 141)

Shortly before his retirement Troup gave a lecture to the Magistrates Association in which he revealed more of his views on probation and the treatment of crime generally. His comments also received a certain amount of rather negative attention in the press, one in particular where he stated:

> The last thing any court should do is to accept evidence from any person styling himself or her self a psychologist or psycho-analyst. Psychology is a great and difficult science; and it is the last science that should be touched by an amateur. Only mischief can come if listening to foolish persons who have dabbled a little in the obscene publications of Freud and his school.[58]

He went on in his lecture to recommend that courts should be given information about a defendant prior to sentence, a practice advocated by Burt. Nonetheless he was hostile to psychologists and to psychoanalysts in particular.

Just a few years after Troup's retirement the Home Office lost another key personality. In 1925 H. B. Simpson retired. He had joined the Home Office in 1884 shortly after graduating from Oxford University and had risen to be Assistant Secretary. His background was remarkably similar to Troup's and the two were contemporaries and longtime colleagues. As these two key personalities retired some new faces arrived that were to loom large in the story of probation over the following decades. In 1919 Sidney Harris (1876–1962) had been appointed Assistant Secretary at the Home Office and placed in charge of the Children's Branch which meant that he effectively ran probation at the Home Office. He shared the classic senior civil servant background where he went to public school, later graduated from Queens College Oxford and became a civil servant in 1900 and then joined the Home Office in 1903.

There were other key significant changes in personnel in these few years. Shortly after the Act the National Association of Probation Officers was radically changed by the retirement of its original chair, Sidney Edridge, and the arrival of three new people to the key posts within the organization. Gertrude

Tuckwell, the first woman Justice of the Peace, became president in 1927. The young Earl of Feversham returned from South Africa where he had worked under another name as a probation officer to be vice president in the same year. The new chair of NAPO was the widely experienced Old Street police court magistrate, William Clarke-Hall. As Bochel comments in her history of NAPO 'he (like the other two) was able to move in social spheres not normally frequented by members of the association' (Bochel 1962b: 53). These were all well connected influential individuals and in Feversham's case had independent income they were prepared to use to help the organization. He used some of his private wealth to secure an office and the services of a secretary for five years. For the post of secretary he recruited his old friend and senior probation officer from his days in South Africa, H. E. Norman, and paid him the princely sum of £1,000 per year for his troubles. From this point NAPO and its senior members in particular, went out of their way to cultivate good relations with the Home Office. Personal relationships were important, as Bochel points out in respect of the NAPO secretary:

> Norman himself appears to have won the respect of S. W. Harris with whom he met frequently for a discussion of probation matters. It was through this informal contact that the Association raised any problems with the Home Office. (Bochel 1962b: 55)

None of the senior officers of NAPO were serving probation officers and it was many years before a serving officer of any grade was to hold such a post but the finances and contacts these new senior officers brought paid dividends for NAPO.

In political and policy terms major political changes of the time like the arrival of the Labour Party in government for the first time ever were probably more significant in respect of the changing attitudes of politicians, the government and the civil service to probation. Nonetheless, it is interesting to speculate on the role of key personalities, relationships and networks generally in the major shift in Home Office approaches to probation's organization that occurred at this particular time.

The *Criminal Justice Act 1925* had many consequences, one of which was The Probation Rules 1926 (which are reproduced in Le Mesurier 1935: 280) which were circulated by the Home Office to all Magistrates in that year. The Rules include instructions that a probation officer should meet with the person on probation weekly for the first month of the order and meetings afterwards should be dependant on the conduct of the probationer.[59] This regulation seems very directive and symptomatic of a central government in the form of the Home Office becoming increasingly involved in the day-to-day working practices of officers.

A perhaps more mundane consequence of the Act was the large amount of correspondence which began between the Home Office and various local authorities around the country. Not only does this correspondence give a picture of the operation of probation outside of London, it also marked a significant increase in the Home Office's involvement in the operation of the probation system outside of the capital. Much of the new correspondence with the local authorities focused on the arrangements for the payment of probation officers which was now the responsibility of the new Probation Committees made up of local magistrates set up after the 1925 Act. The Probation Rules sent out in 1926 also included a provision that the Chief Financial Officer of the local authority should act as Treasurer to the Probation Committee. Many of the local authorities were concerned about the impact of the scheme on the local rates. The Treasury, too, were concerned about the expense of the new scheme. For instance in correspondence between the Home Office and the Treasury on the issue of enhanced salaries for graduate probation officers, the Treasury wrote, 'no extravagant scales would be allowed for persons with University qualifications (should there ever be any)'.[60]

Home Office correspondence with the smaller boroughs outside of London also revealed a range of varying practices that had existed up until then. In a typical instance, magistrates in Maryport in Cumberland wrote to the Home Office asking that they be allowed to keep their existing probation officer even though he/she also served as the local School Attendance Officer. The Home Offices response was to discourage this on the grounds that the latter implied an antagonistic relationship with the local children, which was not seen as appropriate for a probation officer. Following this decision, the School Attendance Officers National Association wrote to the Home Office expressing their disquiet at being excluded from the role of probation officer.[61]

This was not an isolated case as the Home Office found itself far more involved in the day-to-day operation of probation across the country. This would include matters as relatively mundane as probation officers attending at conferences. For instance in October 1922 two of the London children's probation officers went to the Home Office to ask for money to attend at a conference in Hull. The Home Office agreed to pay a half of a third class ticket as '[t]here are no Children's Officers in the big provincial towns (though there ought to be) and it might be a good thing if the London Children's Officers were to show themselves in the flesh to the northerners'.[62] At the NAPO Annual Midland Branch Conference of 1926 one officer, who insisted on remaining anonymous, complained that because he was part CETS funded he was expected to preach on a Sunday and attend various fund-raising activities such as Flower Days, thus leaving him insufficient time to deal with his probation cases.[63] A few years later, in 1929, the Home Office convened a conference for officers to take place in London. A letter of complaint swiftly followed from the Durham County Council saying that they were expected to contribute to the officers' attendance expenses yet had no say in who was to attend.[64]

At the same time more significant issues reached the Home Office. The uneven use made of probation around the country had long been a concern of the Home Office but this new involvement in the day-to-day work of probation brought to light the uneven treatment of women placed on probation. The matter arose in correspondence from an MP received at the Home Office. Sidney Harris, head of the Children's Branch, notes:

> Rescue workers are used as probation officers for women to a greater extent in the country districts and the smaller boroughs than in the large towns and cities. Where the work is small and the pay meagre it is hard to secure the services of qualified social workers without having recourse to those that have some other means of livelihood and that is where the rescue workers come in.[65]

A short report was prepared after a Miss Wall was sent out to investigate; she notes in her report, after visiting one particular rescue home:

> They often take the probation case into the refuge, keep her a few weeks or months and then draft her onto a training home for 2 years at a considerable distance from her home town and from her probation officer. I found that probation officers write occasionally to girls whom they have placed in Homes, but rarely visited them because of the expense.[66]

In Weymouth she found that '[y]oung girls on probation are generally kept a few months at St. Gabriels and then sent to service'.[67] This was typical of other rescue homes. Interestingly Miss Wall also commented, after her visit to the Rescue Home in Salisbury, that '(t)he slightest evidence seems to be accepted that girls are "fallen" and I doubt if any of these younger ones are rightly here'.[68]

Even as these changes were taking place and the Home Office was becoming more and more involved in the running of probation, the CETS and their police court missionaries continued their work in the adult courts of London and many of the major cities. Each Annual Report of the London Diocesan Branch of CETS begins with a breakdown of the work of the missionaries which includes such things as men and lads placed in situations, employees persuaded to reinstate persons charged, women and girls placed in Homes or returned to friends, men and lads placed in Homes, returned to friends or sent to sea, cases provided with clothing, food, tools, etc., pledges of total abstinence taken.[69] These Reports are remarkably consistent and reveal a working ethos and working practices that had altered little since the previous century.

Following the *Criminal Justice Act 1925* there were effectively two systems of probation operating. One was a system of probation officers sponsored by an assortment of religious and voluntary organizations dotted around the country that had remained unaffected by much of the recent debate at the Home Office. Indeed there is some evidence to suggest that even the 1907 Act seems to have had only a passing significance outside of the London juvenile courts. It was based on assumptions about character, influence and saving souls. At the same time there was a smaller system based on a national system of probation co-ordinated by the Home Office and centred in London. Also centred mainly in London were the ideas of people like Burt in particular and the Child Guidance Clinic 'movement' along with advocates of a university trained social work profession. The newer centralized system was clearly expanding but the older missionary system was now fifty years old.

This was referred to as the system of 'dual control' and we can see it in operation at this time from the writings of those actually involved in the courts on a day-to-day basis. In 1922 Albert Lieck, a London court clerk, produced a guide for newly appointed magistrates which was adopted by the Magistrates Association. He comments on probation so:

> The probation system has, at first tentatively, and now frankly and fully, been in operation for forty years and more. It is a great success, and would be a greater if more and better probation officers could be provided. It is somewhat surprising that they are not, for it costs less to supervise a man or woman out of goal than it does in, and he or she is meanwhile, as a rule, doing work, more or less productive, for the community. (Lieck 1922: 19)

Here he is stressing, not only the cost-saving potential of probation but also the fact that is commented on by other magistrates and writers, which is that the system of probation has a long tradition and is already well established. This would seem to imply a probation system based on police court missionaries and rooted in the nineteenth century. His book makes no reference to social work training for probation officers or the impact of psychology on the treatment of juvenile delinquency.

A few years later in 1925 Henry Turner Waddy[70] published *The Police Court and its Work*, which was his reminiscences of seven years of work in the London Police Courts. They reveal a system of probation based on police court missionaries working in the adult courts and children's probation officers working in the juvenile courts. He sees the two groups as quite distinct and lays particular emphasis on the matrimonial and domestic dispute work of the police court missionary (Waddy 1925: 87) which suggests that the police court missionaries were still operating largely as they had at the end of the nineteenth century. Waddy discusses the children's probation officers in his section dealing with the juvenile courts and regards them as more specialized than the police court missionaries. He does not discuss the possibility of training for probation officers; instead he writes:

> The qualifications for the work of probation are very special. They include sympathy, a brave heart in the hour of disappointment, and a tireless patience. (Waddy 1925: 126)

He refers approvingly to the latest review of the training and appointment of probation officers (Home Office 1922). Like Troup he is dismissive of a Freudian approach to the treatment of juvenile delinquency when he writes, 'the introduction of this consideration into the problem of juvenile misconduct is both fanciful and mischievous, and even a trifle nasty' (Waddy 1925: 148).

Portents

In some respects the 1925 Act simply expanded the numbers of probation officers and the made use of probation throughout the country. Beyond that it ensured that central government was to have a much greater say in the operation of the system outside of the city of London. In itself this was no mean feat as many areas had been untouched by the efforts of the Home Office to extend probation. However, if we consider the wider picture, in particular the work of Cyril Burt and the new Child Guidance Clinics and, independently of him, the work of Macadam and other social work trainers we begin to see portents for the future. A more centralized, coordinated and expanded organization creates a great deal of space for these two practices to move into. By the late 1920s these discourses were having only a marginal impact but, as we will see, that was to change.

Taking a step back and looking at the fourteen years we have just focused on we can see that changes in the operation of probation and the treatment of crime generally were hugely influenced by factors outside of the criminal justice process. Between 1914 and 1928 that would have included such things as the economic crisis of the time, the changing relationship between central and local government, changing class relationships as a distinct middle and working class (now enfranchised) emerge at the same time as the aristocracy withdrew from public life. Also significant were the shifts in the social work and psychological discourses at the time as new bodies of knowledge began to emerge. Finally, it is worth keeping in mind changing attitudes at the Home Office and perhaps even something as simple as the retirement of certain key civil servants. The result was the passing of a major piece of legislation in the development of probation which was to impact on both its organization and its practice. Prior to this Act there is a good case for arguing that by 1925 the probation system had moved very little from its origins in the late nineteenth century.

The Creation of a 'Fully Public Service': Probation 1928–1938

The previous chapter described probation enjoying what might be termed a long nineteenth century as its working methods and organization had changed little since the previous century. However, with the introduction of the *Criminal Justice Act 1925* change seemed to be in the air but the major impact of that legislation will only become apparent in this chapter. Indeed the crucial role that the Home Office plays today in probation traces its origins back to this legislation. In the meantime this chapter will look at just how probation officers' practice moved after the Act. However, there is also much movement in probation policy as well in the period covered by this chapter and the Home Office will be seen to play an ever more leading role in probation.

In respect of probation practice it has been argued throughout this work that the twin discourses of social work and psychology are crucial influences on it. We will see how these shifting and competing discourses moved into the space created by the *Criminal Justice Act of 1925* and how those practices evolved over the years covered in this chapter.

The period of time covered by this chapter was crucial in the creation of a modern system of probation as it marks the arrival of a state funded, national and secular system of probation officers. By the end of this period probation had largely lost its religious and voluntary roots. But, as we will see, that shift was anything but smooth. Garland's (1985) work describes the creation of a penal welfare complex between 1906 and 1914 and we will see in this chapter that penal welfare complex making a very significant lurch towards being a modern penal welfare complex.

However, like the last chapter, the changes that we are about to discuss were not always the direct and intended result of Parliamentary activity. Again only one particularly relevant piece of legislation was passed in the time period we are about to consider, that was the *Children and Young Persons Act of 1933*.

This chapter will argue that its role in respect of probation was its building on the *Criminal Justice Act of 1925* and by laying down the guiding principles for probation practice. The two pieces of legislation can be seen as complementing each other with the earlier Act providing the structures for the later Act. As we'll see much of the lead in probation policy during this period was taken by the civil servants at the Home Office rather than Parliament. The *Children and Young Persons Act of 1933* had a major impact on the treatment, generally, by courts, of children and the role of the Home Office in its devising and guiding through Parliament should not be underestimated.

However, to get the story under way we will consider the policy shifts over the ten-year period in question beginning with the impact of arguably the most significant piece of legislation in creating a modern probation system.

The aftermath of the Criminal Justice Act of 1925

It was not long after the passing of *Criminal Justice Act of 1925* that the majority of Petty Sessional Divisions around the country had their own probation officer. Those officers, though, were predominantly part-time and many continued to be at least partially financed by the CETS and other similar organizations (see Home Office 1928). The situation amongst the full-time officers was similar. Writing in 1928 Brockway comments:

> in 1924, 60 per cent of the 250 full-time probation officers were agents of voluntary societies, and of these two thirds were attached to the Church of England Temperance Society. The Act of 1925 has tended to perpetuate this position, because it provides that one-third of the salary of probation officers may be borne by voluntary societies, thus encouraging local authorities to economise by accepting their nominees. (Brockway 1928: 63)[1]

Writing a number of years later the Magistrate Leo Page commented that 'the justices complied with the letter of the law, as they were bound to, but evaded its spirit by appointing persons utterly untrained and, in some instances, perfectly incompetent and unsuitable' (Page 1937: 296). The reason for this, he argues, was that these officers were prepared to work for a low salary. As we saw concerns about the expense of appointing officers dominated debate in Parliament regarding the Act and as Page suggests continued to dominate debate regarding the appointment of officers afterwards.[2] Curiously, a Home Office Minute dated November 1928 points out that there were 172 part-time probation officers dotted around the country, 48 of whom were in Cornwall and 50 in Devon.[3]

Nonetheless, the courts use of probation began to increase following the Act, from 19.6 per cent in 1924 (Clarke-Hall 1926: 281) to 54 per cent in 1934 of all juveniles appearing in court (Bailey 1987: 152). Bailey goes on to note that the use of probation around the country continued to be uneven well into the 1930s. Leo Page[4] quotes concrete examples from the 1935 Criminal Statistics when he writes, 'the Portsmouth justices placed 33.9 per cent under supervision, while the justices of Southampton dealt in this way with only 9 per cent, at Southend-on-Sea the percentage was 37.6, whereas at Blackpool it was 9.7' (Page 1937: 122). Page goes on to point out that the 17 per cent of adults convicted of indictable offences were placed on probation in 1934 (Page 1937: 121).

In the meantime, the uneven organization of probation around the country was brought to the attention of the Home Office when they took on the coordination of the combining of probation areas following the *Criminal Justice Act of 1925*. The Act compelled all courts to have a salaried probation officer and recommended that smaller petty sessional divisions should 'combine' to form probation areas and then appoint officers. A Home Office grant was made available to cover half of the salary of the officer appointed but only when the officer appointed was approved by the Home Office. Prior to this, the Home Office had had very little to do with the organization of probation outside the capital but with the Act and the Probation Rules which followed in 1926 their role was now much expanded.

This was a major, and often overlooked, change in the organization of probation and one that was to create a good deal of work for the Home Office. The Home Office's own records show the difficulties and opposition they faced to their vision for probation. For instance in Nottinghamshire in 1926 the Magistrates Courts around the county were quite happy to combine to form a Probation Area except in Newark where they objected to appointing a full-time probation officer on the grounds of expense. The Home Office file notes curtly that '[I]t has also been in every way a backward and inefficient place'.[5] There was sufficient concern at the Home Office for a senior official to be sent to Nottinghamshire to meet with Magistrates after which the area was duly combined despite the objections in Newark.

In Bury matters became distinctly sour when the *Bury Times* of 4 May 1929 reported the appointment of a full-time probation officer 'contrary to the wishes of both the Borough Magistrates and the Finance Committee'.[6] The paper went on to report a council meeting where one member stated:

The Home Office called the tune regarding the salary, the magistrates had to make the appointment, and the Council had to pay the piper; without any voice in the appointment or the salary to be paid. ... Those who paid the piper should have some voice in the tune.[7]

The Council decided to appoint their own probation officer at the salary they set and with the superannuation arranged by themselves. The Local Clerk to the Justices wrote to the Home Office in a rather indignant tone relaying the decision and noting '[I]f this is allowed then the sooner the Probation Rules are scrapped and the better'.[8] The decision was reversed when the Home Office pointed out that doing so would mean that they would not get the Home Office grant towards the payment of the officer's salary.[9]

Similar difficulties arose in Devon when the Home Office sent a draft Combining Order to Magistrates in the County. The Magistrates in Exeter objected and an article appeared in the local *Express and Echo* stating:

> It would appear from the draft scheme that the Home Office does not agree with the majority and is disposed to insist upon the appointment of paid officers. The draft scheme is elaborate, and somewhat complicated ... but at best it would appear that the County of Devon must be prepared for substantial outlay for probation work.[10]

In the small Devon town of Great Torrington the magistrates wrote to the Home Office saying that they had had one probation case in the last four years and did not see the point of a salaried officer and that 'the effect of the order will cause unnecessary expense to the Local Authority'.[11] In Stanborough and Coleridge they objected to paying for officers as they were able to use the services of School Attendance Officers or the local vicar for probation cases so 'there is no necessity for the appointment of a permanent staff of Probation officials'.[12] These were not isolated episodes, other magistrates' courts in the county wrote making similar objections. The Home Office were not sympathetic and noted:

> all base their antagonism on a love of the present system. As it is precisely to uproot that system that the order is formed, opposition of this kind should clearly be disregarded.[13]

This is not entirely true, as most of the objections to the appointment of probation officers were based on the expense of the scheme. In all, of the thirty areas affected in Devon, sixteen did not reply to the Home Office's proposals, nine agreed and five objected. In 1929 a Combined Area was duly formed though Exeter opted out of the scheme.

These areas were not unique; there is a substantial Home Office file relating to the creation of a Combined Probation Area for Warwickshire which opens in

1929 and finally closes in 1942 when a Combined Area was created.[14] Here the Home Office had a very useful ally in the shape of Mr L. E. Stephens, the Clerk to the Court at Leamington Spa. Mr Stephens had contacted the Home Office regarding probation in the higher courts in the area and the Home Office sent up a representative to meet with him. They described him as 'a young man, only appointed two or three years ago and will I think be of assistance to us in getting the county organisation on a proper footing'.[15] The Home Office representative encouraged Mr Stephens to organize the combining of the petty sessional areas to form a probation committee. Despite his best efforts a committee of magistrates formed to look at the matter of combining decided against it.[16] Their objections were based on the expense of the scheme and concerns that a full-time officer would have to cover such a large area that they would not have sufficient local knowledge. The matter dragged on for over ten years until a Combined Area was formed in 1942; even then it excluded both Coventry and Birmingham.

Similarly, in Flintshire the debate continued well into the 1940s as the local magistrate's courts objected to having to appoint male and female full-time probation officers as ordered by the Home Office, rather than continuing with their own part-time and unqualified officer.[17] Matters reached such a pitch that in 1941 the Home Office sent Doris Rosling, who was the Probation Inspector at the Home Office, to persuade local magistrates of the benefits of full-time probation officers. Magistrates in Flint remained unconvinced and wrote to the Home Office:

> In particular I have to report that such officers would not be able to effectively personally supervise all cases committed to them in this County, and moreover they would have insufficient knowledge of local conditions, which in the opinion of my Justices is essential for the proper discharge of the duties of probation officer.[18]

The Home Office was unimpressed noting, 'there is nothing new in their objections. They greatly overrate both the worth of their present officer and the value of local knowledge'.[19] The final Combining Order was made on 24 October 1941.

The influence of the Home Office was also beginning to be felt in other aspects of probation. At the same time that these administrative battles were being the Home Office was changing its position regarding the treatment of the offender. The gradual creation of a centralized system of probation dominated by the Home Office was to ensure that this newer Home Office view of the correct treatment of crime would increasingly dominate probation practice.

Treating the young offender

The *Report of the Departmental Committee on the Treatment of Young Offenders* (Home Office 1927) and the subsequent *1933 Children and Young Persons Act* had a major impact on the treatment of juvenile crime that lasted for many years (see Bailey 1987). As Bailey points out, youth crime in this period was not perceived as a major problem. We have already seen that youth crime had actually been falling following the end of the Great War. This begs the question, why was the committee appointed in the first place? It was appointed in 1925, very soon after the *Criminal Justice Act* of that year, just as the Home Office was, as we have seen, busy introducing a new nationwide system of probation officers.

Bailey hints at an answer when he writes that:

> the recommendations of the Young Offenders Committee reflected the wide consensus of opinion which had developed on the subject of the young delinquent by 1925. (Bailey 1987: 66)

Bailey goes into more detail when he writes that a 'formidable alliance had been forged' (Bailey 1987: 66), members of which included the newly formed pressure groups such as the Howard League for Penal Reform (Rose 1961). That alliance also included the higher officials at the Home Office. Later in his book he writes that 'the most significant contribution to the genesis of the 1933 Act in these years was made by the permanent officials of the Children's Branch' (Bailey 1987: 110). The retirement of Edward Troup in 1922 and H. B. Simpson in 1925 from key positions at the Home Office led to appointment of new senior officials. It seems that there was a general sense that change was needed and that the time had come for a new set of policies and practices to reflect a new consensus. The work of Cyril Burt was the type of approach that seems to have caught the spirit of the time. In effect, a new administrative apparatus was being set up for probation (following the *Criminal Justice Act of 1925*), now attention turned to how it would operate.

The Departmental Committee on the Treatment of Young Offenders produced its report in March of 1927. In the introduction, after the assertion that reformation of the offender should be the prime objective of the courts, the Report makes a very interesting, and new, assertion regarding the twin concerns of delinquency and neglect of the young. The Report states:

> The two problems are closely connected and can conveniently be dealt with together, because neglect and delinquency often go hand in hand,... there

is little distinction in the character of the young person concerned or in the appropriate method of treatment. (Home Office 1927: 6)

This resonates with the work of Burt who had argued in 1925 that delinquency was simply a response to the quality of a child's environment, the proper response to which was to address the environment of the child.

The Report makes other novel assertions about juvenile delinquency. For example, there is the assertion that the appearance of a child in a criminal court was in itself undesirable. The report comments:

The principle object to be borne in mind is the desirability of keeping the adolescent boy or girl as long as possible from the police court. (Home Office 1927: 24)

The main reason for this seems to be the contaminating effect of appearing in court. Indeed actually having a criminal conviction could lead a young person further down a criminal career. Therefore, the committee recommended that the words 'conviction' and 'sentence' should be used only rarely in the juvenile courts.

It did not end there; there is evidence that the committee had a good deal of sympathy with other proposals that Burt had made. They wrote:

It is essential that the Juvenile Court, ... should have, in all except trivial cases, the fullest possible information as to the young person's history, his home surroundings and circumstances, his career at school and his medical record. (Home Office 1927: 34)

The Report then goes on to recommend the setting up of three remand homes or observation centres, where a juvenile offender could be sent so that detailed enquiries could be made regarding him or her. Thus an 'expert' assessment of the juvenile offender was recommended for the first time in an official Home Office report.

Arguably the most radical aspect of the Report was the suggestion that the juvenile court should no longer be a criminal court but that it should operate much more like a civil court. The Report advocated juvenile courts being furnished simply and being conducted far less formally than an adult court. They also recommend that they be kept quite separate from the adult courts, with magistrates who had some experience of social work involved. At one point the Report commented that juvenile courts should be set up as though 'an enquiry rather than a trial was being held' (Home Office 1927: 36), which indicates a major shift from an accusatorial system of justice to one based around the investigation of the offender.

In respect of the probation system there was evidence of a slightly different approach. The Report comments:

> A criticism which was frequently made to us in evidence was that the term probation often meant to the offender nothing more than being 'let off' and that this notion is common in the minds of the public. There is some truth in this criticism. (Home Office 1927: 52)

Serious consideration was given to the suggestion that conditions should be available to be inserted in a probation order as a means to 'beef up' that order. The committee decided against the idea that a general condition 'to reside as directed by the probation officer' should be made available to courts. The Report asserted that probation was, first and foremost, 'supervision in the open' (Home Office 1927: 56). Borstal was available if residential treatment was deemed appropriate. It is clear that concerns were being raised about probation and that proposals to make it more demanding were taken seriously.

The committee also considered the suggestion that probation officers should be trained for their work rather than basing it on missionary zeal and force of character. Here again, there seems to be a subtle shift in the approach of the committee. The Report states:

> While character and personality are the most essential qualities, and it is also necessary for a probation officer to have some practical knowledge of the conditions of life of those among whom he will work, the breadth of view afforded by a liberal education is equally desirable if the best results are to be obtained.[20]

This was a perceptible shift from the position taken by the 1922 review of probation officers' training (Home Office 1922), a mere five years earlier, and very close to Macadam's (1925) proposals. In a further allusion to the direction that the probation system was taking the Report comments:

> it is essential that the Home Office should take a more active part than it has done hitherto in probation work and should satisfy itself as to the manner in which it is being carried out. (Home Office 1927: 62)

This is a reference to the provisions in the *Criminal Justice Act of 1925*, whereby the Home Office began to take more control over the appointment of probation officers and their work, particularly in the areas outside of London which had until then largely been left to themselves.

Despite these significant changes in approach at the Home Office the report attracted criticism and the Home Office records for the period give a flavour of that criticism. Although it contained much they would have supported, The Howard League for Penal Reform wanted the Report to go further in its recommendations regarding the central role that the Children's Branch should play in the running of the juvenile courts. They also had little sympathy with the argument that residential treatment could be provided via a Borstal sentence rather than as a condition of probation, because 'Borstal treatment is penal in essence, and this will not be altered by camouflaging it as "training".'[21] The Association of London Court Juvenile Probation Officers also wrote, focusing on the debate within the Report regarding the move to a more civil style of justice approach in the juvenile courts. They argue in favour of this.[22]

At the time of the Report's publication the Home Secretary was the Conservative William Joynson Hicks. He had been Home Secretary at the time of the passage of the *Criminal Justice Act of 1925*, though he had not been in office when the original Bill had been drawn up, and it was he who had spoken in Parliament to defend the need for the missionary spirit amongst probation officers when that Bill had been debated. In the year the Report was published he spoke at the Annual Conference of the National Association of Probation Officers. A selection of his comments from that speech reveals his view of probation:

> First and foremost of all, we want to see a probation officer in every court in the land .... I am most anxious not to let that (i.e. missionary) spirit depart out of probation work ... I want you to deal with the souls of these people.[23]

The contrast is striking; these views seem closer to an older version of probation rather than the emerging professional and trained officer envisaged by senior officials at the Home Office and the Report of 1927. However, during the same speech he stated, 'first and foremost of all, we want to see a probation officer in every court in the land' (HO45/13403).

Within the security of the walls of the Home Office, and following the Report, even more radical changes were being mooted. Sidney Harris (Permanent Under Secretary) and Dr Arthur Norris (Chief Inspector of Industrial and Reformatory Schools) set out their respective positions in a number of lengthy internal memos[24] that they exchanged at this time. Under discussion was the very nature of the way that juvenile courts should be conducted and what appeared to be a search for a sentence somewhere between probation and Borstal.

Early in their correspondence Harris advocated the introduction of a new sentence of a probation order with a condition to reside at a probation hostel for six months. He describes this as a compromise but one that would give the courts the power to sentence to what he calls a 'short shock' which is a term we will come across later. Dr Norris took a completely different view advocating the removal of juvenile offenders from the whole criminal legal process. He writes:

> Evidence was being frequently brought to the notice of the Inspectors of the Children's Branch of the Home Office of persistent refusal by magistrates, those responsible for the care and protection of children and by social workers generally to handicap a child's future by involving the aid of the law with such consequences.[25]

Although recorded juvenile crime had fallen by 50 per cent in the years between 1917 and 1926, he was doubtful that this reflected the level of juvenile crime. What was actually happening, he thought, was that the Police were not prosecuting as they believed that the court was not the proper setting to deal with the protection and training of children.

They did reach an agreement that courts should have the power to insert a condition in a probation order that the probationer reside at a probation hostel for a limited period of time. They also agreed that probation was to be 'treatment in the open'. From these discussions there followed a proposal to establish probation hostels around the country which produced a response we have already seen in other aspects of probation work, namely who was to pay for this. Finally, it was agreed that the Home Office would pay half of the cost of the probation hostels and the local authority the other half.

Concerns about the costs of probation and the role of central government, particularly the Home Office, in its operation continued. Local authorities had followed the debates surrounding the 1927 Committee Report and the Home Office file includes an issue of the Gazette of County Councils for November 1927, which included the following observation on that Report:

> nor is it appropriate that any part of the cost of what is a problem of purely national concern should fall upon local education rates.[26]

Considering this was the time of a worldwide economic depression the economic state of the country at the time (Hobsbawm 1969, Taylor 1975) and the heated debate about the respective roles of local and central government raging at the time (Keith-Lucas and Richards 1978) it is not surprising that the question of cost of any new probation linked proposal would prove contentious.

A proposal for legislation in the shape of a *Children and Young Persons Bill* followed the year after the Report. However, due to political events, it did not see the light of day until 1931. The Bill took the novel stance of bringing together neglected and delinquent children, and proposed a juvenile court suitable to deal with both. Meanwhile the Board of Education began to see the treatment of juvenile crime as part of its responsibility. This began with the Board of Education lobbying the Home Office arguing that they should be responsible for the Approved Schools. A memo dated 29 July 1931 from Mr W. Ritchie at the Board of Education addressed to Harris, states:

> the treatment of these children should be regarded as entirely an educational and not a penal problem, and that accordingly the central responsibility for them, as for the ordinary child, ought to rest with the Government Department responsible for education.[27]

Considering what had been said lately at the Home Office about juvenile crime the logic of this argument was quite powerful. There was also the precedent of the Juvenile Offenders Committee Report of 1920 (see above) which had begun at the Home Office but was finally produced by the Board of Education. Nonetheless, the Home Office response to this request was to give short shrift to the argument. The reply stated that:

> neglect and delinquency go hand in hand and that is the main reason why both class of children are properly dealt with by the Juvenile Courts.[28]

The Act therefore remained in the hands of the Home Office but the Board of Education was to return to this argument with the Home Office at a later date.

The Children and Young Persons Act of 1933 and the welfare of the child

This was a major piece of legislation that covered far more than probation. In one account the Bill received a relatively straightforward passage through Parliament (Rose 1961: 163) as more modern ideas about children, their neglect and delinquency had become generally accepted. Although the broad principles were accepted this omits the fact that the Bill was actually subject to much debate. The Bill proposed the abolition of court-ordered corporal punishment for all juveniles but this particular issue divided both the Lords and Commons (see Gard 2009) and proved very controversial. The Bill also attracted criticism regarding the lack of provision for Remand Observation Centres. According to Bailey the Act:

> underlined the principle that the welfare of the child should be the courts uppermost if not exclusive consideration. [However,] Given how closely the Act followed the proposals of the Young Offenders Committee, it, too, had to be a

memorial to limited changes justified by experience, rather than to fundamental
innovations inspired by revolutionary principle. (Bailey 1987: 84)

The move to a full-blooded enquiry based on a chancery type approach in the
juvenile court, as advocated by Norris, was abandoned as being too radical,
though Harris's assertion that the court should remain strictly criminal seems to
have been dented by the new Supervision Order which gave courts the power to
intervene without an offence being committed. The Act gave courts the power
to insert a condition in a probation order that offenders under sixteen could
be required to reside at an approved home for a period of up to six months.
The idea that probation was exclusively supervision 'in the open' was formally
compromised in legislation. There were other compromises; the 1931 Bill had
proposed the establishment of three remand centres to enable courts to assess
children prior to sentence. This proposal was abandoned on the grounds of
cost although it would re-emerge later. The Bill had also proposed that local
authorities should make all enquiries relating to young people appearing in
juvenile courts prior to sentence. Following much lobbying from NAPO to the
Home Office, the Act finally included a provision that probation officers could
also be used for this task.

It is clear that the senior officials at the Home Office shared many of
the views of the child welfare lobby and had a very real vision of how they saw
the juvenile court operating. The difference perhaps is that the officials were
aware of what would be economically and politically acceptable at the time.
They were prepared to compromise even on key principles of their proposals in
an attempt to see progress with the Bill. Bailey refers to 'the hegemony of child
welfare' (Bailey 1987: 91) and the word 'consensus' regularly crops up in his
discussions of the Act, which suggests a real shift in culture regarding juvenile
crime. It seems clear that in a few short years the approach advocated by Burt
and his like to juvenile delinquency formed much of the basis for this welfare
based 'consensus'.

For evidence of this consensus we can actually look to the debates in
Parliament around the Bill. Oliver Stanley,[29] who was Under Secretary at the
Home Office, whilst Herbert Samuel was Home Secretary, introduced the Bill to
the House of Commons. At the Second Reading of the Bill in the Commons on
12 February 1932, Stanley said:

> We recognise that other conditions than mere inherent vice, may have entered
> into an offence; that the childs upbringing at home, the discipline he receives in
> the home circle, the economic conditions under which he lives, the squalor and

misery of his life, even the companions with whom he associates in school or out of it, may have had much more to do with turning that child into an offender than any spirit of natural evil.[30]

One of the genuinely new ideas contained within the Bill was that there was perceived no great distinction between the delinquent child and the neglected child. For Oliver Stanley and the Home Office this meant that the distinction between Industrial and Reformatory Schools was now superfluous and they would henceforth be called Approved Schools:

> The fact is that the distinction between the two is largely accidental. The neglected child may only just have been lucky enough not to have been caught for an offence. The character of the child who has been suffering from a long period of neglect at home, or a long period of evil surroundings is much more likely to have been seriously affected than the character of the young offender who is perhaps in the school as the result of one short lapse into crime. We do not believe that either will suffer from being in the same school.[31]

Equally striking was the response of the Official Opposition in Parliament, the leader of which was Mr Rhys Davies who rose in the House as soon as Stanley had finished to offer his support for the Bill. This is not surprising as he had been one of authors of the *1927 Report on Young Offenders*. His only criticism, and it was one echoed by other MPs who spoke that night, was that the Bill did not include provision for the establishment of Observation Centres where juvenile offenders could be remanded to for enquiries to be made. This was a proposal made by Burt and in his writings on juvenile delinquency. As if to stress Burt's impact on the whole of this debate, at a later stage of the debates one of the Members, Mr Edward Williams, announced to the House:

> If we had better recreational facilities, particularly in our larger cities, boys and girls could be kept off the streets. We have, of course, approved schools, but we ought to have schools under the charge of eminent psychologists. The name of Mr Cyril Burt has been mentioned and I should like every member of the House to read his work, 'The Young Delinquent'. It is the work of one who is, perhaps, the most eminent practical psychologist in Britain.[32]

Although the Lords blocked the Bill's attempt to restrict the use of court ordered corporal punishment, the Bill went through, including the amalgamation of Industrial and Reformatory Schools.

The final Act did attract criticism in some parts largely because it was not seen as going far enough along the welfare route. This was an issue picked up by the Leader of the Opposition in relation to observation centres when he stated:

The Bill fails, really, to come up to the standard of expectation, because it contains no provision for the establishment of observation centres.[33]

The passage of the Bill through Parliament hid much hard work and negotiating by the Home Office behind the scenes.

Senior officials at the Home Office had begun work on the Bill as early as 1928 when a first draft of the Bill was printed. There were to be eleven other drafts before the Bill was finally enacted and there is a three-volume Home Office file on the Bill which reflects the Department's efforts.[34] A Home Office Minute, probably by Sidney Harris, asked:

> Could some words be inserted to suggest that the main objective of the juvenile court is to ensure the welfare and protection of children and young persons?[35]

This 'welfare principle' was indeed inserted as a clause in the Bill, and though rarely commented upon in the debates at the time, it was the first time that it appeared in English law. There was also a good deal of discussion at the Home Office about the ability of courts to insert conditions in a probation order, in particular a condition to reside. The issue had dogged the Home Office for a considerable period of time and it seems that with this Bill they were determined to settle it once and for all. Much of the debate focused on the belief held at the Home Office that probation was 'treatment in the open'. Within the safety of a Home Office file Harris was able to note the more practical reasons for his objections to the proposal that a general and unlimited condition of residence be available in a probation order.[36] He writes:

> But the 'residence condition' is also freely used to send probationers to Homes
> for long periods – sometimes for the whole duration of the probation order.
> In the case of children and young persons the practice has grown up partly to
> avoid the conviction involved in sending a boy or a girl to a Reformatory School
> or the idea of punishment associated in the past with industrial and reformatory
> schools and partly it may be suspected to avoid the cost which falls on the local
> authority when a boy or girl is sent to such a school.[37]

The recommendation that courts should have expert assessments of an offender prior to sentence had already been made by many, including Burt (1925) and the recent review of juvenile crime (Home Office 1927). To provide these an early draft of the Bill included a section dealing with what were termed observation homes where such assessments could be made. The Home Office envisaged them being organized on a regional basis and being funded by the local authority. In London the original plan was that the Home Office would fund the building and operation of the observation home. The draft legislation proposed allowing a court to make an interim order for three months sending a juvenile to such a home prior to sentence and the home would then provide the Court with a detailed report. The draft legislation set out the objectives of the homes as, 'To provide for the custody, medical examination and observation of children and young persons remanded in custody'.[38] The estimated cost of establishing the home in London was £40,000 and it would require £9,000 per annum running costs. Home Office officials clearly expected problems and a Minute notes that 'the local authorities may object to pay but I think we must insist'.[39] Their concerns were well founded as when the Treasury were informed of the proposal, their reply dated 26 June 1931 gave the proposal short shrift, not only on the grounds of cost but also on the grounds that it set a dangerous precedent for the rest of the country if central funds were to be used. The Treasury argued in the same letter that funding should instead be the responsibility of the local authorities[40] in London.

Discussions continued and later that year Sydney Harris and his superior, Sir John Anderson, met with Mr Gater, Education Officer for the London County Council (LCC), to discuss the Bill. The proposal that the LCC fund an observation home in London led to the following note by Harris after this meeting:

> Mr Gater of the LCC said that in his view these proposals might prejudice the attitude of local authorities (and certainly the LCC) to the whole Bill.[41]

That comment suggests a not-so-veiled threat from the LCC Education Department. Relationships seem to have deteriorated such that in December 1931 Herbert Samuel, Oliver Stanley and Sidney Harris, the most senior politicians and officials at the Home Office, met with the LCC in a further attempt to persuade them of the virtues of observation homes and to discuss the financial arrangements for one in London. The LCC remained unconvinced and by January 1932 the clause introducing observation homes had been dropped from the draft Bill[42] of that year. The Howard League, unaware of these efforts, were disgusted, noting, 'the plea that this country cannot afford a single Observation Centre is simply beneath contempt and we make no comment upon it'.[43]

When the Bill finally reached Parliament, the Home Secretary, in a memo to Cabinet dated 8 January 1932, noted that he expected a good deal of opposition and went on to note that the Whips were even doubtful of its success.[44] Their concern focused on the clauses of the Bill dealing with working children. Although the House sat until 4.30 a.m. at the Second Reading of the Bill on 12 February 1932, there were few objections to the broad principles of the Bill. The key battles over the Bill in Parliament were fought over the Bill's proposal to abolish court-ordered corporal punishment. These debates became very bitter and the issue caused a major division between the two Houses of Parliament that moved outside of criminal justice and focused on the very relationship between the two Houses of Parliament. Rather than lose the Bill entirely the government removed the proposal to abolish court ordered corporal punishment. The final Act made no reference to this and it was as if the whole debate had never happened.

The roots of the Home Office training of probation of officers

As the expert psychologist and psychological discourse were gaining an even stronger foothold in the juvenile courts, it is perhaps not surprising that the issue of probation officers' training became important particularly following the changes the new Act brought. We have already detected a shift in the Report of the 1927 Young Offenders Committee on this issue from that adopted by the 1922 review of probation (Home Office 1922). Viewing the *Criminal Justice Act 1925* as providing new space for probation officers to move into around the country and the 1933 Act, with its welfare principle and enthusiasm for experts, defining the guiding principles as to how that space should be utilized then a change in the working practices of the probation officer seems inevitable. The emerging consensus on juvenile crime implied that force of personality and missionary zeal alone were likely to be considered insufficient for a probation officer. Despite the efforts of Joynson Hicks, the Home Secretary, to retain this as the *Criminal Justice Act 1925* went through Parliament, it was an approach that appeared increasingly out of date. This was a view, as we will see shortly, increasingly taken by the major probation officers' organization, that is NAPO.

For many years Elizabeth Macadam (1925) had advocated a system of university-based training for social workers and she was probably one of the first university-based social work lecturers to be appointed in the UK when she took up her post at Liverpool University in 1910. She advocated similar training for probation officers and now took the idea to the Home Office. On 8 December 1925 she and her colleagues representing the Joint University Council for Social Studies (see Yelloly 1980) met with Sidney Harris at the Home Office to propose a training scheme for probation officers. They proposed that the two-year social science training course, which she had described (Macadam 1925), be used as a basis for the training of probation officers. The deputation to the Home Office included a number of university-based social work or social science tutors[45] and Macadam as Honorary Secretary of the organization. A slightly different approach was advocated by

H. H. Ayscough (Secretary of the Central Church of England Temperance Society) who contacted the Home Office proposing a training scheme based on a combination of the CETS short training programme used for the new police court missionaries and the Diploma in Economic and Social Science run at the LSE. The Home Office file also includes correspondence from the Magistrates Association expressing concern at the religious element of the course proposed by Ayscough.[46] There were therefore two quite distinct proposals for probation officer training being discussed at the Home Office at this time.

The proposals were clearly taken seriously and Sidney Harris was sympathetic to the calls for the introduction of a training course for probation officers. Indeed, the Home Office had maintained a register of those looking for work as probation officers since 1923 and had noted at the time, 'if the work is to be done at all I am clear that it should be done by the Home Office and not by an outsider'.[47] The matter of probation officer training was taken up by the Advisory Committee on Probation and After Care, which sat at the Home Office, and of which he had been chair since 1924. This was the committee set up following the 1922 review of probation. The Minutes for the Committees meeting, which took place in November of 1929, included the following comment from Harris:

> For some time I have not felt satisfied that we are getting the best material for the probation service … it is important for the future that we should attract to the probation service persons of adequate education and experience as well as of suitable character and temperament.[48]

At the same meeting Harris proposed an experimental scheme for the training of probation officers. The scheme was part university-based and part practical and in outline at least very similar to the scheme that Macadam had established at Liverpool University. This initial proposal continued to be discussed at the meetings of the Probation Advisory Committee with Harris taking much of the lead in those discussions. At the meeting that took place on 20 February 1930, the committee agreed that the training should include a University Diploma in Social Science if the candidate did not have the qualification already. The proposal was that candidates would attend the courses at Liverpool, London or Birmingham Universities, there were to be seven places available initially and the training would take anything between one to three years to complete. The committee also decided to invite Elizabeth Macadam to join them to help with the selection for, and setting up of the training scheme.[49] From this point on she was very closely linked with the development of the training scheme for probation officers and remained so until well into the 1940s. The weight the

Home Office afforded the views of Macadam suggests, as does Yelloly (1980), that Macadam was a very influential, though now forgotten, figure in British social work during the interwar years.

The recently appointed president of NAPO, the Earl of Feversham, was also recruited onto the Advisory Committee on Probation and After Care in 1930. The Howard League for Penal reform had been agitating for a number of years for a training scheme for probation officers, but now senior officers of the National Association of Probation Officers began to do so as well. With NAPO having a well-connected member on the key Home Office committee dealing with probation they were to have a significant voice on the whole issue.

As we have already seen, the reality of probation practice had long been a mixture of old and new and so it is perhaps not surprising that not all probation officers supported the need for training, particularly a training scheme as envisaged by Macadam and for that matter the Home Office. In fact there is a good deal of evidence to suggest that the issue caused much debate amongst probation officers (Vanstone 2007: 76 detects this controversy too). At the NAPO Conference of 1931, the chair of the Conference, veteran magistrate and longtime supporter of probation, William Clarke-Hall, made the following address:

> It would be the greatest possible disaster to the system were it at any time divorced from the religious and idealistic spirit. If probation officers were to be appointed as mere officials the work would suffer infinitely.[50]

Clarke-Hall (1866–1932) may well have represented something of 'the old guard' having employed some of the very first probation officers in his Juvenile Court at Old Street. On the other hand, Mary Ellison, a working probation officer writing in 1934, whilst noting the usefulness of expert knowledge, went on to note, 'the final determining factor is the personality of the individual appointed' (Ellison 1934: 3). She might have been expected to take the more 'modern' view. The need for a two year training course for probation officers was by no means accepted by all connected with probation.

Nonetheless the Home Office decided to go ahead and in the same issue of *Probation* (the recently revamped journal of NAPO) as Clarke-Hall's comment appeared there was a small advert seeking to recruit applicants for the newly established Home Office training scheme for probation officers. The records show that there were thirty-one initial applicants for the training scheme, of which it was commented that it was a 'rather disappointing field', and, 'As one expected the women applicants are far superior to the men'.[51] A Selection Committee meeting drawn from the Probation Advisory Committee was held at the Home Office on 3 October 1930, after which it was agreed that one man and two women be appointed. Those interviewing candidates also commented on the low quality of the applicants, 'with the men the Committee found it difficult to choose anyone whom they could reasonably appoint'.[52] The appointment committee agreed that the reason for the low quality of the applicants, particularly the men, was the low salary on offer.

The Home Office persevered, and by August of 1931 eleven trainee probation officers had been appointed. In April 1932 the Home Office wrote to many of the petty sessional divisions around the country seeking their views on the training scheme and of the 145 who replied 17 replied that they were opposed to the scheme. It also appeared that most courts were still recruiting their own probation officers or using the local agents of the CETS to act as probation officers.[53] Clearly the views of magistrate around the country mirrored those of the probation officers and they too were sceptical of the need for a probation officer to be university trained. However, in 1933 there was the first contact from courts seeking to recruit from the officers who had been through the new scheme.

It might be tempting to see the creation of the Home Office training scheme for probation officers as an inevitable step in the steady development and professionalization of the service particularly when we keep in mind the recent changes in probation organization and the whole ethos and operation of the juvenile courts. This would be a major over-simplification. The particular training scheme that was introduced was only one option available and by no means the most inevitable, it also appears to have initially encountered very real difficulties.

These major policy and legislative changes were to have a huge impact on probation practice but in the meantime the probation officers 'on the ground' carried on with the day to day work. Here the Temperance Societies continued the work they had begun over fifty years ago and many of the older more experienced officers would still be soaked in the mission spirit. For them a belief in the power of personality, religious faith and character to turn from crime were still working.

Practice in the 1930s

The reality of probation practice as these major changes occurred is reflected in a number of autobiographies written by probation officers and other works on the role of the probation officer that were published in the 1930s. Their variety reinforces how the 1930s were a transitional phase for probation. Perhaps the most widely read publication amongst probation officers was *Probation* which was the journal of the National Association of Probation Officers. In his history of psychology Rose writes that the journal 'became virtually a Tavistock house journal' (Rose 1985: 199). An overview of the early issues of the journal would vindicate that view, but this would be a simplification of a complex situation and it fails to reflect the notion of transition in probation during this period. Vanstone, in his history of probation practice, writes that 'the influence of psychology increased in the second half of the 1920s, and reached new heights in the 1930s' (Vanstone 2007: 75). Later he focuses on the journal itself and writes:

> It is clear from the content of the journal that a range of probation officers through, conferences summer schools, training and reading the journal itself during the 1920s and 1930s, were exposed increasingly to psychological theories underpinned themselves by discourses such as those of psychoanalysis, eugenics and mental hygiene. (Vanstone 2007: 83)

Slightly later in his book he detects in the contributions to the journal 'the resilience of moral judgment, Christian mores and class perspectives' (Vanstone 2007: 87). Vanstone also raises concerns that the journal may not have reflected the reality of probation officer practice (see Vanstone 2007: 85) but this study would contend that the journal simply reflected the competing discourses impacting on that practice and on the officers themselves and the strange mixture of old and new that has always characterized probation.

The journal began in 1929 and the first edition included an article by William Clarke-Hall in which he writes that a probation officer 'must possess that quality so entirely indefinable, the quality of personality'.[54] In the same edition there is an article titled 'The Technique of Probation', in which the author states that 'Probation Officers might compare themselves with doctors'.[55] The two seem quite contradictory as one harks back to the old approach of the police court missionaries, whereas the other reflects the 'new psychology', 'professional' and 'expert' probation officers that were increasingly being written about.

The second edition included an editorial which stated:

> The N.A.P.O. believes most emphatically that the religious spirit is essential to the best probation work and welcomes accordingly members of all religious denominations.[56]

On the other hand, many of the early editions of the journal included articles written by Dr Charles Burns, who worked at the Tavistock Clinic, in which he confesses a debt to the work of Cyril Burt. These articles have titles such as

'The Psychology of the Criminal', and in one he describes the importance of probation officers taking into account the interplay between environment and personality. By environment he means the home, and he goes on to conclude that deprivation will lead to problems.[57] In a later article he writes about the 'young probationer' that:

> We must even take into account such minor points as septic tonsils or teeth because any poison in the body tends to affect the nervous system. We must remember that body and mind are an indissoluble whole and that a disturbance in one provokes a disturbance in the other.[58]

This author at least is very much soaked in a medicalized view as to the causes of crime. It would be interesting to speculate as to how articles like this were received by former police court missionaries, by now working as probation officers, often in the adult courts.

In the following year virtually every edition of *Probation* included an article from somebody working at the Tavistock Clinic. One article focused on hysteria,[59] another described the causes of crime and stated that 'the first cause is mental defect'.[60] It is at about this time that there begins, within the pages of the journal, a lively debate about the need for prior enquiries before any person is placed on probation. This was an issue that was later to concern those who drafted and debated what was to become the *Children and Young Persons Act of 1933*. At the annual NAPO Conference of 1931, William Clarke-Hall proposed a motion that anybody under the age of twenty-one should be subject to 'investigations' prior to sentence. He argued that without such investigations 'the use of probation is often haphazard and indiscriminate and unsuitable cases are placed under supervision'.[61] The motion was carried with the support of Dr Burns who was also at the Conference that year. If William Clarke-Hall represented the 'old school' of probation and Dr Burns the new approach, both agreed that an expert assessment was needed prior to sentence rather than the court simply making its own judgment about a defendant.

A rather strange mixture of old and new, of mission and psychological treatment, continues throughout this period in the pages of the journal. For instance, there regularly appears on the back pages of the journal advertisements for courses of lectures at the Tavistock Square Clinic or the National Council for Mental Hygiene. Some of these even make reference to the work of Freud and other psychoanalytical approaches,[62] though these are given scant coverage in the pages of the journal. The annual conference of NAPO continued to attract some very important speakers and each positioned themselves to some extent in relation to the varying views of probation practice discussed. Feversham, president of NAPO, writes:

> The psychologists have been telling us recently that no system of punishment can be effective which is merely punitive, but that punishment to produce the results that we desire must include re-education of the individual offender.[63]

The debates at the NAPO Conference of 1932 continued this theme of old and new. The key speaker that year was the Home Secretary, Herbert Samuel, who told probation officers that '… you are engaged in one of the most practical forms of religion'.[64] Other addresses at Conference that year included J. R. Rees of the Institute of Medical Psychology on the 'Psychological Causes of Crime' and the Chief Probation Officer of Liverpool, Harry Goldstone, on the 'Economic Causes of Crime'. Later that year the journal carried an article by W. H. Chinn, a probation officer from Birmingham, who as a worker 'on the ground' seems to have soaked up at least some of the writings of Burt. In particular he writes:

> Probation should never be used without first taking into account the social facts, i.e. the personal and environmental history of the offender and his suitability for that kind of treatment.[65]

Here we see a range of people working in different capacities within or alongside probation taking quite different views on the working practices of probation officers.

Subtle changes become evident as the 1930s progressed; the articles appearing in *Probation* continued in a similar vein but with one or two new developments detectable. One of the key speakers at the 1932 NAPO Conference was the London Juvenile Court Magistrate Basil Henriques who stated:

> But if this non institutional training (i.e. probation) is to be effective, it must be in the hands of thoroughly skilled and properly trained officials … The scientific treatment of the offender is the basis upon which probation must be worked today.[66]

The phrase 'trained officials' to describe probation officers is important and it reflects the recent changes in the role of the Home Office particularly in the work, payment and training of probation officers.

In 1934 a lengthy article appeared by Sybil Clement-Brown who was the tutor at what was to become the influential psychiatric social worker training course at the LSE. She wrote that 'delinquency is a relationship between the individual and society, so that our job in its solution will depend partly on modifying the attitudes of others towards him and partly on changing his outlook towards them'.[67] She captures the essence of a new brand of social work that was to emerge over the decade, and one that was reflected within the pages of *Probation*. Its debt to Burt is striking, particularly his view of an individualized social casework. In the meantime, Elizabeth Macadam continued to advocate her own brand of social work training, this time to the NAPO Conference of 1936 when she stated:

> it must be remembered that the object of the course is not to cram a man or woman with the details of everything that he may ever want in his future work but give him a background of knowledge and understanding and a thoughtful approach to his responsible duties.[68]

By this time her programme of social work training had been adopted by the Home Office for their probation officer training course.

In the meantime the religious influence in probation continued to be powerful. For instance at the NAPO Sussex Branch Summer School of 1936 a motion was passed by all the officers attending that 'the religious element is essential in probation work'.[69] The fact that Sidney Harris from the Home Office was also present did not seem to affect the officers.

We have already seen that there was a tradition within probation of officers and missionaries producing their own memoirs for public consumption which continued into the 1930s. Lillian Le Mesurier's *A Handbook of Probation and Social Work of the Courts* is different as it was published under the auspices of NAPO and was a written as a guide for officers. She offers a history of probation before going on to describe the way the probation system operated. It is a work singled out for particular attention by McWilliams in his studies of the development of probation, and he says its view of probation work lacks '… a body of theoretical and empirical knowledge, accessible to the officer (which leads to facts being interpreted via)… application of common sense and moral evaluation' (McWilliams 1985: 267). It might be fairer to see Le Mesurier's work as an attempt to encompass the various and in some respects contradictory approaches to probation practice reflected in the above discussions within the pages of *Probation*.

Vanstone (2007) sees the Handbook as a 'collective aspiration to professional status' (Vanstone 2007: 89). He describes the revamped journal *Probation*, which we have just considered, in similar terms. These publications sought to give probation a professional status. Mair and Burke take a slightly different view and write:

> The Handbook can be seen as yet another step by N.A.P.O. to take full control of probation work, to be recognized as the authorities voice in Practice. (Mair and Burke 2012: 71)

Bearing in mind the tensions within NAPO and its relationship with the Home Office and CETS, this comment would imply a political subtext almost to Le Mesurier's work.

The book looks at probation practice in two distinct sections, one she calls 'probation work proper' and the other more general social work of the courts, which is 'sometimes referred to as missionary work' (Le Mesurier 1935: 52). Probation work she then divides into two parts, the first of which is investigation and the second supervision. The role of the probation officer in the latter is to help the probationer find employment and '... also to place him or her in touch with wholesome influences, either religious social or both' (Le Mesurier 1935: 55). To perform that role a probation officer needs the qualities of 'tact, patience or common sense,...' (Le Mesurier 1935: 58). The officer would also need knowledge of the Law and a local knowledge of services, charitable organizations and the like. Despite the quite specific requirements she places on a probation officer, Le Mesurier makes scant reference to the training of probation officers except to say that it is desirable, and to note the new training course started by the Home Office. Her separation of probation and missionary work is interesting though not new.

On the other hand, she clearly saw a role for the expert as the work of Burt and his colleagues had not passed her by. She writes:

> A study that is becoming increasingly necessary to all engaged in the work of education is that of psychology, and to few it can be more important than to probation officers. (Le Mesurier 1935: 62)

However, there is a particular relationship between the psychologist and officer, she writes:

> It is not to be supposed, nor indeed wished, that they can make a deep and thorough study of this subject, which is one for trained experts. But they can and should learn enough to recognize certain symptoms..., and – above all – to know when it is wise to consult the expert. (Le Mesurier 1935: 62)

The expert was therefore the psychologist and in her view the probation officer would act as a gatekeeper to the psychologist and other community resources. This description of the social worker role is remarkably similar to that of Mary Richmond (1917) who also saw the social worker as a gatekeeper and assistant to the psychologist.

Le Mesurier might have been ambivalent about the training of probation officers but she argued strongly that they make up a professional group. For her, though, this is very much tied in with the fact that many probation officers, even in 1935, were part-time, juggling their work for the temperance societies with their probation officer role, and often poorly paid. She asserts:

> a large proportion of part-time officers still exists and is to be deplored. As a rule the part-time officer means the ill-paid officer, and sometimes the unskilled and inexperienced officer … probation work is a highly skilled, full time profession, for which the best available men, and women are required. (Le Mesurier 1935: 69)

Although she makes reference to university based Social Science Diplomas, which by 1935 were more widely available, many of her comments on the issue make particular reference to practical training. Again this suggests Le Mesurier trying to encompass all probation officers in her account by unifying all probation officers with a claim they can all agree to, namely professional status and better pay.

In a lengthy chapter on 'investigation' Le Mesurier describes environmental factors which are the remit of the probation officer and individual factors which should be dealt with by a 'medical psychologist' (Le Mesurier 1935: 90), again stressing the point about the role of the probation officer in relation to the new psychological expert. Later comes a lengthy chapter on 'probation and child guidance', which again shows the influence of Burt and the new consensus emerging and reflected in the *Children and Young Persons Act*. For instance Le Mesurier writes that '[d]elinquency is not a disorder or entity in itself, but a fact of general maladjustment' (Le Mesurier 1935: 210). The same chapter also discusses the research of Cyril Burt and goes on to argue that probation officers should have a knowledge of mental testing, IQ testing and mental ratio tests. Again, though, it is the psychological expert who would actually carry out that testing.

An alternative perspective on probation is offered by Jo Harris (1937) who published his memoirs of his experiences as a probation officer, titled *Probation – A Sheaf of Memories – thirty-four years work in local Police Courts*. When her work was published, Le Mesurier was working at HMP Wormwood Scrubs in London which was where younger offenders were sent for allocation to one of the Borstals (Benney 1936). Jo Harris had spent all his working life in East Anglia, a long way from the busy capital and the Home Office and as we have already seen there were major differences between probation in the capital and in the more rural parts of the country. Harris's work is more personal and even anecdotal, closer to the work of Thomas Holmes (1908) where he looked back on his work following his recent retirement.

Harris's work is soaked in religious language which is an immediate reminder of an older approach to probation. He describes probation as 'redemption in the open' (Harris 1937: 21) and his opening chapter makes frequent use of words such as love, forgiveness, mercy and justice. He regards the period up to 1925 as an 'experimental' one in probation's development and the *Criminal Justice Act* of that year marking the proper beginnings of a probation system. Unlike Le Mesurier but in common with others he was suspicious of state involvement in probation. For instance, he writes:

> The less officialism that comes into this great work of redemption, the more successful it will be. (Harris 1937: 31)

Unlike NAPO, who saw the Home Office as the means by which officers would achieve their aims of a full-time and professional service, Harris's view may well have been quite typical of many probation officers of the time.

Yet recent developments in probation had not passed him by. When describing the work of the juvenile courts he writes:

> The Probation Officer's reports deal with his (i.e. the juvenile's) home conditions, his leisure life, general behaviour and habits.

He goes on:

> One looks forward to the day when a psychologist shall be attached to every area who will be able to detect these 'minds at mischief', and the many kinks in character will be treated as diseases rather than faults. (Harris 1937: 46)

In a strikingly modern outlook he argues that the chief causes of delinquency are to be found predominantly in the home, particularly a lack of parental control. However, bad housing, bad company, unemployment and gambling also play a role. In common with both Burt and Le Mesurier he discusses the interplay between these factors as being particularly important. He argues that the best safeguard against juvenile delinquency is a good family life, and that can only be provided within a 'traditional' family.

The religious tone is continued in the work of Dark (1939), whose work *Inasmuch… Christianity in the Police Court* is perhaps not surprising as he was editor of *The Church Times* when he wrote it. For example, he claims that 'The probation officer's office is a spiritual dispensary' (Dark 1939: 25). Again he stresses a bad home as the chief cause of juvenile delinquency and then goes on to discuss the influence of bad social and economic conditions as they impact on the home and family.

Out in the provinces the mission was well established. In 1931 H. Courtenay Orchard published his memoirs of nearly thirty years as police court missionary in Walsall. He describes arriving in the town as an evangelist with the Wesleyan Church in 1903 and being appointed police court missionary in 1904. Perhaps not surprisingly his approach to his work harks back to an earlier period. When describing his 'charges' he writes:

> at least seventy-five percent of them are no psychological problem at all. It is more often than not the problem of environment. Take him out of his environment, or if you cannot do that, try to alter it. If you are powerless to do that, which is quite likely, endeavour to counteract the evil of his environment with some such life as a properly organized Lad's Club offers, and then you will go some distance. (Courtenay Orchard 1931: xxxiv)

Much of his time was spent running clubs and societies of an enormous range for the local youth but he was also a man of clear religious conviction which underpinned much of his work. His attitude to the recent changes in probation following the 1925 Act and the Rules which followed is interesting. On this matter he wrote:

> In many instances, to put it quite mildly, it means one third of the salary, and a bit more than three fourths of the control. And it does not make for the efficient working of this beneficent bit of legislation. In fact … (it) has, in some places, turned a creation, which working at its best is pulsating with life and love and vigour, into a machine bereft of a soul. (Courtney-Orchard 1931: 267)

A few years later Walter Stanton published his memoirs of his time as a police court missionary in Worcester. Much of his book focuses on what might be called matrimonial and even more generally social work to the court. Early on he describes a police court missionary as 'a handmaiden to the court, a kind of fairy god mother to all and sundry' (Stanton 1935: 17). It is only in the latter sections of the book that he describes 'probation work'. He describes the juvenile offenders he has met as 'dwarfed in mind and often body … self restraint is entirely unknown … environment and hereditary taint having left its fell mark upon their unstable natures with but faint hopes of eradication' (Stanton 1935: 77). There then follow a number of vignettes of where he describes helping one young man to move into a Home, another to emigrate and another to move to a Reformatory School. The book includes a number of quotes from religious texts and the word mercy is used throughout his account of work with offenders. Like others these are accounts of the role and explanations for crime which have a long tradition.

The works of Harris, Dark, Courtenay-Orchard and Stanton all remind us that the police court mission was still very important to probation around the country well into the 1930s. The *1934 Annual Report of the London Police Court*

Mission showed Church of England Temperance Society to have 64 missionaries working in the courts of London and that new cases for that year were made up of 1,660 men and lads, 351 boys under 17, 565 women and girls and 32 girls under 17.[70] An earlier report notes that:

> The Missionary is the Churches Agent in the police Court to uplift the fallen and to work for the reclamation of those who have been guilty of offences, but, like the great Apostle, the Missionary makes himself a servant to all.[71]

The CETS approach to the *Children and Young Persons Act 1933* is also revealing. They wrote:

> The Act will undoubtedly result in a great many more cases being brought into the Juvenile Courts. This will not seriously affect our Missionaries in the Metropolitan Police Court area as they do not normally attend the Juvenile Courts, but it will bring a great deal of additional work to those who serve the Petty Sessional Courts in Middlesex.[72]

These comments do suggest that little had changed in the adult courts of London. The children's probation officers in the juvenile courts appointed nearly thirty years before continued to work differently from missionary probation officers in the courts of the capital.

The differences between adult court and juvenile court probation practice were often made by practising probation officers of the time. For instance another working officer, Dorothy Eyres, writes in *Probation* about her work:

> That among schoolchildren being mainly preventive, perhaps needs the widest experience of social work to ensure contacts with the numerous agencies already existing for helping children physically, mentally and spiritually, educationally and socially. The work amongst adolescents needs a more specialised training…, and experience in the psychology of the boy or girl who is neither man, woman or child. The work among grown ups needs special gifts of personality and of the spirit, a wide experience of life and a true sense of vocation.[73]

There is a clear suggestion in her work that older versions of probation practice tended to linger in the adult courts. It should be remembered that Burt (1925) wrote about juvenile delinquency and worked for the London Education Committee so it is reasonable to expect his influence to be greater in the Juvenile Courts.

Another officer to describe her experiences in print was Mary Ellison who in 1934 published *Sparks Beneath the Ashes*. At the time she had been working as a probation officer for six years so would have been appointed after the *Criminal*

Justice Act 1925 and the quite radical changes that had followed that. It is curious therefore she makes least reference to the psychologists and actually seems quite sceptical of the profession. In a section dealing with more 'upmarket' shoplifters appearing in court she writes:

> In such cases good psychologists are often invaluable. Choose your expert with caution! There are psychologists and psychologists. (Ellison 1934: 97)

She was also doubtful about the need for probation officers to be trained (Ellison 1934: 3).

Her explanations for crime seem closer to the earlier work of people like Devon (1912) and Bray (1908) rather than Burt (1925) or those working in the Child Guidance Clinics. For instance, she writes:

> Insufficient decent accommodation, overcrowding and insanitary conditions cause the rising generation to grow up enfeebled, degraded from birth. The mental and moral stamina of their parents has suffered a great strain, their nerves in some instances have been fretted to rawness by existence under such disabilities. (Ellison 1934: 40)

In fact this particular quote has echoes with late nineteenth-century concerns about deterioration. Throughout her work Ellison makes regular reference to the police court missionary, but this in the context of an account of her own working day as a probation officer. For her the two roles are distinct, she describes being in court and working alongside the police court missionary.

These books, all published within a few years, describe a cocktail of psychology, social work, mission and religious zeal, professionalism, anti-officialism and sociological explanations of crime. The same mixture in fact that was in evidence in *Probation*. Superficially they seem contradictory yet they did coexist and alliances were forged, probation expanded, the number of full-time officers increased and the probation system spread wider into the more rural parts of the country.

Applying psychoanalysis to the delinquent

The psychology discussed so far has been based on the work of Burt and others who advocated intelligence testing and focused on the interplay between environment (usually the family) and personality. Although Freud's work was being increasingly read and applied in Britain (Hynes 1976) by the mid-1930s, the psychoanalytical approach was rarely applied to the offender. The work of Maurice Hamblin Smith (1922) did not lead to a deluge of writing on the subject. The antagonism displayed by Edward Troup to the work of Freud and described in the previous chapter was not unique. For instance, Edward Glover, a psychoanalyst working with offenders, comments on the Home Office that 'its attitude to psychology, in particular psychoanalytical psychology, has been cautious to the point of neglect' (Glover 1960: 38). He also recalled that as he lectured magistrates in 1922, at least one stormed out in protest (Glover 1960: 12). Valier (1998) points out that Glover and other psychoanalysts attracted a good deal of opposition from other sources including the Fabian Society during this period.

Despite the indifference and occasional hostility, the approach attracted some interest even if it was marginal to the main discourse shifts going on within criminal justice. In 1929 Grace Pailthorpe (1932) submitted her report on the psychology of the delinquent to the Medical Research Council who dithered for three years and insisted on a number of alterations before it was finally published (Saville and Rumney 1991). The Report had been produced under the auspices of Dr Hamblin Smith who supported her research. Pailthorpe's[74] works is based on her study of 100 women and girls at Holloway Prison and in a number of preventive and rescue homes.[75]

Her research did not show psychoanalysis as the answer to all the problems of criminal behaviours but estimated that it could be usefully applied in 19 per cent of cases (Pailthorpe 1932: 96). For the remaining she recommended either permanent segregation, permanent supervision in the community or education. She argued that symptoms of delinquency are evident in early childhood. She writes:

> the earlier young delinquents are studied the better ultimately for the public purse. The so-called criminal is not a person who suddenly crystallizes out as a criminal. His asocial behaviour is traceable back to his childhood days. (Pailthorpe 1932: 90)

To aid in that early diagnosis she advocated the establishing of what she calls a 'central clearing station' to which all offenders would go on their first conviction.

Interestingly Pailthorpe's work borrows freely from the work of both Freud and Burt.[76] She makes much of family relationships as a factor in crime causation, as Burt does, particularly lack of parental love, this in turn leads to a lack of what she terms 'sentiment development'. She makes regular reference to the psychological testing of her subjects, and like Burt advocates a variety of treatments tailored to the needs of each offender. She describes her own method as analytical, the following reflecting the tone of her work:

> But even when, as in the case of my own investigations, the opportunities for formal deep analysis of individual cases are limited, it is nonetheless possible to apply analytical principles. These can be applied, not only in obtaining detailed histories, but in singling out special characteristics to be examined in comparative work. Thus, in detailed individual work the simple but revolutionary expedient is adopted of letting the subject tell their own story, having first of course removed all possible obstacles to or obvious sources of bias in the recital. (Pailthorpe 1932: 10)

At the same time that this work was published, Pailthorpe was busy establishing the Institute for the Scientific Treatment of Delinquency (ISTD) with Dr Edward Glover[77] who had helped her redraft some of the above study so as to make it acceptable to the Medical Research Council (Saville and Rumney 1991). The ISTD was explicitly psychoanalytically based and set itself as an organization using these methods with offenders. Drs Pailthorpe and Glover had begun planning the organization in 1931, and by 1935 were treating their first clients. Their Annual Report for 1935 shows that the ISTD treated 116 referrals, 75 of whom were referrals from courts.[78] At the same time staff at the ISTD, mainly Glover and Pailthorpe, were lecturing probation officers on their work and within a few years commented, '[I]t has been found necessary to organise a more advanced course for those probation officers who have attended lectures in previous years'.[79] In these early days they operated on a financial shoestring, much of the income came from the Poor Box of courts who had received reports from staff working for the ISTD. Most of those working for the ISTD did the work as a sideline to their existing practice, but by 1937 premises were found for the ISTD at Portman Street in London (Saville and Rumney 1991: 14) which became known as the Psychopathic Clinic. Today it is known as the Portman Clinic and deals with a very similar client group.

Despite its rather modest beginnings it is clear that there was a good deal of interest in its work amongst those working in the field. This is illustrated by the names of the early vice presidents of the organization that included Cyril Burt and the Earl of Feversham, not to mention Freud and Jung themselves.[80] It is also apparent, even this early, that there was a great deal of interest in the work and methods of the organization from probation officers. Not only were referrals being made by officers from court but many officers attended courses run by the ISTD. In fact, as early as November 1932 NAPO was in touch with the

ISTD seeking to cooperate,[81] by 1934 there was a meeting between NAPO, the London Police Court Mission and the Principal of Ruskin College to discuss the possibility of establishing a course run by the ISTD.[82] and in the following year the same committee noted more requests from London probation officers for 'practical instruction in psychology'.[83] The ISTD set out explicitly to cultivate a relationship with probation officers and NAPO, who in return were only too pleased to reciprocate.

Although the leading figures in the ISTD were saw their practice as psychoanalytical they were not solely devoted to this particular approach with offenders. Valier describes the work of the ISTD in its early days and writes:

> Psychological treatment at the I.S.T.D. took the form of a range of techniques from pure suggestion and hypnosis to psycho-analysis, and often the use of combined methods, guidance and persuasion. Many cases were only given advice and instruction. Psychological treatment was usually combined with 'environmental handling': supervision and help from a probation officer, or an environmental influence from other social workers. (Valier 1998: 3)

From these small beginnings the organization and the approach it took was to become very influential in the treatment of crime and will be returned to. At this stage though, the Home Office kept a distance (Valier 1998: 3).

Psychological understandings of crime and delinquency were also beginning to make their presence felt in other ways particularly in respect of social worker training and a new course which began to attract the attention of probation officers. This was the one-year diploma in Mental Health Social Work Course run at the LSE, and for a long time organized by Sybil Clement-Brown. The first students were admitted in 1929 but the impetus came from one or two social workers, including Clement-Brown, who had been over to the USA to train (Clement-Brown 1970, Timms 1964: 19).

The syllabus for an early version of the course ran in 1932 included such subjects as general psychology, individual differences, mental subnormality, psychiatric social casework, applied social psychology, psychology of childhood and adolescence, mental health in early childhood (Timms 1964: 301). These subjects contrast with the training course which had just been started by the Home Office based on Macadam's broad liberal education. However, as Yelloly points out, 'The first course was strikingly eclectic in its theoretical content' (Yelloly 1980: 54), suggesting that no particular school of psychology dominated, a view echoed by the Course Tutor (Clement-Brown 1970). The course was designed for experienced social workers and placed much stress on the placement element (Clement-Brown 1970) which usually took place in the Mawdsley Hospital or the London Child Guidance Clinic. A number of probation officers attended the course and for these it operated as an addition to the Home Office training course.

Within the pages of *Probation* there was a good deal of interest, as we have seen, in these subject matters and the course itself attracted considerable interest in probation circles but very much at grass roots level. This support is acknowledged by Glover who a number of years later wrote, 'probation officers provided some of the staunchest supporters of institutes such as the I.S.T.D.' (Glover 1960: 44). Clement-Brown contributed at least one substantial article to the Journal[84] and the course was regularly advertised on the back page of *Probation* throughout the late 1930s, indeed scholarships for probation officers were occasionally offered.[85] Thus the Mental Health Social Work Course at the LSE and the ISTD both began to make small inroads into probation during this period. Both were forerunners of significant shifts in the social work and psychological discourses and were to have a major impact on probation in later years.

Accusations of sentimentalism

Outside of these discussions it became apparent that crime was rising rapidly in the 1930s and this despite the slow move out of economic depression (see Hobsbawm 1969, Taylor 1975). In his survey of juvenile crime between the wars Bailey writes that 'from 1935 a vigorous controversy burst forth concerning the reasons for the upward trend of juvenile crime' (Bailey 1987: 117). He identifies two distinct camps which formed offering different explanations for this increase. One was based mainly around the police and magistrates who put much of the blame on the new 'sentimental justice' particularly following recent legislative changes. The other group was based around what he calls the 'reformers'. Many at the Home Office had argued that 'the abnormal conditions of the thirties – depression, unemployment and poverty – were mostly important for accentuating defective family life' (Bailey 1987: 126) and were the cause of the rise in crime. A third explanation for the sudden increase in recorded crime also emerged later based on the 'net-widening'[86] consequences of the *Children and Young Persons Act 1933* and was used as the 1930s wore on.

Probation was aligned with Bailey's 'reformers' group and there must have been an element of being 'under siege'. Such is hinted at when Sidney Harris delivered the key address at the NAPO Conference as early as 1932, a year before the implementation of the *Children and Young Persons Act 1933*. On that occasion he considered the various explanations offered for rising crime and stated:

> Another possible cause, certainly referred to a good deal, is leniency in the penal methods of today.

Harris continued:

> The Probation System is likely to be blamed for the recent increase in crime, but in this case the criticism ought to fall on the shoulders, not of the probation officers, but of the magistrates who decide when probation is to be used.

After dismissing the cinema and motor car as causes of the increase he concludes:

> When unemployment suggests itself so obviously as the most important reason for the increase of crime, I do not think we need look very much further.[87]

However, as the decade wore on and economic conditions improved recorded crime continued to rise.

The Police did not share this view and by the late 1930s were becoming increasingly concerned by, and vociferous about, the increase in recorded juvenile crime. Information collected by the Metropolitan Police showed a substantial rise in juvenile crime from 1932, primarily offences of larceny and 'breaking'. These figures were sent to the Home Office, the London County Council and to the Board of Education. The Chief Commissioner then decided to make the information public and noted that '[t]he publicity which will be obtained from the Commissioners Annual Report is far greater than will be ever obtained from the Home Office statistics'.[88] He was clearly a man well aware of the headline grabbing possibilities of an increase in recorded crime. The Home Office obviously took the information seriously as Sidney Harris later wrote to the Chief Commissioner asking for further copies of the above statistics.[89]

The Home Office's own research from the Statistical Branch came to the conclusion that the 1933 Act was in fact the main reason for the increase in crime. Their Report of 1937 noted that the increase in juvenile crime had begun to slow down and went on to conclude:

> The only new factor operative in 1934 and 1935 and not operative in the earlier years is the entry into force of the new Children Act in November, 1933. The conclusion seems irresistible that the comparatively large rise in 1934 and 1935 figures was due to the stimulus of the desire to use the new Act

in respect of children breaking the law. This stimulus, it would seem, attained something like equilibrium in 1936.[90]

So by the late 1930s the Home Office used a 'net widening' explanation for the more recent and rapid increase in juvenile crime particularly. Home Office officials and a number of magistrates argued that the *Children and Young Persons Act 1933* had increased confidence in the juvenile courts to such an extent that the police and other public bodies were encouraged to take children to court knowing that their welfare needs would be the prime concern of the court rather than a desire to simply punish for the offence committed.

This had been predicted in the *Report of the Departmental Committee on the Treatment of Young Offender* (Home Office 1927) which included the comment that '[W]hen it is released that these courts are especially equipped to help rather than punish the young offender, we hope that the reluctance to bring such children before them will disappear' (Home Office 1927: 47). Others accepted the netwidening argument; *The Times,* for example, commented on the rise in juvenile crime that 'the statistics really reflect the growth in confidence in the system as reformed' and it is 'not that children have suddenly become more wicked, but that the legal machinery has become more efficient' (*The Times* 4 January 1937 and 25 October 1937). However, the Chief Commissioner of Police in London had little sympathy with the argument when he wrote:

> It has been suggested in the papers and elsewhere that this is due to the fact that, owing to the humane treatment now adopted, the general public is more likely to send juveniles before a court than previously. So far as breaking offences are concerned I do not believe there is a word of truth in this.[91]

The two camps thus remained entrenched throughout the 1930s.

These debates show that despite the consensus being formed on the correct responses to crime and particularly juvenile crime at this time the new system was attracting considerable criticism. It was against this background that the Home Office launched yet another review of probation. In some respects this may seem a little strange as policy and practice within probation appeared rather settled if based on a strange mix of old and new. Nonetheless one issue continued to dog probation and was becoming more controversial in the aftermath of the recent legislative changes. This was the issue of what was known as 'dual control' where the Home Office and numerous societies, dominated by the CETS managed and paid for probation.

For many connected with probation this led to two types of probation which were increasingly seen as mutually exclusive.

The mission under fire

By 1936 the probation system had already been reviewed three times (Home Office 1910a, 1913, 1922) since its introduction, it had also become one of the key disposals available to the juvenile courts, although its presence in the adult courts continued to be based largely on the old police court missionaries. The issue of what was known at the time as 'dual control', where many officers were jointly funded by both religious societies and the state, was being increasingly criticized. These criticisms were not new (for instance see Brockway 1928, Clarke-Hall 1926) but they were increasingly being made, as we shall see, by the Home Office officials. To date these criticisms had not been acted upon because the religious societies were crucial to probation and particularly to probation finance.

Only a year after the *Children and Young Persons Act 1933* the Home Office appointed The Departmental Committee on the Social Services in the Courts of Summary Jurisdiction and it reported in March 1936 (Home Office 1936). In her history of probation Bochel describes its report as 'the blue print for the probation service for the next quarter of a century' (Bochel 1976: 150) and Mair and Burke describe it as 'the most important document in the first fifty years of probation's existence' (Mair and Burke 2012: 73). Ironically, its beginnings were far more modest as it began life as a review of the work of probation officers in the matrimonial courts precipitated by one of the Law Lords drafting a Bill relating to proceedings for matrimonial cases in 1934.[92] When Sidney Harris was appointed Chair of the Committee and the rest of the Committee including the Earl of Feversham were appointed the committee took a much wider view of its role and review the whole of the work of the probation service. Harris particularly seems to have been concerned for probation at this point in time and wrote on a Home Office file that 'the whole system with all its merits may fall into disrepute unless care is taken to provide against obvious difficulties'.[93]

When the London Police Court Mission were notified of the committee's appointment and task they suspected that something was afoot and noted in their annual report that year:

> It was disappointing to us to find that apart from the Chairman, who holds a neutral position, there was not one of the committee who had ever been known as a friend of the Police Court Mission.[94]

Their concerns centred on the role of the missionary spirit and voluntary element in probation. The London Police Court Mission also noted in the same report:

It would be almost incredible that an undertaking which has become part and parcel of our national system of administering justice should be brought to an end in favour of a purely official public service.[95]

Their Annual Report for that year noted that the police court missionaries had been around for 58 years and by 1934 there were 64 missionaries working in the Police Courts of London and Middlesex. The Report for 1936, the year the Home Office Committee finally reported, revealed that the number of missionaries had increased to eighty-one.[96] It is quite clear that the London Police Court Mission was a crucial part of the operation of probation in London and particularly in the adult courts. This position was mirrored around the country where the Temperance Societies still part funded many probation officers.

On the other hand, the National Association of Probation Officers had long lobbied hard for the end the system whereby many probation officers were part funded and managed by one of a large number of voluntary societies including the Church of England Temperance Society. This had been NAPO policy since its formation in 1912 (see Bochel 1962a). Bochel's history of NAPO describes the very good relationships between the organization and senior civil servants, particularly Sidney Harris, at the Home Office. She writes, '[d]uring this period it was consulted by the Home Office in a hitherto unprecedented way' (Bochel 1962b: 55). The president of NAPO, Feversham and the secretary H. E. Norman had lobbied very hard for the committee to widen its original brief and look at probation generally. They were therefore delighted to see the approach the committee took and the inclusion of Feversham on the committee. Bochel goes onto argue that all the NAPO members giving evidence to the committee spoke in favour of the creation of a fully public probation service and against the 'dual control' system. Timasheff writing only a few years after the committee reported notes simply that it was appointed 'in accordance with the wishes of N.A.P.O.' (Timasheff 1941: 75). Many NAPO members may well have been missionary probation officers and so not wildly in favour of the stance that the executive were taking.

The committee took evidence from a substantial number of probation officers and shortly after its Report was published Feversham noted:

in the presentation of that evidence the National Association of Probation Officers played a not inconsiderable part. Thirty nine probation officers were called, most of them elected by their Branch organisations to present the views of their local colleagues in the different provincial areas.[97]

Evidence was also taken from the Chief Constables Association which included a stinging criticism of the police court missionaries:

> It is thought that in the appointment of probation officers too much consideration is given in some cases to their Christian views and outlook, with the result they are sometimes rather trusting, sentimental and unduly optimistic, and that too many persons have received the benefits of probation on the strength of statements made by probation officers.[98]

They preferred the newer officers but commented that 'there is a suggestion that some sort of training is desirable to compensate for lack of experience'. In their oral evidence the Chief Constables Association said:

> The point of view of the newer type of probation officer is more constructive than that of some of his predecessors, who too often regarded themselves as the prisoners advocate, sometimes even to the point of hampering the police.[99]

The 'old chestnut' of the varied use of probation was raised early in the Report, and again the blame was placed on the courts. Interestingly, a new dimension was added:

> On the other hand, there is good ground for believing that probation is sometimes used to excess, especially in the case of the young offender. (Home Office 1936: 42)

The accusations of sentimentalism referred to above and criticisms that probation was little more than a 'let off' were also addressed:

> The disciplinary element in probation needs emphasising, and it should be generally understood that, far from being a sentimental gesture, probation when effectively carried out makes serious demands on the probationer. (Home Office 1936: 43)

This disciplinary aspect might be seen to contradict many of the early pronouncements about probation officers being a friend to the offender (see Home Office 1910a, for example).

The probation officer's role and qualities received a good deal of attention in the Report. Personality on its own was abandoned as being sufficient qualification to work as a probation officer:

> personality by itself is not enough. It must be reinforced by the knowledge and resources which the trained social worker possesses. (Home Office 1936: 58)

The Report then went on to outline its vision for a training scheme for probation officers based on a university diploma in social work. The proposed training included: social administration, industrial conditions and organizations, the work of the child guidance clinics, psychological methods, court practice and procedures and various statutes (Home Office 1936: 132–133). The Report envisaged two methods of probation training, one based on a general social science university diploma and another on a more specific 'probation course'. The Report included only passing reference to the training course which the Home Office had already set up and operated since 1930, criticisms of which were noted. The solution to these criticisms was the appointment of a Central Training Board at the Home Office to recruit and supervise the training of all probation officers.

The Report took the radical step of proposing that probation be now a 'fully public service' (Home Office 1936: 103). The Report claimed that this had been the view of the vast majority of the witnesses who had given evidence and this implied that the religious societies (particularly the Church of England Temperance Society) should no longer have a role in the appointment and payment of probation officers. Early concerns about probation's slide into 'officialism' were now to be laid to rest. In conjunction with this fully public service a Home Office–based system of Probation Inspectors was to be appointed. The Report commented:

> We recommend that the Secretary of State should be given a general power of inspection to satisfy himself that a reasonable standard of efficiency is being maintained before Government Grant is paid. (Home Office 1936: 153)

The debate about dual control was thus resolved. The mission element in probation was finally dead; killed not by the arrival of a new psychological discourse or a move away from mission and personality but by a Home Office and NAPO based alliance to create a public service social work agency. It was primarily administrative concerns about organization, training and funding which dominated the Report of 1936 and which led to this change.

The Home Office very carefully monitored press reaction to the Report and noted that it was 'interesting, and even remarkable that they are without exception favourable'.[100] Perhaps not surprisingly, the CETS did object in their Annual Report for that year:

> In our opinion the great success of the Mission and of the probation system in the past, is that its workers have been drawn into the service by a deep sense of vocation and a conviction that they were doing essentially religious work. Being appointed by a religious and voluntary society, the 'missionary spirit' orientated all their work. They were not Court officers but friends of the people and regarded as such.

> We fear that if probation becomes a public official service the missionary
> spirit will gradually disappear to the great loss of the whole system.[101]

The London Police Court Mission set up a sub-committee to consider the Home Office Report and argued that 'many criticisms contained in the Report were unfair to our Mission'.[102] The staff of the London Police Court Mission hoped that the 'London Police Court Mission will be allowed to carry on her work if she fulfils the standard the Home Office shall require'.[103]

The sub-committee met on 7 May 1936 and was clearly angered by the Report seeing the 'mission ideal under threat'.[104] Sir Edward Troup, who following his retirement from the Home Office was by now chair of the London Police Court Mission, chaired that meeting and felt strongly enough about the issue to write to the Home Office including a copy of the minutes of the meeting. However, higher ranking church officials took a softer line and the Archbishop of Canterbury wrote to the Home Office asking that they receive a deputation, saying that '[t]he object of the Deputation would not be to criticise the recommendations of the Report'.[105] The deputation duly attended headed by the Archbishop of Canterbury on 24 November 1936. Although they accepted the Report's overall direction, they continued to advocate a religious presence in probation work. Further meetings took place and a deputation of the London Police Court Mission attended at the Home Office on 5 January 1937. This one included the former Home Secretary Joynson Hicks. It is ironic to note that two old Home Office stalwarts now sought to defend the old system of probation and were lobbying hard at the Home Office on behalf of the CETS.

The Home Office were clearly being put under a lot of pressure by some very influential individuals yet they did not relent and a Home Office Minute quoting the Home Secretary, Samuel Hoare, notes:

> He is satisfied that the system under which candidates for the probation service
> are nominated, so far as the adult courts are concerned, by the London Police
> Court Mission, can no longer be defended and that there is need to bring the
> whole of the probation staff under unified public control.[106]

It is clear that the Home Office had become anxious that the system for appointment of probation officers particularly for the adult courts was out of its control. Figures showing that the use of probation in the juvenile courts was far higher than in the adult courts, the uneven use of probation and the varied arrangements for probation around the country had all been noted at the Home Office. The fact that the Treasury was contributing to the salaries of the police court missionaries via the grants to the religious societies was a concern to both the Home Office and the Treasury.[107] The Receiver of the Metropolitan Police actually managed the financing of probation and the paying of the grant to the various societies and his concern, judging from the same file, appears to have stemmed from the fact that the Home Office had no control over who was appointed as probation officer in the adult courts and that the state was effectively paying for their missionary work outside of the courts.

So the Home Office decided that it should manage the whole of the probation system in the same way it did the children's probation officers in the capital, and had done since 1907. These officers were centrally appointed and their work was seen as secular in nature. In late 1937, a matter of months after the final Report was published, the Church of England Temperance Society noted, 'we must expect the Home Office to take over the employment of all our Missionary Probation Officers in the Metropolitan Courts in the near future'.[108] In effect a national system of probation was to be created.

Shortly after the publication of the Report, Sidney Harris was promoted to Assistant Under Secretary at the Home Office and a new Probation Branch was created at the Home Office on 26 January 1937 thus taking probation out of the Children's Branch. Its first principal was B. J. Reynolds[109] who had in his department one Deputy Principal, one Chief Clerk, two Clerical Officers and a Probation Inspector. The day after the creation of the new Department Sidney Harris delivered the Clarke-Hall Lecture where he reiterated many of the themes included in the 1936 Report. His lecture makes regular reference to probation as a public service and probation officers as skilled professionals. He also referred to the perception of probation as an option only for juveniles:

> The mention in the statute of age as a factor which a Court must consider before releasing an offender on probation has given currency to the idea that probation is a method only for the young, and it is true to say that at this day many courts never or hardly ever apply the probation system to adult offenders. This is a serious and even tragic mistake. (Harris 1937: 24)

He also pointed out the huge regional differences in the use of probation. In the same lecture Harris stated:

> A high percentage of failure, so far from casting any reflection on the value of the probation system, may indicate that some offenders by lack of enquiry or for some other reason have been wrongly placed on probation or that the method of supervision is at fault. (Harris 1937: 36)

This belief in the value of the probation system helps explain the commitment to the scheme by the Home Office in the face of criticism from the Metropolitan

Police and others. Assuming that Harris reflected the views of the Home Office in his lecture it is quite clear there was a view of how probation should operate held at the Home Office and a determination to establish such an agency. Probation could now no longer be left to the whim of individual or groups of magistrates and was to be controlled by central government via the Home Office.

As probation was to have its own branch at the Home Office the final *Report of the Children's Branch*, which concerned itself with probation, was published in January 1938 (Home Office 1938b). The previous Report had been produced ten years before so this Report reviewed the developments over a period of rapid change. The Report makes regular reference to the *Children and Young Persons Act of 1933*, in particular the provisions contained within it for a court to order that children beyond parental control, or in need of care and protection, 'be given the same friendly assistance and guidance as those who are placed on probation' (Home Office 1938b: 3). The Report also states that plans were afoot to 'extend probation methods still further by applying them to truant children' (Home Office 1938b: 35). The suggestion was clear; probation was likely to be expanded beyond working with the convicted criminal.

As for probation officer practice, the Report includes a section on 'psychology in relation to juvenile courts' and notes that 'psychological advice is being increasingly sought by juvenile courts' (Home Office 1938b: 17) but continues:

> The attitude of the ordinary member of the public to medical psychology is perhaps not yet one of complete confidence … aware that so-called 'psychological' jargon and catchwords are nowadays currently and widely used. He is given to understand that there are stray individuals holding themselves out as experts who may perhaps be possessed of a certain sympathetic intuition but who have had no serious scientific training or experience – of them he is suspicious and not without reason. (Home Office 1938b: 17)

Unease with the 'psychological expert' within the Home Office has already been noted and it seems that even now the Home Office could not shake it off. Psychology's domination of probation was far from complete and its main enthusiasts seemed at least to be primarily at the grass-roots level.

Like the review of probation just completed the Report was concerned that there was 'a good deal of unevenness throughout the country in the use of different methods of treatment' (Home Office 1938b: 27) and suggests that smaller courts might learn from those on London and other larger cities:

> those courts which make relatively little use of probation might take judicial note of the fact that the busiest and most experienced courts use it freely. (Home Office 1938b: 34)

The creation of a national system of probation to counteract its uneven use around the country was now underway. The determination of the Home Office to address it suggests how little confidence they had in magistrates to make the right decision for each child appearing in court and reflected their exasperation with magistrates, particularly in the more rural areas.

The final report of the Children's Branch to deal with probation also reminded its readers that courts now had the power to insert a condition of residence in a probation order but only in a place approved by the Home Secretary and then only for a period of six months. A place suggested by a probation officer was not suitable, so a system of Home Office inspected and approved hostels or lodgings was established. The new Probation Branch created at the Home Office also had amongst its staff a Probation Inspector to do this work. It is doubtful that one individual would have made a lot of impact but the principle of Home Office inspection of aspects of probation was a new and significant departure and reflected the central role that the Home Office intended to take in probation. Ironically, the first Inspector was Doris Rosling,[110] a former Police Court Missionary at Old Street Police Court in London.

The Emergence of a Modern Service: Probation 1938–1948

This chapter will describe the final move towards a noticeably modern probation system. By 1948 offenders could either be placed on probation (with or without conditions) or be ordered to perform an Attendance Centre Order, whilst remaining in the community. These two were the community based options available to the court in the period seen by many as the arrival point of the rehabilitative ideal. It is the decline of this modern edifice that has attracted a lot of criminological writing over recent years (see Brake and Hale 1992, Cohen 1985, Garland 2001, all of which start from this point); this chapter will chart the debates and manoeuvres that led to its arrival.

In the meantime this work will continue as before; that is, our focus will be on both the practice and policy of probation over the time period in question. However, this chapter will argue that policy settled after 1948. In terms of probation practice the social work and psychological discourses that we are about to consider came gradually to dominate the field well into the late 1970s.

The period of focus is bookmarked by a Bill and an Act of the same name; however, the ten-year period between them saw some very important shifts for probation. As we have already seen, legislation did not occur in isolation and its consequences have also been surprising sometimes even to those actually devising the legislation.

The Criminal Justice Bill 1938 and the 'short shock'

At this particular point in its history discussions about probation tended (very briefly) to get caught up in discussions about court ordered corporal punishment primarily because a Bill was in the process of being drafted that dealt with both. The Home Office's exhaustive review of probation (see Home Office 1936) had been followed by major changes in probation's organization.

The aim was to expand and centralize under Home Office control a national system of probation officers. Shortly after the review of probation had been published the Cadogan Committee was appointed to look at the issue of court ordered corporal punishment. Until this point courts had been able to impose a sentence of corporal punishment on any boy under the age of fourteen convicted of an indictable offence, on any boy between the age of fourteen and sixteen convicted of one of a very specific list of offences and any adult male convicted under the so-called *Garrotters Act of 1864* or *The White Slave Traffic Act 1912* (see Gard 2009, Gibson 1978, Pearson 1983).

The issue had been particularly divisive during debates on the *Children and Young Persons Act 1933* when a government proposal to abolish court ordered corporal punishment had failed. The response of the Home Office was to appoint the Cadogan Committee in 1936. It in turn produced the *Report of the Departmental Committee on Corporal Punishment* (Home Office 1938a), which recommended the abolition of corporal punishment and so gave the government and the Home Office the ammunition to make another attempt to abolish corporal punishment. The fact that the Report had been unanimous, well argued and had received a generally positive press had all helped considerably to embolden the Home Office.

Nevertheless nagging doubts remained, perhaps not surprisingly considering the emotions that the subject had provoked. For this reason a Conference was convened soon after the Cadogan Report was published to consider what to offer to replace corporal punishment and to consider the proposal made by the Cadogan Committee to set up 'Deprivation of Leisure Centres' as an alternative. A memo to the Secretary of State commented:

> We have all felt that there was a certain weakness in our proposals relating both to Deprivation of Leisure and Howard Houses schemes because neither of these proposals has been examined by a committee. They represent ideas generated in the Home Office and not supported by any Report which has been published.[1]

The second proposal, that of Howard Houses, originated from the Howard League and entailed establishing hostels where defendants could be sent as a sentence of the court for a short period of time (Rose 1961).

The Conference met on 7 April 1938 and included the Magistrates Basil Henriques (who had suggested deprivation of leisure centres to the Cadogan Committee) and Margery Fry from the Howard League for Penal Reform. Feversham from NAPO was also there as were a number of senior Home Office civil servants including Alexander Maxwell, Sidney Harris and Frank Newsom (later to be Permanent Under Secretary). After the meeting Harris noted:

Opinion at the Conference was divided but there seemed to be general agreement as to the need for some method between probation on the one hand and sending away to a school for training on the other. Something 'short and sharp' was thought to be needed for those who are too troublesome for the probation officer, but not so ill-disciplined as to need a long and expensive training. Some of those at the Conference thought that detention in a remand home or, still better, in a place specially provided for the purpose of detention, would meet the case. Others thought that such places if used solely for purposes of detention, might develop all the evils of prison. Greater support was shown for the suggestion that there should be power to deprive a young offender of his leisure on Saturday afternoons, which was one of the suggestions of the Committee on Corporal Punishment.[2]

Feversham (of NAPO) was concerned that such a centre on Saturday afternoon would be imposed as part of a probation order but was reassured by Maxwell that it would be a separate order of the court.

The Conference's proposals were taken up at the Home Office where legislation was being discussed to reform criminal justice. However, abolishing corporal punishment was not going to be easy, a Home Office Minute noted, 'the most convenient procedure would be to include the necessary procedures in the forthcoming Criminal Justice Bill where they will fall into their proper perspective. A separate Bill would concentrate attention on one controversial aspect of penal reform'.[3] The following month a Memo to Cabinet noted:

> We are satisfied that the great body of enlightened public opinion endorses the recommendations of the Departmental Committee and that a substantial majority in the House of Commons would be in favour of legislation to implement those recommendations and will bring considerable pressure on the Government to introduce legislation for the purposes as soon as there appears to be any Parliamentary time available.[4]

Thus the proposal for a short sharp shock of deprivation of liberty on a Saturday was offered as a substitute to the supporters of corporal punishment.

The Criminal Justice Bill 1938 was first presented to Parliament on 10 November 1938, and received its second reading on 29 November. The Home Secretary with the job of guiding it through Parliament was Sir Samuel Hoare, who said, when introducing the Bill of Home Office enquiries that:

> They go to show that today the young are not more wicked than they were, but that they are less controlled by their parents. They go to show that it is not so much films and shilling shockers that make juvenile crime, but broken homes, indulgent mothers, unkind step mothers or unemployment.[5]

Hoare went on to elaborate the proposals contained in the Bill, the government's main objective being, 'reducing the possibility of imprisonment and abolishing corporal punishment for the young' and 'in substitution of these out-of-date methods we are proposing' to introduce the Compulsory Attendance Centre. These would operate on a Saturday and courts would be able to sentence a defendant to attend for up to sixty hrs. Hoare describes the regime as 'within, of course, more rigid rules, that of a well ran boys club or similar institution'. The Bill also included provision to set up Howard Houses which Hoare described as 'a new form of hostel', where defendants could be sent for up to six months.[6]

The debate, which followed Hoare's speech, was strikingly measured in comparison to other Bills that had sought to abolish corporal punishment. Crucially though corporal punishment was now seen as out of date in the face of the more modern treatment–based alternative of probation. In essence the Bill sought to promote one sentencing option as it abolished another. Yet an alternative to that older option was deemed to be necessary.

The relative calm of the debates in the House hid a degree of controversy, which the Howard League for Penal Reform did not miss. They highlighted the clause in the Bill which proposed allowing a court to impose a probation order with a 'condition of mental treatment' (see below), and noted of it:

> The effectiveness of this clause will depend on the courts, the probation officers, the public attitude, which may stigmatise or popularise psychotherapy, and the supply of qualified practitioners which is at present small.[7]

The clear suggestion here is that the new clause would be used with the psychological and psychoanalytical professionals who, as we have seen by the late 1930s, were becoming increasingly influential in probation circles and within the social work discourse generally. As for Compulsory Attendance Centres the League criticized the government for not seeming to have thought the proposal through properly. They commented:

> It may turn out to be that almost mythical thing, an effective deterrent to the youth of abounding and lawless energy; it may provide gathering grounds for the law breakers; it may provide places were they will learn some useful discipline; it may be stupid and cruel if it is used to deprive the overstrained lad of his freedom and fun, and to take away Saturday football from those whose bodies need more exercise.[8]

The League was very supportive of the plan for Howard Houses. The same article also goes on to note that the Standing Committee which considered the Bill spent eight hours debating the corporal punishment clause and eighteen debating the other thirty-one clauses. During these debates 60 members attended at the Committee and the public galleries were full. At the next sitting the Committee was barely quorate and the public galleries almost empty.

By June of 1939 the Bill had passed through its Committee stage but world events then took over. By November of 1939 Hoare was compelled to announce to the House that the bill had to be dropped as time had run out,[9] as the Howard League commented, '*The Criminal Justice Bill* was the first and most important legislative casualty of the war'.[10]

Crime and the Second World War

Although a detailed survey of crime in the war is not the place of this work, a few comments would be pertinent as it was to have an impact on probation.[11] Smithies (1982) argues that wartime conditions saw the arrival of particular crimes. For instance he argues that theft offences became particularly rife, not just at work where, for example, 'every moveable object in a dockyard risked being stolen' (Smithies 1982: 26), but throughout the country where the Black Market provided temptation for many, not all of whom would have been considered dishonest in peacetime conditions. Smithies goes on to argue that the Black Market was so significant that 'by 1941–1942 serious strain had begun to develop in the country's distributive system' (Smithies 1982: 59). Rapid rises in crimes of theft and the creation of a Black Market obviously also had an impact on the system of rationing which covered most goods by 1942.

Other offences became rife in wartime conditions. Smithies argues that white-collar crime rose, particularly amongst local government officials who, because of their positions, had access to many opportunities for dishonesty. Other crimes were seen as related to a general breakdown of morals and standards of behaviour; here Smithies points to offences related to betting, gaming and drinking (Smithies 1982: 107) along with prostitution, which was rife during the war. A similar picture is painted by Pearson (1983) who remarks that 'epidemics of looting in London, Sheffield, Manchester, Coventry and elsewhere in the aftermath of air raids also excited considerable alarm' (Pearson 1983: 241), reminding us that the problem extended well beyond the capital.

However, as for the figures, Smithies points out that after an initial rise at the start of the war, the rate of juvenile crime actually fell after 1941 (Smithies 1982: 180). He accounts for this so, 'The war saw in many towns (though by no means all) a marked shift in police policy away from prosecutions to cautioning' (Smithies 1982: 181). Thus a picture emerges of a rising crime rate dominated by an increase in offences of dishonesty committed by older offenders. In fact Smithies argues that it was the 17–20-year-old young adults who attracted the greatest wrath of the courts during the war.

Sentencing figures for the period reveal that amongst the 17–20-year-old age group the numbers sentenced in the Magistrates Courts to probation fell by 19 per cent between 1938 and 1946, whereas the numbers sent to prison increased by the same percentage points. As for the 14–16-year-old age group, 9 per cent fewer were put on probation, whereas 9 per cent more were fined. The bare numbers for those placed on probation between 1938 and 1945 are shown in Table 5.1.[12]

Table 5.1

	Boys under 17	Girls under 17	Males over 17	Females over 17	Total
1938	14,980	1,134	10,469	3,445	29,758
1939		No records			
1940	19,983	1,916	6,051	3,445	31,395
1941	19,751	1,923	4,584	3,125	29,383
1942	17,142	2,168	4,942	3,705	27,957
1943	17,445	2,241	4,315	4,145	28,146
1944	18,144	1,989	4,964	4,124	29,221
1945	19,609	1,820	4,875	3,620	29,924
Average for 7 years	18,151	1,884	5,743	3,620	29,398
	62%	6%	20%	12%	100%

The figures reveal that overall the use of probation remained fairly constant over the war period with the exception of adult males many of whom would have been in the armed forces at the time. They also show that the use of probation amongst males under seventeen rose significantly over the whole period in question and reflects the increase in crime amongst that age group. The other sentences remained stable over this period. With adults all the sentencing options fell as a proportion (including probation by 7 per cent) except the fine which rose by 19 per cent.[13] Curiously, juvenile crime did not seem to attract the same concern it did in the First World War. These general trends should be borne in mind as we watch events unfold.

As with the First World War there were those who concerned themselves with crime in wartime conditions. However, by now the first criminology academics had been appointed and one or two wrote on the matter (Garland 1988, Hood 2004). Herman Mannheim had arrived in England in 1934 after he had been stripped of his professorship at Berlin University in 1933 (Hood 2004). By 1941 he was Lecturer in Criminology at the LSE and published *War and Crime* in which he attempted to draw conclusion from the last War pertinent to the war raging as he wrote. Mannheim was not optimistic; he wrote:

> That the present epidemic of war will bring in its wake, in most countries touched by it, an enormous outbreak of lawlessness nobody can doubt. ... [And]
>
> That a rigidly enforced black-out cannot fail in the long run, to bring about an increase in various types of crime will be obvious to everyone. (Mannheim 1941: 129 and 132)

Mannheim also discussed juvenile crime and evacuation of children from the larger cities, noting 'figures which have been published from evacuation and neutral areas seem to show substantial rises in juvenile delinquency, due to the absence of compulsory school attendance or effective substitutes' (Mannheim 1941: 142). As we will see the issue of evacuated children was to loom large in probation work during the war. As for probation, Mannheim expected its use to fall in the war; he wrote:

> For the choice between making a Probation Order and committal to an Approved School, the home conditions of the offender will inmost cases be decisive, and it has already been indicated that the absence of fathers and elder brothers, the war work of mothers, and similar factors frequently force the Juvenile Courts to prefer Committal to a Probation Order. (Mannheim 1941: 144)

Mannheim also pointed out that during the last war the use of corporal punishment rose as probation fell, but he did not seem to expect the same this time. As Smithies' work shows, some of Mannheim's predictions turned out to be wrong, but his work reflected the concerns of the early war period.

In the same year Bagot published his *Juvenile Delinquency – A comparative study of the position in Liverpool and England and Wales* under the auspices of Liverpool University. Although much of his work related the pre-war period, he writes in his conclusion of the current war:

> On this occasion, however, large numbers of children have been without school discipline for many months, and have thus missed what to many is the only beneficial influence on their childhood. In addition to its effect on discipline, a state of war produces nervous and emotional conditions in may children which have a detrimental effect on their behaviour. (Bagot 1941: 90)

The similarities with Mannheim's predictions are striking with both expecting juvenile crime to be a major problem in wartime.

Probation on a war footing

Until now probation's organization had been remarkably 'flat' with one or two of the larger urban areas promoting an officer to be Chief or more usually Senior Probation Officer. In 1936 the Metropolitan Police Court District appointed its first Principal Probation Officer. As probation in London was run directly by the Home Office, it was their responsibility to make the appointment. However, as Reynolds, the new Head of the Probation Branch, noted, 'I should have like to have seen the appointment filled by the promotion of an experienced probation officer, but I am satisfied that there is no one of the calibre required'.[14] In December of 1936 Mr Arthur Guy Clutton-Broch was appointed. He had been educated at Rugby and Magdalene where he achieved a second in the History Tripos. In 1933 he had been appointed Assistant House Master at Feltham Bortsal and by the time of his appointment as Principal Probation Officer was Deputy Governor of Portland Borstal. The dominance of public school and Oxbridge in much of the criminal justice sector already referred to in this work, and in the work of Mangan (1986) and Cannadine (1990), seems again demonstrated.[15]

It soon became apparent that the relationship between the Principal and his superiors at the Home Office was uneasy. The key issue was that the Home Office appeared reluctant to relinquish control of probation in the capital. In a letter sent in May 1939, Clutton Broch complained:

> The chief trouble is the delay which is very inconvenient, and the time taken in explaining to members of the Probation Branch, either on paper or verbally, something in which quite a simple decision is involved.[16]

By the time this letter was sent, five Assistant Principal Probation Officers had been appointed in London one of whom was Miss E. R. Glover (see later). A management structure was rapidly being created. Interestingly, Martin Page, while researching his work on probation in London, managed to have some communication with Guy Clutton-Broch who told him:

> I, as the Principal Probation Officer was the least qualified of all. In social science, I had neither degree, diploma nor training. I was one of the last great untrained. (Page 1992: 150)

Relationships between Clutton-Broch and the Home Office remained strained and Page (1992) says that this was the main reason for his resignation in February 1940.

In the meantime probation officers were planning for war. In November of 1938 the secretary of NAPO wrote an article titled 'Scattering the Children' which stated:

If it is hoped to preserve the moral and mental balance of the next generation all the essential services that have been built up for child welfare would have to be evacuated with the juvenile population.[17]

This was the first mention of evacuation in the journal. The second major issue of concern facing the service as war became more likely was:

In any national emergency a large number of probation officers will be called from post. A half of the full-time officers have joined the service in the course of the last two or three years and fully this proportion are of military age. The withdrawal of so many skilled workers will be a serious matter but it is clear that the problem can only be met by the provision of suitable substitutes ... This calls for more or less urgent consideration.[18]

The Home Office shared these concerns and wrote to every Probation Committee in the country to find out how many officers were of military age and how many in the Reserves. In August of 1939 the Home Office wrote again to Probation Committees suggesting part-time officers be asked to go full time and that less matrimonial work be taken on. A list of retired probation officers who might be able to help was also compiled, those turned down for the Probation Training Scheme in 1939 were contacted and a list of women 'with general social work experience' who might help was prepared.[19]

By 1940 the strain was beginning to tell on probation and NAPO sent out a questionnaire to officers to elicit views on the problems they were facing. Based on this a Report was produced in May 1940. It notes the increased workload of officers as juvenile crime had risen and that children evacuated out of the cities were often lost contact with if they were on probation. Norman, Secretary of NAPO, concluded:

The real strain will be felt by the country in these evacuation problems when the time comes for resettlement of the population in their old haunts when demobilisation is taking place and unemployment may be rife.[20]

It was therefore apparent that during the early stages of the war the service was facing a good deal of pressure, increased work loads due to rising juvenile crime, a shortage of officers and pressure in rural areas with the newly evacuated urban children.

As the war continued other pressures emerged. For instance in 1942 the War Office asked NAPO if its members would make enquiries on behalf of serving soldiers regarding 'estrangement and alleged misconduct' of their wives.[21] Many probation officers served in the Home Guard or worked Fire Watching. The Army Welfare Service also used officers to make enquiries on their behalf.

Probation officers also worked under the Defence of the Realm Act and a Home Office file makes reference to them persuading those who had refused to be conscripted and found themselves in court because of it. Under the same rules officers were also used

> to assist young people suspected of subversive activities and subjected to restriction under Defence Regulation 18B, women who failed to comply with directions for examination and treatment under Defence Regulation 33B and aliens under restriction orders.[22]

Probation officers from London sometimes found themselves seconded out to the rural areas to work with evacuated children. Despite the extra workload the Home Office estimated that by 31 December 1942, seventy-three probation officers were in the forces.[23]

Perhaps because of this pressure of work and scarcity of staff the issue of conscientious objectors working as probation officers received a good deal of consideration. Interestingly, the Home Office expected the problem to be particularly significant in probation. B. J. Reynolds, Head of the Probation Branch, wrote in 1940:

> In selecting candidates for training the probation Training Board looks for a strong desire for social service and some evidence of this desire is accomplishment. It is perhaps to be expected that a man who is working from such motives there should be a proportion who are unwilling to accept combatant service and a few who may perhaps refuse the alternative service offered.[24]

The decision was 'that unless or until cause is shown to the contrary it would be well to endeavour to keep these officers in probation work'.[25] However, rather sinisterly, the Home Office maintained a list of officers with 'pacifist views'. In London there were three conscientious objectors working as probation officers, one of whom was liable for military service. There were also a number of trainee probation officers registered as conscientious objectors. The Home Office seemed satisfied by assurances from the Principal Probation Officer that they were not attempting to spread anti-war propaganda.[26]

The difficulties faced by officers were also reflected within the pages of *Probation*, the NAPO journal. Here the issue of evacuation often dominated. Late in 1939 H. E. Norman wrote in *Probation*:

> Amongst the main troubles which have arisen from this new war experience has been a certain amount of delinquency amongst the wilder lads and a remarkable amount of enuresis amongst the younger children;... both enuresis

and delinquency have a relationship to emotional unhappiness and a sense of insecurity. The delinquency has not been of a serious character – mostly petty larceny.[27]

The same journal also commented:

The evacuation has caused many emotional problems among children and mental health social workers have been sent to several districts, where they are working in close cooperation with probation officers.[28]

By the following year circumstances had changed:

It is now openly admitted that the evacuation scheme has broken down, not from any grave defect in the way the scheme was put into operation, but from omission to evaluate the intangible factor of family unity in this country.[29]

These discussions simply mirrored a phenomenon that dominated much public debate at the time. The evacuation of urban, usually working class children, was a massive operation with major repercussions. In his history of wartime Britain, Calder writes:

It is estimated that between the end of June 1939 and the first week of September some 3,500,000 or 3,750,00 people moved from the areas thought to be vulnerable to those considered safe. Population movements in September alone affected a quarter to a third of the population. (Calder 1969: 35)

For all those involved it was a swift and shocking exercise in experiential education. Tales of working class children encountering for the first time indoor toilets, vegetables, cows, beds and the like reinforced the sense of shock. Accusations of city parents neglecting their children and passing on the cost and responsibility for their feeding and clothing to the rural population were common in the press (Calder 1969: 43). Nonetheless, by the early months of 1940 many parents had collected their children and only a small proportion were still away from home by mid-1940. Evacuation continued to be a talking point and smaller scale schemes continued through much of the war (Calder 1969).

Discussions about the rise in juvenile crime during the opening years of the war often included reference to the peculiar circumstances of war. Basil Henriques was a Juvenile Court Magistrate in London when he wrote in 1941:

There are several new factors aggravating juvenile delinquency today. The lack of parental control in the reception areas; the inability of some city bred children to find satisfying occupations in the strange environment of the countryside; the extremely unsatisfactory and irregular school attendance, often, but not always due to the neglect of parents; the great temptations to take away apparently abandoned articles from bombed premises and to break open gas meters from partially destroyed empty houses; and the spirit of daring adventure which is everywhere fostered and which is being admirably shown for rightful purposes by fathers and older brothers.[30]

The same explanations were also offered by the Home Office and the Board of Education in a memo sent to NAPO and discussed in the editorial of *Probation* stated:

relaxation of home discipline resulting from military service of the father, or war work of one or both parents. Interruption of school life through evacuation or enemy action, new temptations facing boys and girls on leaving school for work, high wages, unwholesome recreations, the excitement and unsettlement of war, and the spate of stories of high adventure by land, sea and air.[31]

As for individual probation officers the war brought similar and other problems; Miss E. Inman, a Probation Officer in London, described to the NAPO Conference her enormous difficulties in tracing children evacuated out of the city. On many occasions no sooner had she traced a child than the child returned to London only to be evacuated again shortly afterwards. If a child appeared in court in the rural areas it would then normally be returned home if placed on probation. In many cases mother was working and father was in the forces and many of the schools were closed. Children spent a great deal of their lives in shelters, and in periods of heavy bombing the family virtually lived underground. Added to all these problems was the fact that her office had been bombed.[32]

It was not just the work with juveniles that was affected by the war. S. A. Gwynn, Principal Probation Officer in Middlesex, addressed Conference stating that officers had received a massive increase in 'applications for domestic advice' and that more generally there had been a huge increase in 'domestic and kindred social work' for officers.[33] As for those working in the adult courts, Kenneth Fogg, an officer in Croydon, found many probationers were working long hours and were therefore often difficult to find. Air raids added to his difficulties in finding people and made visiting probationers a dangerous activity.[34]

What is apparent from these accounts of the work of officers and more general accounts of the increase in juvenile delinquency during the war was that there were both similarities and differences with experiences of the First World War. Explanations of an increase in juvenile crime sound remarkably similar, based on breakdown of family discipline, the excitement of war, etc. However, the fact of evacuation and the air raids combined with the expected invasion meant that there were material differences, particularly in the day-to-day work of individual officers. This War touched the lives of the clients and officers themselves more than the previous war.

One new explanation for crime was based on the role of the mother in a child's development. For instance NAPO conducted its own survey of officers' explanations for the increase in juvenile delinquency. They conclude:

> the primary cause of the trouble is to be found in the home. We think, however, that such loose terms as 'lack of parental responsibility' and 'lack of parental control' are misleading because they convey a false impression of the ability of parents to control rather than a wilful refusal to accept responsibility.... The influence of the father in the family is far less important than that of the mother.[35]

The same article also made reference to a mother creating a sense of insecurity and confusion, which she unwittingly communicated to the child. This could create delinquency. This hints at a move away from Burtian psychology to something that at least acknowledges a subconscious motivation for offending. This merely reflected similar ideas which were gaining ground within the psychological and social work discourses, that is, a Freudian based understanding of the human psyche. In many respects this idea that early parent and child relationships had consequences for the child's future behaviour was a novel idea but it had conservative undertones. For example, one probation officer wrote:

> Nature herself has ordained that the mother shall be dominating influence on a child's life. The mother makes or mars the character of her child. If only more mothers realised the power entrusted to them.[36]

With many women at the time working in munitions factories that clearly had implications for their children and their children's behaviour.

Changing explanations for crime

As we have seen, mainstream explanations for crime had moved very little over the previous fifteen years or so. The work of Burt (1925) still dominated the approach of many in probation and Macadam's (1925) 'broad liberal education' approach to social work training still dominated the Home Office training scheme for probation officers. However, the ISTD and others advocating a

Freudian based approach to working with juvenile offenders had begun to make inroads into probation work by the mid-1930s.

One former Southend probation officer was, in 1943, working as a social worker at the ISTD and wrote in *Probation*:

> I am indebted to the Mental Health Course, for the opportunity it offered for giving some insight, slight though it be, into the mysterious, unconscious mechanisms of the mind and the cross currents of instinctual desires upon which human activities mainly depend for their direction and drive. In the first place it gave me a faint clue to the age-old puzzle of the irrational, apparently purposeless crimes which are frequently committed.[37]

On the very same page is the by-now regular notice of scholarships being available for probation officers to attend the Mental Health Course based at the LSE.

It wasn't only probation officers who were showing an interest in the new Freudian influenced psychology. Claud Mullins (1943)[38] published *Crime and Psychology* complete with an introduction by Dr Edward Glover (of the ISTD). Mullins was no fringe eccentric but a Metropolitan Police Court Magistrate and a veteran of a number of Home Office Committees. For example, at the time this work was published he was a member of the London Probation Committee which advised the Home Office in its running of Probation in London. In the preface to the work he thanked the ISTD and the Tavistock Clinic for 'their prolonged help in difficult cases that I have had to deal with in court' (Mullins 1943: ix). In his introduction to the work Glover wrote:

> Mr Mullins was not indeed the first lawyer to accept with enthusiasm the teachings of modern psychology, but he was the first magistrate in this country to apply them systematically in ordinary police court work.[39]

In case there was any doubt about what Glover meant by 'modern psychology' Mullins opens his book with a section 'Principles of Modern Psychology' which is based on Freudian ideas and includes the following:

> Therefore the purpose of psycho-therapy is to return to health those whose lives are being adversely affected by their unconscious conflicts. This is done by helping them to gain insight into the causes of their condition. When faulty repressions giving rise to mental symptoms are corrected, the emotional tension is released. (Mullins 1943: 4)

As for probation, it 'has done far more good than harm; it provides the machinery ... whereby psychotherapy can be given to the delinquents while they remain at liberty' (Mullins 1943: 108). He goes on:

I would recall that since I was appointed a metropolitan magistrate in 1931 I have used the probation law to send many scores of delinquents to medical psycho-therapists. The results... have been on the balance most encouraging... But I have never yet had to fetch back to court, for either warning or punishment, anyone who was undergoing psycho-therapy. (Mullins 1943: 121)

Not only was psychotherapy particularly beneficial for delinquents, but Mullins also argues that 'it would be better if those on the Bench could submit themselves to a prolonged course of psycho-analysis' (Mullins 1943: 218).

Mullins' work also includes a number of case studies and descriptions of his day-to-day work in the courts. Psychotherapy was usually offered after an initial remand for enquiries to allow an assessment at the ISTD or at the Tavistock. If treatment was thought appropriate it was offered by way of a probation order. Treatment was the sole responsibility of the psychotherapist but when it came to the probation order, 'the probation officer and the court must accept the exclusive responsibility for his (the probationers) obedience to the terms of the probation order' (Mullins 1943: 53). Mullins also makes reference to war conditions and argues that evacuation could often be more traumatic than air raids for children. He writes:

If then, natural development can have a deep psychological; influence, probably unrealised at the time, it is obvious that any unusual or catastrophic experience at any time of life may have a far deeper influence. (Mullins 1943: 12)

This view was to become more common as the war progressed.

Mullins represented one, or what might be termed the new approach to psychology; the traditional approach was epitomized in the work of W. Norwood East whose mammoth *The Adolescent Criminal – A medico-sociological study of 4,000 male adolescents* was published a year earlier. Norwood East was Lecturer on Crime and Insanity at the Maudsley Hospital and had been at one time a Prison Commissioner, Medical Inspector of H. M. Prisons and Senior Medical Officer at HMP Brixton. The introduction to his work was provided by Sir Alexander Maxwell, Permanent Under Secretary at the Home Office, and the book was published under the auspices of the Home Office.

Norwood-East's approach is rooted in the statistical approach to psychology which can trace its roots back to Karl Pearson and Galton (1869/1978) and through to Goring (1913) and later Burt (1925). Norwood-East collected vast amounts of data on his subjects and with the aid of a statistician calculated what influence these factors had on the child's likelihood to offend. He therefore has lengthy chapters which deal with such things as 'hereditary and family factors', 'character disabilities', 'mental disabilities'. He then goes on to consider environmental factors which include the largest section on the home. In a section that has echoes of Burt's (1925) earlier work he writes:

> Crime frequently results from a failure to control instinctive action and from negligence in directing the emotions towards purposes which are socially useful. The home should be the first training ground but some adolescent offenders appear to have received no effective social guidance until they are sent to a training or penal institution. (Norwood-East 1942: 123)

Other sections deal with the influence of school and employment. Norwood-East then goes on to consider the impact of physical condition before embarking on a section that includes much intelligence testing of his subjects (Norwood-East 1942: 221).

Although Norwood-East's and Mullins's works were produced within a year of each other, their approaches are radically different. The contrast between the works reveals one of the key themes of this work, that is the competition not only between but crucially within the key discourses. Freudian based psychology was, as we have seen already, beginning to have an impact on social work and the treatment of crime. In some ways Norwood-East could be seen as rooted in the old early twentieth-century approach and Mullins's work heralding the arrival of the new psychodynamic approach to the criminal into the mainstream. It was the latter Freudian based explanations that were to dominate after the war and to have a major impact on probation practice.

Reactions to the two works were interesting. For instance the Howard League for Penal Reform commented that 'nothing very fresh or unexpected emerges'[40] in Norwood East's work. Mullins, meanwhile wrote in *Probation* in the same year that his book was published, arguing that the relationship between the parent and child was a prime cause of juvenile delinquency.[41]

As the war progressed the ISTD enjoyed a period of rapid expansion. Early 1942 found them discussing salary increases for staff and planning to recruit a new social worker.[42] By this time Dr Kate Friedlander had arrived at the ISTD and she and Dr Glover were providing courses on 'Freudian Theory of Delinquency' to the University Extension Course in London. At the Home Office, Probation Branch, W. G. Minn[43] was organizing the training of probation officers and the ISTD noted that:

> Conservations with Mr Minn at the Home Office had shown that he would be interested in some lectures in General Psychology for Probation Trainees[44]

In the summer of 1943 the Church Army made a group subscription and asked for a member of the ISTD to come and lecture their staff.[45] A few months later Dr

Friedlander lectured trainee probation officers at the same time that the number of cases that the ISTD was working with reached its highest level of 186, after low points of 102 in 1941 and 113 in 1942.[46] By early 1945 Council noted that 'the clinic had been working at full pressure since the last Council Meeting'.[47]

Money for the work of the ISTD came from a number of sources including subscriptions, life memberships, etc., but Dr Friedlander and her colleagues were also paid for their teaching. For instance she gave courses to social workers at the request of Eileen Younghusband in 1942 and received 25 guineas for the work.[48] Other organizations requested speakers from the ISTD; in 1942 these included the Rotary Club, Housewives Clubs and an Occupational Therapy Centre and each made a contribution to the Centre. Amongst the list of those paying five or ten shillings to become members were a good number of probation officers.[49]

Saville and Rumney's (1991) history of the ISTD describes regular moves and only shortened therapy being available as a result of War conditions. The Council Meeting Minutes show that whilst this may have been the case a knack for self-publicity and sheer hard work in spreading news of the organization and its work began to pay real dividends in the war. This is illustrated in the growing closeness between the ISTD and those in the Probation Branch at the Home Office, particularly those involved in the training of probation officers.

Probation and the outbreak of peace

Over the last few years of the war and the first few years of peace probation experienced a number of changes. B. J. Reynolds was still in charge of the Probation Branch but during the war he appears to have taken a sabbatical sometime in 1942 and 1943 when Doris Rosling[50] ran the department. This being the case she was probably the first woman to head a Home Office Department and interestingly Jarvis writes of her that 'she became something of a controversial figure, epitomising in the eyes of probation officers a new directive approach' (Jarvis 1972: 61). In May of 1943, on his return, Reynolds was a keynote speaker at NAPO Conference and commented that the war had created a 'growing sense of unsettlement in the Service'. He went on to comment that following the review of probation in 1936 (Home Office 1936) there were now twelve Principal Probation Officers throughout the country and sixty-five Senior Probation Officers. He went on to comment that 'combined areas scarcely rank as a major feature of the re-organising work of the Probation Branch'.[51] This last point hides the fact that combination of areas was still creating headaches at the Home Office. For instance in Cheshire a Probation Branch Inspector noted in 1938:

> There is every argument for the County becoming a combined area as there is a good deal ignorance, lassitude and dilatory organisation hiding behind the insularity of the several municipal units.[52]

Almost nine years later a further Home Office visit to the County produced the following comments:

> The work of Mr Hughes at Stockport showed many of the effects of isolation; he is stale and unimaginative while his manner is over confident … we were not able to see Mrs Jones at Runcorn until she had returned from her full-time work as signal box operator, and both she and her colleague Mr Cooper carry out no enquires for the courts, nor, could they take on these duties.[53]

This goes on to demonstrate that probation remained a very varied organization, with some rural areas still working as they had at the turn of the century.

Meanwhile in the capital the work of probation was dominated by the Home Office aided by three important committees. The London Probation Committee had been set up following the review of probation in 1922 (Home Office 1922) and advised the Home Office as it ran probation in London. It was revamped in 1936 following the review of probation that year (Home Office 1936) but by 1942 Sydney Harris and others questioned its usefulness as much of its work was done by the Home Office. One of the Committee members was Claud Mullins who wrote to Harris saying that 'it always seemed to me that you as chairman, gave the Committee no scope'.[54] The Committee survived despite continued criticisms of its usefulness from the Home Office and in 1948 Miss Goode acknowledged that 'this somewhat torpid body has suddenly began to take a critical interest in certain aspects of the administration of the London Probation Service'.[55]

The largest of the Committees advising on probation matters generally was the Probation Advisory Committee which was made up of magistrates, civil servants and one NAPO representative. The Home Office view of this Committee was:

> Experience has shown the value of the Advisory Committee. It is useful for the Home Office to be able to discuss questions of policy with a committee on which the Justices who control the probation system are largely represented. By this means we are more likely to ensure the acceptance of a policy by the Justices generally when it has been considered and approved by the Advisory Committee. In addition the Advisory Committee should serve as a useful vehicle of propaganda for the advancement and improvement of the probation service.[56]

Significantly, neither of these Committees carried any decision-making powers; they simply facilitated the Home Office's smooth running of probation. They show probation to be in some respects highly centralized in the capital yet the discussion of events in Cheshire (and other areas) reveal a provincial service very resistant to change. This ambiguity was noted as early as 1907 when the Home Office first became involved in probation; it is shown here to be still a very important issue forty years later.

The one committee with any real power set up in 1937 as a sub-committee of the Probation Advisory Committee was the Probation Training Board. Its job was to recruit for and manage the Home Office training course for probation officers which had started so inauspiciously in 1930. The Board appointed in 1937 included Magistrates and Justices Clerks along with Macadam and Carr-Saunders from the academic world. It was chaired by Sidney Harris. Macadam immediately set to work writing a recruiting brochure in which she stressed the importance of university training yet stated 'much depends on the influence of a probation officer on those who are placed under his care and no amount of training or education can supply the personal qualities which alone make for the best and most permanent success'.[57] This suggests that old ideas about personality were still considered important.

In these early days the bulk of the training was provided by court clerks, prison governors, senior probation officers and magistrates, though Macadam also did some teaching. By 1943 W. G. Minn appears to have had key responsibility for the course that the Home Office ran and it was he who had been in contact with the ISTD. It was only in the war years that more modern psychoanalytical approaches appeared in the course. The LSE evacuated out to Cambridge in the war which is where the Home Office course went too. The course was shortened considerably due to the shortage of officers, nonetheless it continued.[58]

By early 1945 there were two settled routes to train as a probation officer. One involved a two-year Diploma in social sciences or similar at a university followed by the Home Office three-month theoretical course. The other required twelve months' practical experience of social work followed by the Home Office theoretical course. The theoretical course included psychology, probation casework, law, medicine, ethics and social and economic conditions.[59] The official view though was that the specialist training by the Home Office was over a six- to twelve-month period, and interestingly, that 'personality is of the greatest importance'.[60] The circumstances of war may well have resulted in the course being shorter than intended.

Probation training was a radical departure at the time for a number of reasons; Macadam writes, 'perhaps the most outstanding advance in social training during the brief peace years is to be found in connection with the probation service' (Macadam 1945: 84). This was, she argues, not only because the training was university based but also because 'the Home Office was the first Government Department (apart from the Board of Education training of teachers) to seek the help of the Universities and become responsible for the cost of training' (Macadam 1945: 84). Macadam goes on to point out that probation offered 'opportunities which unlike most branches of social work required men in larger numbers than women owing to the preponderance of male over female offenders' (Macadam 1945: 84). The financial support offered to trainees by the Home Office, it is worth stressing, was a radical departure.

W. G. Minn and Elizabeth Glover,[61] both Probation Inspectors, ran the Home Office course and acted as tutors to the students during the three-month theoretical training. The Training Board was attempting to recruit graduates into the Service but in late 1945 Glover was forced to concede:

> The group of trainees for the present theoretical course has been the most depressing I have yet dealt with. They are a group of good hearted, well-intentioned, deeply conscientious men who yet fail continuously to show any insight into human nature or to grasp the fundamental principles of practical casework.[62]

The same Home Office file also notes that three of the group were dismissed from the course. An interesting development at this time was that the National Institute of Industrial Psychology began to advise the Home Office on their interview technique and also provided intelligence testing of candidates.[63]

Minn later wrote a short review of his work in which he noted that between 1930 and 1936, thirty-nine men and nine women were trained by the Home Office. Between 1937 and 1939 (after the Training Board was established) 117 men and 40 women were trained. He also went to argue that the then modern training course emerged in about 1941 (Minn 1948: 168). His view of the probation officer role was as a gatekeeper to various resources rather than providing that expertise herself. He also wrote, that though an officer would not be a psychologist his training should involve 'the study of elements of psychology, followed by study of the character problems arising in the courts' (Minn 1948: 170).

In the following year the other key Home Office official involved in probation training, Elizabeth Glover, wrote *Probation and Re-Education* in which she argues that probation 'is an educative process' (Glover 1949). She discusses the role of family relationships referring to Burt (Glover 1949: 55) and the importance of youth clubs (Glover 1949: 133) but much of her work stresses the role of the probation officer in building up the self-esteem of the young criminal. A typical comment she makes is 'one wants to build up the child's damaged self-confidence and self-respect' (Glover 1949: 108).

Her views on psychology are interesting. She writes:

> The great contribution which psychology has made from the point of view of probation is that it has led us away from the purely legal or moral approach to delinquency to the scientific or curative one. It has taught us that all conduct, good or bad, has a reason, and that if the conduct is bad, one must first look for and find the reason before one can correct it. (Glover 1949: 19)

However, she continues that 'psychoanalytical treatment is only rarely either suitable, available, or recommended' (Glover 1949: 96). A little later she writes 'intelligence tests administered by a qualified psychologist are necessary to assess scientifically a child's intellectual ability' (Glover 1949: 106). All of this leads to the conclusion that Glover's view of psychology in relation to probation is closer to Burt's rather than any of the new psychoanalytical ideas interesting a number of probation officers.

During the last few years of the war and those immediately after, the pages of *Probation* continued to reflect this meeting of the old and new amongst probation officers and their practice. In 1943, J. H. Cottam, a probation officer in Tynemouth and Wallsend, wrote:

> We agree that the primary course of the trouble is in the home. The broken home where parents have little idea of discipline, being too strict, or too lenient, or alternating between the two. Parents who entirely lack the ability to be parents to their children. Overburdened mothers who have little energy or time for their children. Parents who fail to give their children any religious instruction, or elementary sex teaching. Homes where the child fails to get the love and affection he so much needs. Competent parenting is the first need.[64]

This whole section could have been taken directly from Burt's (1925) work, published nearly twenty years earlier.

Other articles reflected different traditions within both the psychological and social work discourses. For instance one officer writing of her work in Liverpool reflected the approach advocated by Attlee (1920) and discussed earlier. She writes:

> it is vital that the probation officer should have direct contact with those members of the community who have a say in the management of local affairs,

and who, to some extent, have power to influence committees responsible for any change or improvement in local conditions.[65]

In the same journal an officer from Bradford wrote:

> I trace the primary course of juvenile delinquency to faulty education in the early years, and especially in the home. … I am convinced that the time is more than ripe for a campaign to educate parents in the bringing up of their children – not from the material standpoint, but, for the want of a better word, from the spiritual standpoint.[66]

In some respects the above quotes seem to contradict each other but as we have seen many times probation was a site for the meeting of competing discourses and emerging and declining strands within those discourses. These last two quotes merely reflect that tradition.

At the same time there appears a slight concern that probation practice was getting a little out of date. For instance in 1947 the editorial in *Probation* commented on a visit to the Conference of Social Workers that:

> Unless we can keep abreast of modern developments in training particularly – we shall be different, very different, from other social workers, but the difference will not be to the advantage of those whom we are trying to help.[67]

Later that year an officer working in North London wrote that 'many experienced probation officers can recall associations with the older missionary officers who laid the foundation of the probation service' before going on to state that 'the probation officer requires not only the right personality but also the right technique'.[68] The same author described an officer that was friendly, had local knowledge, was professional and qualified but with a 'calling' as being the modern ideal probation officer. Again the combination of old and new is striking, and again a 'main grade' officer is voicing it, even though the editorial, quoted above, seems to suggest that some of it was out of date.

One new trend does emerge at this time and it is highlighted by Vanstone when he writes of 'the beginning of a growth in confidence of the profession is evidenced by an increase in papers from within the Service' (Vanstone 2007: 95). He too notes the psychological explanations of crime these articles contain but also notes religious motivations in some of the writing. This trend of different strands of the psychological discourse dominating the writing of probation officers published in the journal is one that was to continue for many years and reflects the confidence shared by many about the efficacy of probation practice.

'The psychiatric deluge'

In her history of social work in the UK Woodroofe (1962) argued that there was a 'psychiatric deluge' experienced by social workers in the interwar period. This work, like Yelloly (1980), has argued that it would be more accurate to see it as a 'psychiatric trickle'. In fact it was only after the Second World War that psychoanalytical ideas really entered mainstream social work. As we have also seen, in many respects, probation lagged behind in adapting to many of the changes in the social work discourse.

Two significant (for social work) books were published in the years immediately after the war, one author has already been referred to in this work, and the other was to become very important to British social work. Both were intimately connected with psychoanalytical approach to the treatment of the offender. Kate Friedlander published *The Psycho-Analytical Approach to Juvenile Delinquency* in 1947, when she was described as Honorary Psychiatrist at the ISTD and Director of the West Sussex Child Guidance Service. She had been involved in running short courses for probation officers for almost ten years by this time. Her work is soaked in Freud and the application of his methods to juvenile delinquents. She writes:

> Not until the psycho-analytical method made it possible to study the unconscious (that buried part of the mind which reaches down into the early years of existence) could a comprehensible picture of the emotional development during the first years of life be obtained. Deep down in the unconscious these old antisocial impulses which we have seen expressed in the toddler are still alive, and influence the thoughts and actions of the adult. (Friedlander 1947: 14).

She then offers a Freudian analysis of child development which includes an oral phase, the Oedipus Conflict, the formation of a Super-Ego, the latency period and puberty (Friedlander 1947: 17–64). Early in her section on treatment she asserts that 'the diagnosis of the delinquent can be satisfactorily undertaken only in clinics specially adapted for this purpose' (Friedlander 1947: 195) the aim of which is:

> The fundamental process in psycho-analytical technique, therefore, is to bring into consciousness those unconscious drives or conflicts which have caused the neurotic illness thus making possible a further process of modification of hitherto repressed drives. (Friedlander 1947: 207)

The methods by which this was to be achieved, as described by Friedlander, include free association or suggestion under hypnosis, or suggestion and persuasion when awake (Friedlander 1947: 224). She also describes environmental methods of treatment by which she means working with the family, primarily with the mother, to rebuild mother–child relationships thus aiding the development of the super-ego of the delinquent (Friedlander 1947: 238).

The role of the probation officer in this is to establish a relationship with and between the family members. She writes:

> The task of the probation officer is to grasp the emotional undercurrents in a home, to evaluate their importance for the special problem of his charge, and to find a way of modifying the faulty attitude of the parents. This is difficult, and becomes possible only by means of transference. Not only with the child, but first and foremost the parents will establish an emotional relationship with the probation officer which will correspond to their own personalities. The probation officer must help to develop this relationship. (Friedlander 1947: 248)

When the child is older then the relationship with the child rather than the parents is more important, argues Freidlander. Perhaps because of her approach Friedlander takes a very different view to Girls and Lads Clubs than that taken by many contemporary probation officers. She writes, 'the antisocial child cannot get on with other children of the same age, … Club life, at a time when the child is not yet able to form friendships will add a further burden and not relieve its difficulties' (Friedlander 1947: 250).[69]

Friedlander's approach therefore implies a radical departure for many probation officers who remembered the influence of Cyril Burt and probation in the 1930s. Not only in what they recommend for their younger charges but also for the very relationship that they have with the youngsters and their parents.

In the same year John Bowlby published *Forty-four Juvenile Thieves: Their Character and Home Life*. At the time Bowlby was Psychiatrist in Charge at the Child Guidance Unit of the Tavistock Clinic. The premise from which he worked was that:

> The correct approach to the problem of human behaviour – the recognition of its unconscious springs and the profound influence of early inter-personal relations between infant and parents – belongs, of course, to Freud. (Bowlby 1947: 2)

His work then recounts a number of case studies to illuminate his conclusions crucial to which is that most came from a broken home. This is a term we have come across before and dates back to the early days of probation. However, Bowlby states:

The concept 'broken home' is a derivative of sociology not psychology. An adequate psychological study must first analyse the situations jumbled together under one heading and select each for special study. (Bowlby 1947: 37)

Bowlby goes on to provide more detail when he writes:

Thus there can be little doubt that prolonged mother-child separations are associated to a high degree with chronic delinquency in general and with certain types of chronic delinquent in particular. (Bowlby 1947: 38)

Equally crucially for Bowlby was that this separation of mother and child occurred 'during his first five years of life' (Bowlby 1947: 36). The conservative implications of this writing are interesting, particularly views about a 'woman's place being in the home'.

Both these works specifically addressed juvenile delinquency and both were based on Freudian understandings of child development. As probation was the central agency dealing with juvenile delinquency it would have been one of the prime target audiences of both writers. As we have seen, the ISTD and Child Guidance Clinics were beginning to have a greater impact on probation and probation officers and links between these agencies were strengthening all the time. These two substantial works would have fed into and supported an emerging interest in psycho analytical explanations of delinquency attracting the attention of many in probation.

For anyone reading the book at its time of publication the immediate and obvious conclusion to be drawn was that evacuating children from the cities to the safety of the countryside during the early stages of the war was completely counter productive. Indeed such is referred to by Sybil Clement-Brown in her own reminiscences as a social worker in the early part of the war. She writes:

In the weeks and months that followed never had there been more dramatic demonstration of the meaning of family separation or the impact of differences in ways of living. Painful experiences, with groups of children emerging with a kind of atrophy from residential nurseries drove in upon us the stultifying effect of impersonal care.

These were experiences common to all social workers.

As time went on it was inevitable that those with special experience of mental disturbance should be called upon often without medical support, to take, as individuals, responsibilities never faced before; a crucial test of accountability. (Clement-Brown 1970: 166)

The trauma of separation due to evacuation is also referred to by Calder who writes, 'at the beginning of September (i.e. 1940), from Aberdeenshire to Devon, countless numbers of children wet their beds' (Calder 1969: 41). In fact enuresis was often said to be the practical manifestation in children of the shock of separation from parents, particularly mothers.

Yelloly's survey of social work history also stresses just how important the war and the experiences of evacuated children were to the work of social workers. She writes:

> War had many lessons for social workers. Perhaps for the first time it showed how vital was a knowledge of child development to the work of all social workers, not merely those working in clinic or psychiatric settings. (Yelloly 1980: 76)

She also reminds us that it was not just Bowlby who based his research on Freudian ideas about child development and the importance of the mother–child bond in that. She refers to the work of other psychoanalysts working in Britain at the time, these included Anna Freud and Melanie Klein. Their writing, she argues, pointed in the same direction:

> these studies highlighted in an unmistakable way the crucial importance of understanding and meeting the emotional needs of children, and of endeavouring to structure inevitable separation experiences so that the child was helped and supported through them. (Yelloly 1980: 77)

In fact, Yelloly argues that 'there is evidence that after the Second World War marked changes took place in British social work' (Yelloly 1980: 2), the key to which was a 'new professional culture' of which psychoanalysis formed a major part (Yelloly 1980: 2). Like earlier in the twentieth century, war, and on this occasion evacuated children, proved a major stimulus for shifts in the psychological and social work discourses. Probation was not immune from these shifts and as we have seen much of this new writing was actually aimed at them.

The Criminal Justice Act 1948 and its impact on the probation service

As these debates in social work theory and practice were taking place and in turn having a major impact on probation practice other moves were afoot. As the war ended and peacetime conditions slowly returned, more 'normal' politics was resumed. In 1945, as the new post-war Labour Government settled into office, the Home Office dusted down *The Criminal Justice Bill 1938* and took a number of important ideas from it and included them in *The Criminal Justice Bill 1947*. However, the nine-year gap had precipitated some changes as

Rose (1961) comments, 'the experience of the war and post-war years sharpened the feeling that punitive measures were needed' (Rose 1961: 232), particularly following increases in juvenile crime in the early part of the war (Smithies 1982). One result of this was that the new Bill included a provision for a Detention Centre Order, which would be a 'short sharp, shock' in custody for those under twenty-one. In fact there was a good deal of support for the Detention Centre amongst arguably more enlightened Magistrates. For instance Watson (1942) writes 'what is needed is a small local establishment in which discipline of the sternest, the food is of the plainest, where everything is done "at the double", and where there is the maximum of hard work and the minimum of enjoyment' (Watson 1942: 143). A. E. Jones (1945), an experienced court clerk, makes similar points whilst also referring to a regime that should be 'like that of a military barracks' (Jones 1945: 165). Basil Henriques thought that the Centre could 'combine punishment with deterrence and also some character training' (Henriques 1950: 161).

The main reason the Detention Centre appeared in the Bill, argues Bailey (1987), was that Howard Houses and Attendance Centre Orders proposed in the 1938 Bill were gone. As the Bill included the abolition of corporal punishment a punitive alternative had to be offered but as the Bill progressed through Parliament the Attendance Centre Order was reinstated, Rose claims, by the former Home Secretary Samuel Hoare (Rose 1961: 233).[70] Therefore, almost by accident, two alternatives to corporal punishment were available.

These differences between the two Bills were the result of much behind-the-scenes work at the Home Office. In December of 1945 the influential and powerful Parliamentary Administration of Justice Standing Committee produced a Report prepared by a Sub-Committee it had appointed to consider Compulsory Attendance Centres. The Sub-Committee set out to discuss how a scheme of Attendance Centres might work. It regarded the aim of such a centre as to deprive attendees of their leisure time, however:

> We have assumed that the method should not be regarded as merely punitive but that, within the limits prescribed, an attempt should be made to apply some form of reformative influences.
>
> It has the advantage which appeals to common sense, of punishing the offence without taking the offender away from his work or interfering with his education.[71]

They were agreed that the Police should not run such a centre nor should it take place on Police premises. In fact they envisaged the Centre being ran by a probation officer and that attendees would remain subject to probation supervision after their time at the Centre was over. The tone of the Sub-Committee was sceptical at one meeting; it noted:

> Difficulty was found in deciding whether the object of compulsory attendance should be wholly or mainly punitive, or to what extent attempt should be made at training and reformative treatment in the very brief time available.... There seemed to be a good deal of doubt whether there was a real need for compulsory attendance centres.[72]

The Sub-Committee therefore decided to discuss the idea with a group of invited Principal Probation Officers at the Home Office on 2 November 1945. The notes from this meeting state:

> As the Principal Probation Officers were so opposed to the scheme it was thought unnecessary to spend much time in discussing with them the practical difficulties of administration.

Sidney Harris, who had chaired the meeting, was forced to conclude that the whole 'project was by no means free from difficulty'.[73] It was largely because of these practical issues that the Sub-Committee was unable to support the introduction of Attendance Centres despite the fact that this would mean 'no disagreeable alternative to whipping would be available'.[74] Despite the problems the proposal to introduce a new community penalty in the form of the Attendance Centre was, as we have seen, hastily included at the last minute with little thought given to who might actually run them.

As for the Bill itself, the key changes proposed for probation are included in clauses 3–11, 35–37 and in the 1st and 5th Schedules. Section 3 stated that a court could make a probation order after 'having regard to the circumstances, including the nature of the offence and the character and home circumstances of the offender'.[75] The Bill also introduced a probation order with a condition of residence in a hostel or home approved by the Home Secretary for a maximum of twelve months. The Bill introduced a probation order with a condition of mental treatment. Such a condition could be imposed on the evidence of a 'qualified medical practitioner'.[76] The treatment could last up to twelve months and could be either as an inpatient or an outpatient in an approved institution. The Bill also empowered the medical practitioner to alter that treatment so long as he notified the probation officer and court. The Bill also proposed that the probation officer supervising the probation order would no longer be named on the order, instead the responsible petty seasonal division was to be recorded.[77] The schedules to the Bill included some detail of changes to the administration of probation. Some of these were quite significant and included the creation of probation committees for each probation area whose role was to appoint, manage and arrange for the payment of the probation officers. It was also their duty to make sure that there were sufficient probation officers and that there was at least one male and one female probation officer for each area. The Bill also introduced case committees which were to operate at the petty sessional division level. Their role was 'to review the work of probation officers in individual cases'.[78] At a national level it was the role of the Secretary of State to devise the constitution for probation committees, to define the roles and responsibilities of probation officers and to regulate the qualifications and appointment of probation officers. It is also worth adding that the Home Office would be responsible for approving probation hostels and homes and would also be expected to inspect them too. Finally, the Bill also allowed for the Home Office to use a statutory instrument to bring petty seasonal divisions together to form a probation area with a probation committee. Clearly lessons had been learnt from struggles over the previous twenty years or so and the Act allowed the Home Secretary to do this without consultation if it was necessary.

The change that attracted most attention in Parliament was that individual probation officer should no longer be named on an order. A number of speakers commented similar to Mr Dumpleton on the importance of:

> the establishment of a close and helpful relationship between the probationer and the probation officer as a person, not merely as an official appointed by the court and the authorities. That personal relationship would be much better secured if the probation order were to name the probation officer.[79]

This accusation that probation officers were increasingly becoming state officials was, as we have seen, far from new. However, the changes to probation that were introduced were accepted relatively smoothly by Parliament. Despite the occasional complaint corporal punishment was finally abolished at the same time that the Attendance Centre was introduced along with the 'short sharp shock' of the Detention Centre. Interestingly attempts by the Home Office to involve probation in one of the simple restrictions of liberty options proposed had been swiftly fended off by senior probation personnel and NAPO. It has to be said though that the Home Office never seemed wildly convinced in the first place.

The new Attendance Centres were dealt with in Sections 19 and 20 of the Act, which noted that they were to be available for 12–21-year-olds, committed of summary offences. They were not to interfere with school or work and they were to be run by an 'Officer in Charge'.[80] It was the job of the Secretary of State to notify the availability of such centres as well as actually providing the centres in liaison with the Police and local authority.[81] Probation was not to be involved in their running and, despite the objections of the Home Office, the Police were.

Probation officers in the form of the National Association of Probation Officers seemed more than happy with the Act. The pages of *Probation* are not full of debate and criticism of the Act. The most damming criticism is saved for the removal of the supervising probation officer's name form the order. In his editorial, the NAPO Chair (S. Farmer, Principal Probation Officer in Berkshire) commented:

> The proposal that a probation order shall in future name, instead of the probation officer, the petty sessional division in which the offender resides, is unchanged. This is perhaps the feature that we most regret, as we must regret anything which might weaken recognition of the importance that personal relationships between probation officer and probationer which is fundamental to the probation idea.[82]

The theme is returned to on a number of occasions and the National Executive Committee which met on 4 March 1948 notes that 'the amendment to name the probation officer had been lost' (*C. E. Troup, in HO45/16515* 1920: 190). Presumably this refers to the debates in Parliament. The new power given to courts to insert a condition of mental treatment did not attract a great deal of comment. One speaker at the 1948 NAPO Conference, Basil Neald (barrister and MP), did point out courts now had the power to order a defendant to reside in a mental institution on the recommendation of only one doctor, whereas in the past it had required two and that there was now no provision in the Act for the court to cross-examine that doctor.[83]

Ironically, one of the severest critics of the Act was Edward Glover at the ISTD who wrote:

> There is no sign that those who framed the Bill have been converted to the psychological point of view, or that they are prepared to strike at the roots of the problem. On the contrary the new Criminal Justice Bill is largely a measure of prison reform,…, a timid, unimaginative and cheese-paring measure. (Glover 1960: 29)

Even if Glover's assertions about the timidity of the commitment to psychology in the Bill are questionable, his view that the Bill actually introduced nothing wildly radical is one shared by many observers at the time. For example, a well-established member of the legal profession said as much, F. Coddington was Stipendiary Magistrate in Bradford and wrote on the Act, that if pushed 'he would have to admit that few alterations in power and procedure have actually resulted from the sections of the Act, and the two schedules, which concern probation' (Coddington 1950: 21). He also uses the phrase 'tidying up' (Coddington 1950: 23) to describe the provisions of the Act.

When the Bill passed into law, it was well into 1949 before many of the provisions relating to probation came into affect. It also very quickly became apparent that section 56 of the Act had the potential to create a great deal of work for probation officers. This clause stated that any offender under the age of twenty-one could be released early from custody and placed under the supervision of 'an approved society or person'.[84] This would require probation officers being far more involved in the supervision of people subject to prison licenses and prison aftercare generally. On a different note, shortly before the Act there had been a major review of the divorce courts and probation officers were finding that their matrimonial work had increased rapidly. It is clear that across a range of functions probation was expanding and what later became known as family court welfare work and prison aftercare had a major impact on the probation officers' work in the late 1940s in particular. Both areas of work expanded over the following years until they became substantial parts of the probation officer role.

The keynote speaker at the 1949 NAPO Conference in Scarborough was the Home Secretary whose speech is reported almost verbatim in *Probation*. It actually provides a convenient snapshot of where probation was at the time, certainly in terms of policy if not practice. Chuter Ede was the Home Secretary at the time and he had been in post four years by then. The combining of petty sessional division to create probation areas that began with the *Criminal Justice Act 1925* was clearly still exercising minds at the Home Office. Chuter Ede commented that probation areas in Lancashire, West Riding and Lincolnshire were about to be created which would leave just two counties in England without their own combined probation area. The issue of probation officer training had also been concerning the Home Office for a number of years by this time. Chuter Ede pointed out that the Probation Training Board 'had ceased to function effectively during the war'[85] but was to be combined with the probation Advisory Board. Since his arrival at the Home Office 277 new officers had been through the Home Office training course and 87 of those had also completed a full-time university diploma in social sciences. His view of the role of the probation officer's role is one that is referred to by many writing in the journal at this time. He comments:

> The essence of probation work is the personal contact of the probation officer with the probationer and his home. A sound basis of the theoretical knowledge

is needed for yours as for other professions.... I do want to emphasize the fact that while theoretical training is of great value in work of the kind in which you are engaged, it is the practical experience which makes the theoretical training worthwhile. (*HO45/11152* 1919)

Like much that we have already seen about the role of the probation officer there is a mixture of old and new. Training is now accepted as necessary for probation officers, even by the Home Secretary but personal relationships are paramount. The Home Secretary did comment on one of the radical departures included in the Act, namely the rapid increase in the aftercare work of probation officers. He urged probation to 'seize the new opportunity' (*HO45/11152* 1919).

The Act was fully implemented towards the end of 1949 with the production of new set of Probation Rules. NAPO's response was remarkably sanguine. S. R. Eshelby, Principal Probation Officer in Essex, reviewed them in *Probation*.[86] He saw nothing very novel in them and wrote, 'only now has much of the present day practice and organisation of probation received official recognition' (*HO45/16515* 1919) and later points out that '[r]ead as a whole the 1949 rules give the impression of giving directions for an adult service ran by adults' (*HO45/16515* 1919). As an example of this he contrasted these rules with those of 1926 and wrote that the current rules did not prescribe what a probation officer should not wear. The guidance for probation officers, 'whilst if anything is less precise than the 1926 rules in prescribing what he shall do with and how often meet his cases' (*HO45/16515* 1919). In regulating the work of a probation officer Eshelby saw the only extra demands placed on that officer being in terms of record keeping.

The general impression is that NAPO were rather pleased with the Act. It seemed to vindicate much of what they had been arguing for and the increased role for the Home Office which was explicit in the Act seems to have caused little consternation. It was very much welcome and Chuter Ede's speech at Conference went down very well. He later spoke at individual Branch Conferences as did a number of the higher civil servants at the Home Office. Miss Goode, for example, seems to have travelled the length of the country talking about her role. It is hard not to share the view of many at the time that the Act simply confirmed what was already good practice. However, the Secretary of State and the Home Office had now taken over some major powers in respect of probation, in terms of local arrangements and nationally for practice, recruitment and training. Its powers of inspection only introduced in 1936 were widened even further. It is easy to forget that debates in the previous decade about CETS and anti-officialism in probation had been very heated. Mair and Burke regard the Act as a watershed in probation's development and write:

> With the passing of the *1948 Criminal Justice Act*, the first phase of probation's development came to an end. (Mair and Burke 2012: 83)

By about 1949 there was in place a particular type of probation with a particular structure and set of working arrangements. There was a clear hierarchy emerging as more areas appointed principal probation officers and senior probation officers and the proportion of full-time officers over part-time officers increased and more and more of those officers had been through some training. The Home Office's figures show that in 1939 there were 659 male probation officers and 408 females, 509 of whom were full time. By 1946 there were 1,052 officers – 543 men, 409 women but crucially 764 were full time. A Report of the time noted, 'The Home Office has continually encouraged courts to employ full time and trained officers instead of part time officers who seldom had the training or qualifications for the work'.[87] In effect the structure and policy of probation, for the time being at least, seemed settled. Indeed, the structure that the Act introduced was to remain in place for many years. On the other hand, probation practice continued its strange mix of old and new and that is the focus of the next and final chapter of this work.

6

Probation, Social Work and Psychoanalysis: Into the 1950s and Beyond

If a probation officer working in 1948 had had the benefit of a time machine and so could travel freely across the years, what type of probation service would they find? If they went back forty years to 1908 when the Probation of Offenders Act was implemented, Miss Croker-King and Miss Ivimy had just taken up their posts in the new children's courts of central London, how would it all seem to our 1948 officer? They would not recognize what they saw as the service they worked for as the structure, management and organization of the service had changed almost beyond recognition. *The Criminal Justice Act 1948* was the final piece of legislation that established a service unrecognizable to that of 1908.

On the other hand, if our 1948 probation officer got back in their time machine and travelled forty years forward to 1988 they would see some remarkable similarities in the structure. They would find a service controlled and inspected by the Home Office, they would encounter probation committees where they would meet regularly with magistrates. They would supervise probation orders, some with conditions and they would have a caseload made up also of aftercare work and matrimonial work. Regular court duties, written reports for court, home visits and clients reporting to see them would be a part of their work. They would work for a probation area, be managed by a senior probation officer who in turn was managed by a principal or deputy principal probation officer (though the word 'chief' rather than 'principal' would be used). Tim May's (1991) detailed survey of probation policy and practice includes a wonderful account of the reality of the probation officer's world at about this time and it is a reality that would be recognizable to a probation officer from 1949.

Having said that probation practice had moved enormously, it is to probation practice and particularly its link with the psychological and social work discourses that this work will now turn. We have already traced the trajectory of shifting and competing social work and psychological discourses in probation practice, from those early ancestors in the police courts using faith, the pledge and character to turn their clients from crime. As we move into the 1950s and beyond we will see how the practice of probation officers moved into a distinctly modern phase based on a modern view of how the rehabilitation of the criminal should be done. The new structures and legal framework introduced by the legislation we have just considered provided the 'space' for these discourses and practices to move into and to operate in.

Probation practice, still a mixture of old and new

We have already characterized probation practice as a mixture of old and new, how particularly strands of the social work and psychological discourses rose and fell over time, how they co existed and on occasions actually competed for the attention of probation officers. The previous chapter contrasted the work of Friedlander (1947) with that of Glover (1949), described the arrival of Bowlby (1947) and discussed the social work training envisaged by Elizabeth Macadam (1925 and 1945). Burt (1925) was still considered a key author in this field and his work continued to be republished and updated well into the mid-1940s. At the same time we have seen Chuter Ede's approach to probation practice in the speech he gave to the NAPO Conference which harked back to an earlier version of probation.

These contrasting approaches to the correct responses to crime are mirrored in probation practice. To see those discourses in action we can, as Vanstone (2007) does, look in *Probation* which offers a useful cross section of probation practice. In the late 1940s this journal reflected the influence of those differing approaches in probation officers' practice. For example, the president of NAPO spoke to the 1946 NAPO Conference saying:

> I would ask probation officers throughout the length and breadth of the country to 'liaise' as closely as they can with the psychiatric social worker and with any avenues which will permit greater advances to be made in the question of the working of the mind in infancy, and in adolescence so that we can get, at normal age, men and women to full maturity of mind.[1]

This is an approach that would have been mirrored by many psychiatrists, particularly those working in the Child Guidance Clinics, and is strikingly modern. In his address to the 1949 Conference, the Home Secretary attended and Feversham is reported as being able to 'underline a point he had managed to [make] ... to the Home Secretary – that economic policies which drive mothers into the factories may bring into the country the needed dollars but lose for it much precious wealth'.[2] In fact, Feversham's speech that year bemoaned the increase in 'broken homes' and the divorce rate which 'would leave us with an enormous problem of unhappy childhood with its consequent results in anti-social behaviour'. Although this may seem a plea for traditional family arrangements, it is a view that Bowlby's (1947) work on maternal deprivation might also support. However, in the same speech Feversham alludes to an older incarnation of the psychological discourse when he points out that 'retarded' children make up 20 per cent of children in Rotherhithe, Lambeth and Southwark but in more prosperous parts of London like Dulwich and Hampstead make up only 1 per cent.[3]

There are also distinct flashes of an anti-psychology outlook within the pages of the journal and this is a view we have already come across. For example, the 1945 the Clarke-Hall Lecture was delivered by Lord Roche, a former Lord of Appeal and at the time chair of the Oxford Combined Probation Area. There is a scathing tone in the report of his lecture but it does note:

> The speaker next referred to the part that psychiatrists may play in the treatment of delinquency and while agreeing that juvenile courts can get valuable help in some cases, pointed out the risk of making psychiatric treatment a 'fashion' which becomes a master.[4]

The head of a local approved school addressed the North Wales branch and when discussing psychology was far more unequivocal; he said:

> It should be considered an adjunct rather than as be-all and end-all of the work. There was no hard and fast rules, and the semi-Nazi idea of one method being better than another must be dispelled.[5]

There are very few explicit references to Freudian psychology or standard Freudian concepts like subconscious, unresolved conflict, ego, super ego, psychoanalysis within the pages of the journal in the late 1940s. In fact the one explicit reference to this approach is in a report of a conference on juvenile delinquency convened by the Home and Education Secretaries. One of the speakers, Dr G. Heuyer, specifically refers to psychotherapy and recommends for many delinquents treatment that is 'psychological as psychoanalysis to bring to light the emotional complexes which project themselves in the form of delinquency'.[6]

Most of the articles in the journal which deal with psychology or psychiatry were written by doctors at the various child guidance clinics and seem strikingly similar to the methods proposed by Cyril Burt nearly twenty-five years before.

For example, P. D. Scott[7] who was a psychiatrist at the Stamford House Remand Centre was invited to write three articles in the journal in 1949, entitled 'Psychiatry and the Remand Home'. He describes his role as working as part of a team made up of psychiatrists, educational psychologists and a psychiatric social worker. The examination of each child included a routine medical examination, psychological testing, observation of behaviour during the remand and then a personal interview with the psychiatrist. On the latter he is rather vague but writes that given time the child will tell the psychiatrist the truth about his home and family though the child's first inclination would be to lie. A study of the child's home background is also made. When the data has been collected a case conference is convened.[8] In his second article Scott writes:

> The vast majority of cases represent maladjustment of potentially normal children and home; it is only in the widest sense they can be called medical problems at all.[9]

Simey, who was professor of Social Sciences at Liverpool University (he also sat on the Probation Training Board) at the time, lectured the North Wales branch of NAPO on the causes of delinquency. He covered a number of possible causes which included the material conditions, family conditions (here he refers to Bowlby), the school and the personal by which he meant 'personal weakness'[10]. Dr Denis Carroll of the ISTD in the same year lectured the Surrey branch of NAPO on psychology and psychiatric treatment describing young offenders so:

> innate lack of ability and weakness of character .... [the] main lines of character are laid down by the time a child is 5 years old ....Other disadvantages were caused by domestic unhappiness, bereavement, overcrowding etc. Delinquent tendencies and bad environment are together a common cause of young offenders. There are also physical causes, such as under-nutrition, as well as the stress of puberty.[11]

Like many of the articles on the causes and treatment of delinquency, even those from organizations that are in many ways avowedly psychoanalytical in approach, Dr Carroll takes a multi-layered approach to his account. Offending is a combination of factors, physical and social, with the subconscious playing a relatively minor part.

The national NAPO conferences were mirrored by local events where many of the branches organized conferences and invited speakers or arranged visits for members. The final edition of *Probation* in 1949 includes news from branches around the country. The East Lancashire and North West branch combined for a conference at which a Chief Assistant School Medical Officer spoke on psychopathic personality. The Teeside branch visited a local Mental Hospital and discussed IQ testing. The East Yorkshire branch invited Dr Carroll of the ISTD to speak. The Northern branch also discussed psychopathic personalities that month.[12] The reason for this enthusiasm and these events is suggested by the Medical Director of the National Association for Mental Health who wrote:

> In a recent questionnaire completed by Branches of N.A.P.O., the overwhelming concern shown by members has been with mental deficiency and sub normality and in particular with the quality and quantity of the social work among mental defectives.[13]

Many editions of the journal included notification of lectures and courses run by the ISTD, often with some impressive speakers, including Hermann Mannheim. At the same time though every regional and national conference included attendance at a Sunday morning church service and there were regular religious contributions to the journal. For example, P. D. Scott, the Bishop of Wakefield, was commissioned to write a series of article for the journal. Religion, and particularly Anglicism, still played a vital role in the work of probation officers. The combination of old and new in the journal is striking but also striking is their happy coexistence. The one thing that all the contributors seem able to agree on is that probation officers are both professional and qualified, the post requires training and that training includes at least some element of psychology and social work. Probation officers also need personality; morality is also referred to on occasions as is 'calling' but that alone is not sufficient.

Change

It is clear that ideas about the correct responses to crime underwent change at some point in the 1950s. Pinpointing the date is impossible but as before there is evidence to suggest that probation practice lagged behind the new ideas. Moving outside of probation circles for a moment the relatively new (in the UK) academic discipline of criminology arrived prompted primarily by the arrival of major academics removed from their homeland by the German Nazi Party. Morris's (1988) history of British criminology between 1935 and 1948 refers to the arrival of Max Gruenhut and Leo Radzinowicz at the LSE and Cambridge, respectively, as the first specific criminological appointments at British universities. Garland (1988) produces a history dealing with the period before 1935 and points out that most research and writing on crime causation came from within the prisons and other penal institutions. Indeed many that we have already come across are from that tradition. Garland selects Norwood-East as one of the earliest proponents of a psychoanalytical treatment of crime causation but Garland notes:

> East was himself a proponent of a psychological approach to crime, but he viewed its scope as being largely delimited, and consistently warned against the dangers and absurdities of exaggerating its claims. (Garland 1988: 9)

The more avowedly committed to the psychoanalytical approach like Hamblin Smith and his student Grace Pailthorpe, Garland argues, were far more marginal and attracted a good deal of criticism from within the criminal justice establishment; again we have seen evidence of that. On the other hand, Cyril Burt's work which saw crime as 'a combination of factors – typically as many as nine or ten – operating at once upon a single individual' (Garland 1988: 13) was much more popular and as Garland writes, 'seems strikingly modern' (Garland 1988: 12). Garland concluded his essay by arguing that there was no major narrative or dominant discourse in criminology before the war. Garland concludes his essay by pointing out that:

> Insofar as they had expertise or a knowledge base it was a detailed knowledge of the institutional terrain and its requirements, together with a general training in medicine or psychiatry, and later, psychology. (Garland 1988: 14)

This is an account we have seen mirrored in probation officer's practice well into the late 1940s. It was eclectic, drawing from psychiatry with elements of eugenics even, a splattering of psychoanalysis, a lot of psychiatry but very much influenced by Burt's approach to the causes of crime. At the same time we have seen echoes of the late nineteenth century with prominence given to personality, morality and religious calling. The structure and management of the service may have changed enormously but probation practice was still a mixture of competing, rising falling, strands within the psychological and social work discourses some of which dated back to the early part of the century.

However, further essays on a history of criminology in the UK describe an academic discipline that was very different as we moved into the 1950s. Martin's essay in the same series focuses on British criminology from 1948 to 1960. He notes:

> The intellectual concerns of criminology at the end of the 1940s were dominated by two major themes: capital punishment and psychoanalysis

He continues:

> For at least a decade psychoanalytical principles were at the heart of the training
> of social workers and probation officers despite the fact that the method of
> treatment could only be applied to a handful of individuals, while in any case its
> efficacy was unproven. Not for the first time treatment was dominated by what
> powerful clinicians wanted to do. (Martin 1988: 38)

There is clearly a sceptical tone in Martin's writing and he later describes a lecture
by Edward Glover, 'who addressed the group at extreme length and tended to
assume the privileges of primacy' (Martin 1988: 42). The primacy of this new
strand within the psychological discourse and the implications for probation
are explicit in his account. It is mirrored by D. J. West, a hugely experienced
criminologist who wrote:

> In the late 1940s psychoanalysis had considerable influence on British
> criminology and on social work with offenders. Psychodynamic explanations of
> delinquent character formation were widely read. (West 1988: 84)

If debates about crime causation within criminology were moving rapidly in the
1950s, then it would be reasonable to expect those debates to impact on probation
practice. Experience though has taught us that probation practice tended to lag
behind the new ideas and it tended to remain loyal to its old methods. As time
wore on, these new approaches to crime causation and treatment did have an
enormous impact on probation practice and we can see that in some accounts of
the training that officers experienced in the 1950s.

Accounts of individual officers' view of their training are few and far between
but the reminiscences of five women probation officers who trained in the
1950s and 1960s have been published and are revealing. Molly Webb recounts
her experiences in the late 1950s when she was accepted for probation officer
training and then attended the London School of Economic Certificate in
Applied Social Studies, of which she says:

> The Jungian basis of the course meant that students were expected to find
> significant factors in the most insignificant behaviours. Phallic symbols
> abounded. (Webb et al 2001: 281)

Barbara Jacobs describes beginning the Home Office's own probation training
course at Rainer House in 1960 where:

> The tutor in charge was a psychiatric social worker by training and, I think
> brought into the Home Office Inspectorate to add a bit of academic clout with

a psychoanalytical bias to the training. We had visiting psychiatrists as well as Home Office Inspectors to instruct us and we learnt criminal law, case work and child development. (Webb et al 2001: 283)

Mary Blumenau trained at the LSE in 1955 and then went to work in London as probation officer. She writes that 'I had been trained by supervisors steeped in the Freudian concepts of transference and one to one relationships' (Webb et al 2001: 284). Another officer described her placement at the Clapham probation Office as she trained to be a probation officer, saying, 'I sometimes felt I was being psycho-analysed by Mollie Samuels, my supervisor, but I survived' (Webb et al 2001: 286). Clearly by the late 1950s the psychoanalytical approach loomed large in probation training, four of the five former officers make explicit reference to it in their accounts.

By the late 1950s the journal *Probation* also began to reflect this shift and certainly by the early 1960s articles appearing in the journal refer to psychiatry, psychodynamic understandings of delinquency and the term 'social casework' is used to describe the methods used by probation officers. For example, one of the few articles written by a serving probation officer describing their practice comes from R. Golding who describes his work with a client in Oxfordshire as 'treating him psycho-therapeutically' and the articles goes on to discuss the conscious and subconscious world of the client before looking at client transference onto the probation officer.[14] By the mid-1960s probation practice is referred to as social casework not just by officers but by the chair of the Advisory Council for Probation and After Care.[15]

The subject of probation officer training and the probation officer role generally also attracted the attention of the *British Journal of Delinquency* (later to become *The British Journal of Criminology*) which had been instigated by the ISTD in 1950. For example, F. J. Macrae, who had been Principal Probation Inspector at the Home Office since 1950 wrote:

> Without being a trained psychologist, the probation should officer should have sufficient knowledge of psychological methods to enable him to detect cases which would benefit by expert diagnosis and to follow up any line of treatment recommended by the specialist; such knowledge might also assist him to exercise in the most effective way his own personal influence. (Macrae 1957/8: 210)

The relationship between the psychological expert and probation officer we have come across before but the reference to a relationship between probation officer and client is new. A little later he makes reference to a 'a more conscious use of personal relationships' (Macrae 1957/8: 214). A similar theme is explored in an article which appeared in a slightly earlier edition of the journal written by George Newton. At the time of writing he was Assistant Principal Probation Officer in London and also lectured on the Applied Social Studies course at the LSE. He detected an unease with probation officers that the training they received was not preparing them for practice. He describes that training as focusing on 'manipulating the environment' (Newton 1956/7: 124) of the offender. Students felt this was insufficient:

> They regarded the use of services or manipulation of the environment as only part of the contribution they should have been making and felt that the job of improving personal adjustments by helping probationers to make improved relationships with others was of major importance. (Newton 1956/7: 125)

This interest in the personal relationships of probationers meant that 'probation officers have turned their attention to the motivating forces of behaviour. In this search, with the help of dynamic psychology, an old half-understood truth had been reiterated, i.e. that feelings influence behaviour and that how a person feels about his situation or himself will influence what he does, how he does it and how he will allow others to help him' (Newton 1956/7: 126). The damaged relationships experienced by the offender on probation thus can be healed by a positive relationship between the person on probation and the probation officer. However, it is very doubtful that Newton is referring to a befriending relationship. He describes the relationship so:

> The skilled and conscious use of an emotionally satisfying relationship with the probation officer becomes the medium through which the probationer is helped to find himself and can begin to plan his future and act responsibly. (Newton 1956/7: 130)

In an explicit reference to psychodynamic understandings of offending he writes that if emotional needs are 'unmet at the right stage of development [they] affect adversely the process of maturation and limit the sphere of rational conduct leaving crippled personalities' (Newton 1956/7: 127). Newton's article includes a number of case studies where the focus is on the relationship between the probationer and family members. Offending is a result of failed relationships and further offending is prevented by enabling satisfying relationships. Helping to repair relationships is the role of the probation officer and Newton goes on to discuss how this may affect the probation officer themselves particularly as they are in a position of authority. In this analysis the probation officer uses themselves as a tool in building the relationship with the probationer; it is effectively a self-conscious use of self in a therapeutic relationship.

In summary then, although the policy framework which the *Criminal Justice Act 1948* introduced remained in place for many years, there is evidence to suggest a distinct shift in practice particularly as we moved into the later 1950s. As we have seen much writing and probation officer training was increasingly influenced by Freudian understandings of human nature and crime. It is a shift commented on by nearly all the histories of probation though there is no consensus as to exactly when this happened.

Probation's zenith

The third of McWilliams's (1986) celebrated essays on the history of probation deals with the service between the 1930s and the 1960s and refers in its title to the 'diagnostic ideal'. Early in his essay he writes:

> Between the late 1930s and the 1960s the probation system in England was transformed from a service devoted to the saving of souls through divine grace to an agency concerned with the scientific assessment and treatment of offenders. (McWilliams 1986: 241)

As evidence for the phase of diagnosis he points to the reports prepared by probation officers and he sees these moving to become a professional assessment or appraisal. However, 'the essence of social diagnosis is imposed meaning' (McWilliams 1986: 242). Essentially probation officers were interpreting the actions of offenders and describing to courts (and offenders) what those actions meant. He is very sceptical about these imposed meanings and argues that they merely give gloss to old fashioned moral judgements that the first probation officers made. He actually describes diagnosis as:

> an interaction between social facts and moral evaluations, and treatment is a moral prescription of what ought to be done in the light of the moral evaluations made. (McWilliams 1986: 246)

Crucially for us though, McWilliams was able to get hold of probation officer reports from across this thirty-year period and he detects a pattern contained in them. The changes in the contents and concerns of these reports mirror many of the changes we have just been considering. For example, the reports he read from the 1930s he describes as 'lay documents written for a lay audience' (McWilliams 1986: 249). In the reports from the 1940s he detects a slight shift and although they are still full of common sense analysis, he notes a Freudian slant, for example, where observation and assessment are proposed. In a report from 1958, 'the language of psychoanalysis is well represented' (McWilliams 1986: 253). He sees elements of Freud, determinism and a casework analysis of a problem that is not necessarily shared by the offender. By the time we get to the 1960s, 'psychoanalysis has swept aside many (although not all) of the earlier understandings, and "explanations" based on causal concepts hold sway' (McWilliams 1986: 255). Later, he writes, '[I]t seems that the apogee of the phase of diagnosis was reached in the mid-1960s' (McWilliams 1986: 255).

It is interesting that McWilliams cautions that the dominance of psychoanalysis was not total. Again this would support much of what we have already seen where probation practice is a site for competing discourses and competing strands within a discourse. The combination of old and new in probation practice is a theme running right through this work and it remains valid even at the zenith of psychodynamic social casework in probation officers' practice.

Vanstone's (2007) approach to probation in the 1950s and 1960s is slightly different. He focuses very much on social casework in probation and the training course for probation officers run by the Home Office at Rainer House. He spends some time looking at the Rainer House course content in the late 1940s and into the 1950s and notes students being taught social casework underpinned by both a psychological and psychoanalytical understandings. The course included material from Burt and the child guidance movement with its pre-war origins. The course also made reference to Freud and Bowlby's ideas about attachment which reflect the more modern post war approach (see Vanstone 2007: 97–106). Vanstone's chapter is subtitled with the phrase 'the heyday of treatment' with clear resonances back to McWilliams's work. On the other hand, Vanstone detects an almost high-handed confidence in probation practice at this time. For example, he writes:

> It was an era of confidence. The papers presented to a European Seminar on Probation in 1952 represent a confidence best seen as part of the period of renewal after the second World War. Despite the fact that there was no research evidence that probation or the psychodynamic model on which probation was purportedly based reduced offending, these commentaries ooze a sense of certainty. (Vanstone 2007: 106)

That confidence spread beyond the shores of the UK. Post-war Germany was divided into four sectors and in the British Sector the British system of probation was exported to this part of Germany. Smith (1994) describes British experts being sent out to implement almost wholesale the principles of *The Children and Young Persons Act 1933* into the British Zone along with a system of child guidance and the decarceration of juvenile offenders. These practices often went against local practices and as Smith (1994) points out were not always well received by a local population many of whom were starving and homeless.

Interestingly, Vanstone's (2007) survey suggests that social casework and psychodynamic interpretations of probationer's offending may not have reflected the actual practice of probation officers confronted with the reality of real live clients. In their day to day work more common sense approaches may well have been equally influential (see Vanstone 2007: 107 for example). There is some evidence to support this in the memoirs of Marjory Todd (1963 and 1964) who worked for a number of years both in the juvenile and adult courts of London. In neither of her books is there any explicit reference to Freud or psychodynamic explanations of offending. Instead the books are full of more common sense understandings of behaviour and focus on the reality of her day to day work. In many respects they are far closer to the work of Thomas Holmes (1908, for example) produced at the very start of the century.

Mair and Burke's (2012) account of probation in the 1950s is titled 'a golden age?' (Mair and Burke 2012: 84) and the question mark is crucial as they suggest that this was not necessarily a golden period for probation. There is less emphasis in their work on probation theory and more on the reality of the job. They use accounts of the work of officers of this period to show that caseloads were high, officers were dealing with fairly intractable offenders, crime was rising and officers were under a good deal of pressure. The prison aftercare work and the increase in matrimonial work that the *Criminal Justice Act 1948* had created meant that officers were being asked to perform many roles and there was a shortage of officers to do the work.

Throughout its history probation has been the subject of a number of key texts that review its development and describe its contemporary operation. We have already seen Leeson's (1914) early account and Le Mesurier's (1935) description of probation practice in the 1930s. The next major review of probation was Joan King's (1958) survey of the service. Like Le Mesurier's (1935) earlier work it was produced in behalf of NAPO but King was merely the editor of this work, the bulk of the material was provided by those working in probation. Perhaps the first thing to say about King's work, and it is picked up on by both Vanstone (2007) and Mair and Burke (2012), is that it includes a lot of discussion about the nature of social casework. Vanstone in particular writes that about a quarter of the book is given over to this topic and he goes on to argue that it 'gives explicit recognition to the Freudian school of psychology' (Vanstone 2007: 110). The term 'social casework' is noticeably absent in Le Mesurier's (1935) earlier survey of probation.

King (1958) writes at some length about the nature of social casework and sees it as a solution to many of the difficulties of contemporary living. She discusses Freud and his ideas particularly about child development and then writes:

> This body of knowledge has become available to social caseworkers at a time when external pressures on their clients have been lessened by greater national prosperity and the Welfare State but when the increasing complexity of modern life has created new stresses, making it necessary to focus more attention on internal conflicts and personal problems. (King 1958: 49)

She goes on to elucidate on casework in a way that McWilliams (see above) would recognize when he comments on officers assigning meanings to their clients' actions. King writes:

> The caseworker has learnt to recognise that the problems which brings the client to his attention, or about which the client expresses most concern, may or may not be what is troubling him but is often an expression of unsatisfied desires or unresolved conflicts. (King 1958: 59)

King also makes much of 'diagnosis' and 'social diagnosis', the importance of planning casework and she stresses the importance of keeping accurate records of the casework done. These are all aspects of probation practice that McWilliams (1986) identifies but they have a long tradition and formed a key part of Mary Richmond's (1917) description of casework written over fifty years earlier. King then moves on to look at social casework specifically in respect of probation. On this matter she writes:

> All that has been said about the general principles of casework applies with certain modifications to the work of the probation officer whether it be with child or adult, first offender or old lag. (King 1958: 71)

For King the key difference is that probation officers need to resolve the difficulties of 'practising casework in an authoritarian setting' (King 1958: 71). This places special pressures on the probation officer and requires the fostering of a good relationship between officer and client where the client is happy to talk and the officer is perceived as caring and warm. This is a professional relationship; not only is the officer helpful and understanding but they can also provide insight into the true motives for their client's action. Again, King writes:

> The professional relationship thus provides the clients with a medium within which they can find themselves, particularly that part of themselves which they were uncertain about or afraid to face alone. (King 1958: 53)

When it comes to working with children the social caseworker's role is much less about the environment of the child, which is where probation officers had traditionally focused their efforts, particularly with the younger clients. Now officers should focus on the feelings of the child; King writes:

> Unless these feelings are shared, and the child helped to understand them, the child will either repress them or act them out in more delinquent behaviour. (King 1958: 94)

The difficulty with this approach to probation officers' practice is the potential for conflict with those longstanding supporters of probation, namely the magistrates. The problem is compounded by the fact that with the creations of probation committees and case committees by the *Criminal Justice Act 1948* magistrates now had a substantial supervisory role over the work of probation officers. It is a problem King also identifies:

> In some ways recent advances in casework training and the tendency to a more 'psychological' approach have tended to widen the gap between the probation officer and the lay magistrates. The latter regard their common sense and practical experience as an important part of their equipment in fulfilling their judicial duties, and may therefore tend to accept the idea, so tenaciously held by public opinion as a whole, that common sense alone will solve all human problems including those of delinquency. (King 1958: 176)

This is a view of probation practice that contrasts sharply with earlier accounts and it allies probation officers with those providing 'expert assessment' to the courts.

King's account of the probation officer role, particularly the use of social casework, owes a heavy debt to the insights provided by Freudian psychology. This is in contrast to the more social psychology that Burt describes over thirty years earlier. What is striking in King's account of the probation officer role is the confidence with which she describes the social casework method and the efficacy of the body of knowledge and expertise on which it is based. The histories we have just discussed all refer to some degree at least to the 'golden age' of probation at about this time and in many respects that is in evidence in King's work. Probation is now a highly skilled, professional occupation clearly dominated by a particular strand of a psychological discourse and employing an expertise misunderstood by many.

By the 1960s researchers were becoming interested in the reality and particularly the effectiveness of probation practice. Mair and Burke (2012: 95) actually use the phrase 'enter research' and see its origins in the late 1940s.

They discuss at some length a project undertaken by the Cambridge Institute of Criminology in 1958 which they note 'was very positive about probation, but there was a serious limitation insofar as probation's success was not compared with any other court sentence which made it difficult to judge just how effective probation was' (Mair and Burke 2012: 99).

A slightly later study of probation officers' practice was conducted by the Home Office Research Unit in 1966 (see Folkard et al 1966). Folkard's study was one of the first to attempt a 'scientific' study of the effectiveness of what probation officers actually did. The very framework of the study is interesting, it is described as using a social psychological framework for the study of personality and social environment (see Folkard et al 1966: 6) and 'the main purpose of the project is to evaluate the results of treatment' (Folkard et al 1966: 9). The study itself was carried out in the Middlesex Probation Area. Of the probation officers they interviewed they found that they 'agreed about the high importance of the offenders personality, of his emotional adjustment, and of his family' (Folkard et al 1966: 24) which would seem to support the contemporary descriptions cited above. On the other hand, researchers also noted that officers with over eleven years service tended to stress practical help and helping clients finding jobs (Folkard et al 1966: 25). Later they write, '[t]he older officers who have been in the service for a longer period of time tended to do more home visiting and to use other agencies more frequently' (Folkard et al 1966: 41).

These observations suggest that probation practice continued to be a mixture of old and new. At one point the study notes that 'it seems fairly obvious that one of the main determinates of the type of treatment which is given is the probation officer who gives it' (Folkard et al 1966: 35). As we have seen before, competing social work and psychological discourses are in evidence in probation practice. The study concludes with a rather disconcerting comment:

> The development of casework theory has been influenced to a considerable extent by psychological theory, where the main concern is the treatment of individuals suffering from psychological disturbance. Even in these type of cases the effectiveness of treatment techniques derived from this theory remains to be established. (Folkard et al 1966: 42)

The discussion of the effectiveness of probation was to continue, and still does continue right up to the present day. These doubts about the effectiveness of probation practice were to attract far more attention as we moved into the 1970s and what later became known as the period of 'penal pessimism'. Nonetheless this confidence in the efficacy of social casework and probation was to continue for the time being.

Policy, a settled consensus

Probation practice moved substantially in the 1950s and early 1960s and although it is a slight simplification, a social casework based on a psychodynamic understanding of the reasons for delinquency dominated much of probation practice or at least the rhetoric of practice. In sharp contrast the policy and politics of probation during this period, particularly following the 1948 Act, remained strikingly uneventful.

The trend was clearly towards a more hierarchical and professionally qualified service. The highest ranking Home Office civil servant, Sir Frank Newsam, wrote an account of the work of his department in 1954. In this he pointed out that forty-two of the larger probation areas now had a Principal Probation Officer. In 1938 there had been 400 full-time officer and 600 part-time officers; by 1954 there were 1,191 full-time officers and 75 part-time officers. The training scheme for officers was now well established with two recognizable routes into the service but both requiring completion of the Home Office's own course at Rainer House (see Newsam 1954: 140 and 141). In the meantime the National Health Service, created by the 1945–1950 Labour Government, incidentally led by a former social worker (Clement Attlee), had taken over the management of the Portman Clinic and the Tavistock Clinic. As we have already seen, these were two centres focusing on the psychodynamic based treatment of delinquency.

When the Conservatives found themselves back in office, led briefly by Churchill, in 1950 the newly created welfare state was left intact and so began a period in British politics referred to by many as 'Butskellism'. This was named after R. A. Butler, Tory Chancellor of the Exchequer and the Labour Leader Hugh Gaitskill and indicating a period of political consensus where the 'mixed economy' of a private and state sector was accepted by both major political parties. This consensus is generally agreed to have held until 1979 and the election of Margaret Thatcher as prime minister. This consensus also held in the field of 'law and order' and into probation policy.

In 1946 the Conservative Party published *Youth Astray: A Report on the Treatment of Young Offenders*. The Report was produced by a sub-committee of the Conservative Party Committee on Policy and Political Education. The majority of the committee's membership were barristers and prison visitors; curiously nobody from probation was involved. In the forward R. A. Butler wrote, '[t]he Committee have realized that the young are very often offenders through no fault of their own' (Conservative Party 1946: 1). Indeed the basic tenants of much recent legislation addressing juvenile delinquency are accepted by the Party. The Report comments:

> The misbehaviour of boys and girls is mainly the outcome of conditions, social, economic, and to some extent hereditary, for which they themselves cannot be blamed. The blame – that there is – rests largely upon society. (Conservative Party 1946: 45)

The Report also recommended the abolition of custody for all children. In respect of probation the Report supports NAPO's stance that probation officers should write all court reports rather than those on younger offenders being allocated to the Education Department. On the issue of probation training they write, '[t]he personal qualities of the officer depend upon careful selection and adequate training' (Conservative Party 1946: 19). Indeed the whole stance of the Report is very supportive of the changes being proposed by the government of the time and about to be published in the Criminal Justice Bill. Such is noted by NAPO in their rather indignant review of the Report which notes:

> One may doubt the desirability of bringing this subject into the field of political publicity – and one's doubt is not removed by the fact that there is much in this report with which one can whole-heartedly agree.[16]

This lack of political controversy in the area is really quite striking and seems to support the notion of a 'golden age' for probation. Certainly in terms of the policy and politics of probation it enjoyed much support.

As we moved into the late 1950s the policy consensus remained intact despite crime starting to steadily increase. Right at the end of the 1950s the government produced two documents which directly referred to probation. The first of these, *Penal Practice in a Changing Society* (Home Office 1959), is primarily concerned with the prisons and other custodial sentences but makes explicit the major impact the *Criminal Justice Act 1948* had had on the work of probation officers who were now required to work with discharged prisoners. The report comments, 'provision was made for the field-work of statutory after-care to be undertaken by the only nation-wide network of qualified social case-workers available to do it – the probation service' (Home Office 1959: 20). The Report also shows that it was not just in the probation service where psychology and psychiatry had made great inroads. The Report discusses adult offenders in prison where 'methods of training have been progressively extended and improved, notably in the application of psychiatry and psychology' (Home Office 1959: 12). As if to stress the point the Report discusses psychiatric and psychological services in the prisons commenting that 'A modern prison service requires an adequate specialized service of doctors with psychiatric experience, psychologists, and such other qualified persons as go to make up a psycho-therapeutic team' (Home Office 1959: 18).

In the same year that this report was produced the Home Office appointed what was to become known as the Morison Committee which was the first full review of the probation system since 1936 (see Home Office 1936 and earlier in this work). Like the earlier review of probation NAPO had lobbied hard for the committee's appointment. In 1957, Frank Dawtry, the General Secretary, wrote:

> the Probation Division of the Home Office is not a remote civil service department, it is closely associated with the daily work of the Service it administers. This is a condition much appreciated by probation officers, but one which means that the administrators may not be able to see the total situation or to see this as objectively as might be desirable. The work of the division itself may not have kept pace with the times and could usefully be reviewed. (Dawtry 1957/8: 186)

He goes on to write that 'the time has now come for a new departmental committee or royal commission to examine all aspects of the Probation Service' (Dawtry 1957/8: 187). Bochel's (1962a and b) history of NAPO describes the role of the organization's officials in persuading the Home Office to appoint and widen the brief of the least committee to review probation by the Home Office. It would seem that NAPO continued to enjoy the sympathetic ear of the responsible government department.

The Report was finally published in early 1962 and like much that we have come across is a mixture of both old and new concerns but also a very interesting reflection of where probation was at the time. Its remit was very wide but right at the start the 'old chestnut' reappears: 'the misconception, that a person placed on probation has been "let off" has not, in our experience, yet been wholly dispelled' (Home Office 1962: 3). When it comes to the methods to be used by probation officers the report is deliberately unspecific but begins from the traditional premise of 'advise, assist and befriend' (Home Office 1962: 22). The Committee does stress that '[t]oday the probation officer must be seen, essentially, as a professional caseworker, employing, in a specialized field, skills which he holds in common with other social workers' (Home Office 1962: 23). The Report also stresses a disciplinary role of probation officers particularly in their responsibility when prosecuting breaches of any order and so that the public are protected.

The Committee were quite happy to leave the probation officer with much flexibility in their work; for example, there is an acknowledgement that some cases would be more complex than others and they could 'be identified only by the operation of the probation officer's diagnostic skill' (Home Office 1962: 24). The closest the Committee got to a definition of social casework was to say that it 'is the creation and utilization, for the benefit of an individual who needs help with personal problems, of a relationship between himself and a trained social worker' (Home Office 1962: 24). The Report continues:

> The caseworker thus needs the fullest possible insight into the individual's personality, capacities, attitudes and feelings and he must also understand the influences on the individual's history, relationships and present environment which have helped to form them. (Home Office 1962: 24)

The key to successful casework is the relationship between the probation officer and the person placed on probation; the 'casework relationship' and this is a theme the Report returns to regularly. It should be 'a positive influence, counteracting the ill-effects of past experiences and of irremovable factors in the present. Such a relationship is founded upon the sense of mutual acceptance between the caseworker and the person to be helped' (Home Office 1962: 25). Mere material help may be appropriate but the Report sees the casework relationship in these terms and the aim of the relationship is to enable the probationer to help themselves.

Beyond this the specifics of supervision should be left to the probation officer; the Report noted that 'the probation officer, in our view be conceded reasonable discretion to use the supervisory techniques he thinks fit' (Home Office 1962: 26). There is then a discussion about the use or mix of home visits and office visits when supervising those on probation. Again, discretion is left to the probation officer:

> It is for him to decide, from the knowledge of the whole situation, how frequently visits to and by the probationer are required.

The reason being:

> both these practices play a part in the casework relationship. (Home Office 1962: 26)

There are some significant developments noted in probation since the previous review. The Report noted that since that Report there had been the final and irreversible emergence of the probation service as a profession, requiring professional training and skill (Home Office 1962: 26).

Reaction to the Report was remarkably sanguine; Mair and Burke comment on how 'uncontentious the 177 conclusions and recommendations' (Mair and Burke 2012: 112) were. Vanstone (2007) is a little more sceptical and saw portents for the future particularly in respect of probation practice and the dominance of social casework. In respect of the latter he noted that the Morrison Report 'showed no inhibitions in endorsing it as an approach to working with offenders' (Vanstone 2007: 113). However, slightly later he writes, 'during this period debates about casework whether within groups or with individuals tended to be about its details and occur within an acceptance of the basic validity of the model' (Vanstone 2007: 116). Thus highlighting the fact that there was no evidence to suggest that social casework turned offenders from crime, that is, that it worked, although (as we have already noted) there was an emerging interest in probation's effectiveness.

The development of the probation 'operation' at this time was quite remarkable, in terms of numbers of offenders supervised, the number of officers, the number of trained officers, the rise of a hierarchy within probation itself and the expansion of the Probation and After Care Branch of the Home Office. Those changes are reflected in statistics collected by the Home Office and published in the *Report of the Probation and After Care Department 1962 to 1965* (Home Office 1966). This Report opens by noting the huge increase in work for the probation service as it had taken on all the supervision of post custodial licences, hence the change in name of the service to the Probation and After Care Service. In addition the Prison Welfare Service was to be taken over by probation and staffed by probation officers. When the Divorce Court Welfare Services are added into the mix then we can see that by the mid-1960s the reach of probation officers had extended well beyond their early days in the magistrates courts.

A few simple statistics from the Report place the scale of the probation operation into perspective. In 1950 there had been 656 male and 350 female (making a total of 1,006) probation officers. In 1966 there were 1,765 male and 653 female (making a total of 2,417) probation officers (Home Office 1966: 12). The expectation was that these numbers would increase. In 1966 there were 69 Principal Probation Officers, 24 Deputy or Assistant Principal Probation Officers and 286 Senior Probation Officers (Home Office 1966: 13). The Probation Inspectorate at the Home Office now had a staff of twenty-six. The first Principal Probation Officer (Clutton-Broch) and the first Inspector of Probation (Miss Rosling) had been appointed in 1938 shortly after the last review of probation. A further change of note was the increase in the number of qualified probation officers, though definitions of what qualified meant were not specific. The Home Office recorded the number of officers appointed without training to be 63 per cent of male officers and 33 per cent of female officers in

1960 but by 1965 only 16 per cent of male officers and 22 per cent of female officers were unqualified on appointment. The Home Office training scheme continued to recruit students with a social science diploma or qualification. The scheme included three months of theoretical training and eight months practical, in the field. Over 100 officers were trained annually between 1963 and 1966 and the numbers were expected to increase (Home Office 1966: 48). The numbers of offenders found guilty of indictable offences and placed on probation had increased from 39,723 in 1961 to 42,650 in 1965 (Home Office 1966: 21). As if to emphasize the sense of probation having 'arrived' the final combining order was made in March 1966 (see Home Office 1966: 5). This was the process originally began back in 1925 with The Criminal Justice Act of that year which ordered that all petty sessional divisions should be combined on a regional basis to form probation areas with probation committees. A project which had created a good deal of work and controversy for the Home Office for many years was finally complete.

Probation's peak

With the benefit of hindsight we can now look back and know what lay in store for probation in the years that followed. Nonetheless, the evidence that the late 1960s represented something of a peak for probation is really quite powerful and this is reflected in the more recent histories of probation written by Vanstone (2007) and Mair and Burke (2012). We have seen that the probation service was expanding. The number of probation orders made was increasing and the number of probation officers was increasing. Crucially though the number of full-time and qualified probation officers were increasing. The scope of probation was increasing with matrimonial work becoming an ever larger part of probation's workload. Probation officers were seen as the most appropriate people to take on the expanding work with those recently released from custody and probation officers were also moving into the prisons. Probation was also developing a structure with a new set of managers and middle managers being appointed. There were real prospects of promotion. Interestingly the Probation Branch at the Home Office was expanding as was the Probation Inspectorate. The Reports we have just been considering also refer to the growth in the academic discipline of criminology which was beginning to research into probation.

Probation also enjoyed a great deal of support, particularly political support. The changes since 1948 had not needed legislation and the political parties seemed to share the same view of probation. The Reports we have looked at in this chapter were produced by both Labour and Tory governments and were ordered by a number of Home Secretaries yet the consensus between them is remarkable. What also stands out is the flexibility; perhaps it would be better described as the professional discretion, the Home Office were prepared to allow probation officers in the way they worked. This was not just in terms of the demands officers placed on their clients but also in the social casework methods that officers used. The Morison Report (Home Office 1962) made much of social casework and a social casework relationship but beyond that they were nor prepared to go; that was a professional decision to be made by individual officers. Note too that it was probation officers, not their managers, who were allowed that discretion.

It has been a theme throughout this work that probation was a site for competing discourses in respect of the treatment of crime. By the mid-1960s particular strands of both the social work and psychological discourses dominated probation practice, some rising and some falling, coexisting and consisting of a mixture of old and new. The attitude of the Home Office and probation management, and by this time we can talk of such a beast, was that it was up to the individual probation officer to decide which method was appropriate to which client.

The problem with a peak of course is that there tends to be a trough and on this subject there is a good deal of literature. Downes and Morgan's account of the politics of law and order describes a major shift and notes that 'the 1970 election was a watershed which, by 1979 had swept away the main supports of non-partisanship' (Downes and Morgan 1994: 225). They then go on to describe what they call a 'second phase consensus' following the 1979 election absent from which was any commitment to rehabilitation of the criminal as a policy aim. In this new consensus the Home Office became central as it was the source of policy and as May (1994) wrote, 'changes in the criminal justice system in recent times have been not only rapid, but chaotic' (May 1994: 861).

At about the same time that the political consensus began to break down probation's methods were found to be largely ineffective. Vanstone writes that 'in retrospect the 1960s can be seen as the zenith of the casework method (and by implication the treatment model)' (Vanstone 2007: 113). That shattering of confidence in social casework is usually attributed to Martinson's (1974) celebrated essay though as we have already seen there were some seeds of doubt already. Simply put, Martinson produced a meta-analysis where he gathered the results of 231 different studies of various programmes that sought to reduce an offender's likelihood of reoffending. These covered a huge range of programmes, some in custodial establishments and some not. Of those in the community he writes:

> In sum, even in the case of treatment programs administered outside penal institutions, we simply cannot say that the treatment in itself has an appreciable effect on offending behavior. (Martinson 1974: 48)

Put crudely, he found that 'nothing works', though to be fair to Martinson he did point out that the majority of the programmes he looked at did not make offenders any worse (see Martinson 1974: 48).

In the years that followed, the political consensus shifted enormously and probation's political support, in what Garland (2001) terms a 'punitive society', plummeted. Brake and Hale (1992) provide a fascinating account of the politics and policy of law and order and describe a new environment for probation. Tim May's (1991) detailed account of probation in the very early 1990s is based on his observations of, and interviews with, a number of probation staff as they grappled with huge legislative changes affecting their work at a key point in probation's history. He paints a picture of a service faced with Home Office directives and instructions, a hostile political environment and an emerging top-down public sector management approach. This happened at a time when its working methods were facing much criticism as being ineffective. All of this, of course, is another story.

The final irony is that as this work is slowly completed the latest proposal from the Home Office, the organization that created the probation system we have, is that this system is to be dismantled. Proposals to privatize or contract out much of the work of the service are being discussed (Guilfoyle 2013). Probation is now simply facing up to current attitudes and knowledge of what the correct responses to crime should be just as it did when it was originally established. It is, and was, a product of its time and place.

Notes

Chapter 1

1 The Memo and the responses are held in *Mepol 2/1267 police court missionaries – review of the value of their work* at the National Archive. The emphasis is in the original.
2 The letter is dated 22 October 1907 and held in *Mepol 2/1267*.
3 All these responses are dated 22 October 1907 and all are held in *Mepol 2/1267*.
4 Helen Bosanquet, born 1865 and died 1925 was the long time Secretary of the Charity Organisation Society. She was also a member of the Poor Law Commission which reported in 1909.
5 To many, a year or two at the settlement was considered the final part of a young gentleman's complete education. Toynbee Hall includes many famous people amongst its former staff including Clement Attlee and William Beveridge. The former Tory Cabinet Minister, John Profumo, worked there for many years following his fall from grace.
6 See Briggs and Macauley (1984). Clement Attlee's first taste of elected politics was whilst working at Toynbee Hall when he was elected to the London County Council. By the turn of the century many industrial cities (Liverpool, Manchester, Leeds, Birmingham, for example) had a university settlement; there were also others in London.

Chapter 2

1 The later measure referred to was the *Probation of Offenders Bill of 1906*, another Private Members Bill of Vincent's. This time the government took the measure over with a scheme of its own; see below. Incidentally, a more modern and critical survey of the Massachusetts Probation System can be found in Platt (1969).
2 These quotes are taken from *The Probation of First Offenders Bill 1886*.
3 The debate in the Lords is recorded in *Hansard Lords*, 3rd Series, Vol. 307, col. 176.
4 Letter to the Editor of *The Times*, 26 July 1886.
5 *Hansard Lords*, 3rd series, Vol. 316, col. 1766.
6 Howard in a letter to the Editor of *The Times*, 1 December 1904.

7 See *Annual Report of the Howard Association*, October 1881. The money saving potential of probation was noted this early and we will return to this view.

8 Home Office Circular dated 15 October 1880 held in *HO45/9593/93897 Observation of Magistrates and Others as to the Treatment of Juvenile Offenders 1880–1887*.

9 Francis Galton (1822–1911) was a nephew of Charles Darwin, and wrote extensively on the science of eugenics. In 1905 he established a laboratory at London University to study eugenics.

10 Karl Pearson (1857–1936) was Emeritus Professor of Eugenics and one time Director of the Francis Galton Laboratory for National Eugenics at London University.

11 *Report of the Inter Departmental Committee on Physical Deterioration*, 1904, p. 13 para. 68.

12 *Report of the Inter Departmental Committee on Physical Deterioration*, 1904, p. 55 para. 282.

13 Charles Masterman (1873–1927) enjoyed a public school education followed by degrees in moral sciences and natural sciences at Cambridge; he was elected to Parliament in 1903. After the Liberal Party's success in 1906 he held a number of Junior Minister posts but lost his seat in 1914. For a while he was considered a rising star of the Liberal Party (Hay, J. R. 1975). He returned briefly to Parliament in 1923 but died in 1927.

14 Bentley Gilbert, p. xxvi in Masterman (1901/1973).

15 Like many Victorian young gentlemen Masterman spent a year or so at one of the Settlements following his time at University. Much less is known of Reginald Bray. It was at his instigation that Masterman went to work at the Settlement but unlike Masterman he stayed in Camberwell at least until 1914, working for and with the poor of the area and serving on the London County Council. He published a number of works on the urban working class; see Bray (1907, 1908, 1912). These works reveal him to be a deeply religious and committed man.

16 Indeed, Baden-Powell wanted to call them 'Imperial Scouts', but was dissuaded by his publisher and mentor Arthur Pearson (Pearson 1983: 112).

17 Indeed, many of these concerns are reflected in Thomas Holmes's later writing (see Holmes 1908) as discussed by Vanstone (2007).

18 Herbert Samuel (1870–1963) was the son of Liverpool banker, and member of a 'political family'. He studied at Oxford then worked as a barrister before entering politics. He was elected to Parliament in 1902. He was Leader of the Liberal Opposition in the 1930s.

19 See *Juvenile Offenders – A Report Based on an Enquiry Instituted by the Committee of the Howard Association – 1898*.

20	See *HO45/10291/112648 Information on New Zealand Probation System*, where both reports are held.

21	Letter received at the Home Office sometime in 1906 and held in *HO45/10349/146626 Probation of Offenders Bill 1906*. The same file also shows a number of Temperance Societies lobbying the Home Office for an extension of the existing *Probation of First Offenders Act*.

22	Home Office Minute dated 23 October 1890, held in *HO45/9970/X30078 First Offenders Act – Disregard of Act in Manchester*.

23	As commented by Godfrey Lushington (Permanent Under Secretary) in a letter dated 25 April 1892 held in *Mepol 2/525 Probation of First Offenders Act*.

24	*Probation of First Offenders Bill 1906*, p. 1.

25	Home Office Minute by Herbert Samuel, dated 22 February 1907 in *HO45/10346/142801 Probation of First Offenders Bill 1906*.

26	See *HO45/10349/146626*. Herbert Samuel quoted from a Minute dated 14 March 1907.

27	This was presumably a reference to the power the court had to release a defendant on his own recgonizances which was included in this Act (see above).

28	Two Probation Orders made in London Juvenile Courts early in 1908 show the Court Clerk had crossed out whichever of these items the Court had not deemed applicable in the case. See *HO144/1023/163781 Children-General File for the Working of the Probation Act*.

29	To be fair there are some who do not take this position, Jarvis (1972) for example.

30	*Hansard*, Vol. 179, col. 1487, dated 5 August 1907.

31	*Hansard*, Vol. 174, col. 294, dated 8 May 1907.

32	Again see *Hansard*, Vol. 174, col. 294–5, dated 8 May 1907.

33	Mr Lief Jones MP, in *Hansard*, Vol. 179, col. 372, dated 26 July 1907.

34	Both worked for many years as probation officers and developed formidable reputations. In 1919, Sidney Harris, at the time still in the early stages of an illustrious Home Office career (see later) noted that 'Miss Croker-King is an Irish woman who has a habit of trailing her coat and is apt to say much more than she means'. Home Office Minute, July 1919, held in *HO45/11912 Appointment, Salary of Women Probation Officers*.

35	See *HO330/71*. They had been nominated by Miss Humphrey Ward who was an anti-suffragettist campaigner of the period, and were to be paid 40 pounds per annum.

36	Home Office Minute sometime late in 1907 by C. E. Troup (Head of the Children's Branch and in 1908 appointed Permanent Under Secretary) held in *HO45/10369/159319 Appointment and Payment of Probation Officers*.

37	Home Office Minute dated 29 January 1908 in *HO45/10369/159319*.

38	The correspondence took place in February 1908 and is held in *HO45/10369/159319*.

39	Letter dated August 1908 in same file.

40	See *HO45/10369/159319*.

41 Note on file dated 2 November 1908, in *HO45/10369/159319*.

42 Memo dated 29 March 1910 held in *HO45/10594/186854 Arrangements for Police Courts and Juvenile Courts*.

43 Home Office Minute dated 19 November 1908 in *HO144/1023/163781 General File for the Working of the Probation Act*.

44 Home Office Minute by Edward Troup, dated 14 November 1910, in *HO144/1023/163781*.

45 The Report from the Birmingham Magistrates is also held in *HO144/1023/163781*.

46 One other example of the work of the Oxford Idealists was the Settlement Movement already described.

47 Home Office Minute dated 3 December 1908 by Troup, shortly after his promotion to Permanent Under Secretary, held in *HO45/10369/159319*.

48 Letter from C. E. B. Russell to the Home Office dated 13 March 1913 held in *HO144/1116/203154 Probation of Offenders Act 1907*.

49 The letter is not specific as to whether Russell was writing privately or as a representative of this committee.

50 The letter is not specific as to whether Russell was writing privately or as a representative of this committee. Russell had also written extensively on crime and its causes; see Russell (1906 and 1910). He served as Chief Inspector of Industrial and Reformatory Schools until his death in 1917.

51 Home Office Minute dated 24 March 1913 held in *HO144/1116/203154 Probation of Offenders Act 1907*.

52 Letter dated 23 July 1913 held in *HO45/11912 Appointment and Salaries of Women Probation Officers 1913–25*.

53 See *HO45/10572/176696 Probation of Offenders Act 1907*. For instance the *Daily Telegraph* of 3 January 1913 included comments from the Recorder at Croydon criticizing the arrangements for probation.

54 Copies of the Report are held in *HO45/24660 CETS work in probation* and *HO45/22773 Probation Officer Duties*.

55 Letter is dated 1 July 1914 and held in *HO45/22773 Probation Officer Duties Including Record Keeping*.

56 The connection between the new probation officers and the Boys Club movement was a long one and will be returned to. It is regularly referred to in the Boys Club movement literature (see, for example, Russell 1910 and 1932 particularly).

Chapter 3

1 See *Report of the Commissioner of Police of the Metropolis for the year 1915 (Cd 8405)*.

2 *Report of the Commissioner of Police of the Metropolis for the year 1916 (Cd 8827)*, p. 8.

3   See Clarke-Hall (1917). William Clarke-Hall (1866–1932) from 1913 was a
    Magistrate sitting in the busy Old Street Magistrates and Children's Court in
    London. He was an early supporter of probation and Children's Courts and one
    time Chair of both the Magistrates Association and of NAPO.

4   See *HO45/10790/301145 Increase in Juvenile Crime 1915–17.*

5   Letter to the Home Office from William Clarke-Hall, dated 22 February 1916 in
    HO45/10790/301145.

6   See *HO45/10790/301145.*

7   Figures taken from *First Report of the Work of the Children's Branch, April 1923*
    (Home Office 1923), p. 110, table xi.

8   Figures are taken from the *27th Annual Report of the London Diocesan Branch of
    the Church of England Temperance Society, 1919.*

9   These figures are taken from Clarke-Hall (1926: 281). The same figures show that
    juvenile crime fell sharply after World War One, so by 1924 those on probation
    make up a higher proportion of those convicted.

10 The Memo and notes of the meetings are held in *HO144/1116/203154 Probation of
    Offenders Act 1907.*

11 Home Office Minute dated 24 July 1917 in *HO144/116/203154.*

12 Home Office Minute dated 20 August 1917 in *HO144/1116/203154.*

13 See *HO45/10790/301145 Increasein Juvenile Crime 1915–17.*

14 Letter from Commissioner of Police for Metropolis to the Home Office dated
    1 June 1916 in *Mepol 2/1699 Juvenile Offenders, Increase 1916.*

15 Letter to Home Office dated 28 January 1916 in *HO45/10798/307268.*

16 Letter to Home Office from Baden Powell dated 7 October 1916 in
    HO45/10790/301145.

17 He had worked as a Boys Club leader in Manchester, written about his experiences
    in a number of books, see Russell (1906, 1910) and served on the Departmental
    Committee on Industrial and Reformatory Schools between 1911 and 1913 before
    being appointed to his current position.

18 See *HO45/10790/301145.*

19 *HO45/16515 Juvenile Delinquency – Juvenile Organisations Committee 1920.*

20 Home Office minute dated 11 May 1920, probably by C. E. Troup, in *HO45/16515.*

21 Troup's notes are dated 11 May 1920 and included in *HO45/16515.*

22 See *HO45/11033/438693 Probation, Certified Schools and Borstal Institutions Bill – 1921.*

23 *Times Educational Supplement* dated 2 October 1919, in *HO45/11152.*

24 Letter from the Home Office to the War Office dated 22 March 1919 *in HO
    45/16515.*

25 Letter from E. Ruggles-Brise to the Home Secretary dated 16 December 1919 in
    HO45/11074/395473 Development of Probation, p. 5.

26 Letter from E. Ruggles-Brise to the Home Secretary dated 16 December 1919, in
    HO45/11074, p. 4.

27 See HO45/24660 for this and other examples of similar correspondence between the Home Office and the CETS working in London over the financial arrangements for the payment of salaries for the Police Court Missionaries in London.

28 Minutes of the London Diocesan Police Court Mission Committee dated 15 December 1920.

29 The correspondence is contained in *HO45/11912 Appointment, Salaries of Women Probation Officers 1913–35*. This saga continued for nearly three years, 1919–1922, and on occasions became quite bitter and personal; at one point the Home Office were forced to initiate an internal inquiry. The voluntary officers scheme collapsed in 1923, and the Home Office had to appoint temporary officers.

30 Letter from William Clarke-Hall to Sidney Harris at the Home Office dated 14 September 1920 held in *HO45/11912*.

31 Indeed this is the very phrase used by the Home Secretary when he agreed to the appointment of the Committee in 1920. See Home Office Minute dated 3 May 1920 in *HO45/11074/395473*.

32 Home Office Minute dated 30 January 1922, signed by C. E. Troup, in *HO45/11074/395473*.

33 Both from *Annual Report of the Howard League for Penal Reform 1921–22*, p. 11.

34 *Annual Report of the Howard League for Penal Reform 1921–22*, p. 12.

35 See *Annual Report of the Howard League 1922–23*.

36 *30th Annual Report of the London Diocesan Branch of CETS and Police Court Mission*, pp. 10–11.

37 Attlee (1920) p. 1. Clement Attlee (1883–1967) studied at Oxford and went to Toynbee Hall in about 1909. He was elected Mayor of Stepney a few years after the publication of this book; he was also MP for the area between 1922 and 1950. He played a huge role in the creation of the welfare state as prime minister between 1945 and 1950.

38 See Macadam (1925). She was later to work as a special advisor to the Home Office on the training of probation officers. Macadam was also very active in and one time chair of the Joint University Council for Social Studies. She was appointed Warden at the Victoria Settlement in Liverpool in 1903 and in 1911 was appointed as the first university based Social Work Tutor (at Liverpool University).

39 Macadam (1925) p. 92. The notion that experience of working class conditions was essential was one of the ideas behind the Settlement movement of the nineteenth century as exemplified by Bray (1908) and is part of a long tradition of social work being done by the middle classes to the working classes.

40 Although the subject matter has changed social work training followed a very similar pattern until recently. It is a model pioneered by Macadam.

41 Cyril Burt (1883–1971) Read Classics and Mental Philosophy at Oxford. Appointed Lecturer in Experimental Psychology at Liverpool University (1909–1913) before his move to London.

42 See Burt (1925). The last edition of this work was published in 1944. Burt's work was regularly quoted well after the end of the Second World War. Incidentally, as Rose (1985) points out, questions were later asked about his conclusions when Burt admitted to falsifying some of the results of his research.

43 Numerous histories on the subject. Foucault (1979), Rose (1961), Radzinowicz and Hood (1986) point out that many of the earliest criminologists like Lombroso were prison doctors. Other well-known British examples would include Devon (1912) and Goring (1919).

44 Hamblin Smith (1922) in the preface. At this early stage Hamblin Smith acknowledges a debt to Dr W. Healy, an American psychologist, who ran a clinic attached to the Chicago Juvenile Court (see Bennet 1981). He is usually said to be the first psychologist to work with offenders and to use the case study method to describe treatment (Bennet 1981: 112). Richmond (1917) also makes regular reference to his work.

45 Burt (1925) pp. 96 and 98.

46 It was at this time that psychologists began using tests on various groups to determine their particular aptitude for various tasks or jobs. It later became known as industrial psychology. Today we might term it 'psychometric testing' by would-be employers.

47 Rose (1985) p. 197. The impact of the 'new psychology' on other branches of social work was far reaching. Indeed it introduced a whole new field for social workers, that of the psychiatric social worker, the first of whom were sent to the USA to train in the 1920s; see Timms (1964) and Clement-Brown (1970).

48 Figures taken from Home office (1924) pp. 9 and 10.

49 *Criminal Justice Bill 1924*, dated 25 February 1924, memo attached.

50 *Criminal Justice Bill 1924,* sections 4 and 5.

51 *Hansard,* Vol. 183, col.1610.

52 *Hansard*, Vol. 183, col. 1610.

53 *Hansard*, Vol 183, col. 1621.

54 *Hansard*, Vol. 183, col. 1622.

55 *Criminal Justice Bill 1925*, dated 5 March 1925, section 4(I).

56 *Hansard*, Vol. 188, Col. 123.

57 Information from Home Office (1928), *Fourth Report of the Children's Branch.*

58 Edward Troup to the Magistrates Association (1923) quoted in *HO45/17943*. A Home Office Minute comments that 'the remarks which seem to have attracted he most press attention were those about "psycho-analysis"'.

59 *Probation Rules (1926)*, dated 4 June 1926, reprinted in Le Mesurier (1935), p. 284.

60 Letter from the Treasury to the Home Office dated 21 June 1926 in *HO45/13386 Development of Probation.*

61 See correspondence in *HO45/13386*. Incidentally the probation officer for the neighbouring area was a representative of the RSPCC, thus indicating that outside London a varied selection of organizations sponsored probation officers.

62 Home Office Memo dated 20 October 1922 in *HO45/16194 Probation Officer Conferences – Proposal etc.*

63 Home Office Minute from Home Office representative who had attended at the Conference, dated 16 February 1926 in *HO45/13386*.

64 The letter of complaint is held in *HO45/16194*.

65 Home Office letter dated 25 July 1927 signed by Sidney Harris, held in *HO45/13219*. In fact many Rescue Workers of the time were trained by the Church as Moral Welfare Workers.

66 Internal Home Office Report, p. 5 held in *HO45/13219*.

67 Internal Home Office Report, p. 24 held in *HO45/13219*.

68 Internal Home Office Report, p. 22 held in *HO45/13219*.

69 This list was actually taken from the 27th Annual Report of the London Diocesan Branch of CETS (1919), though a similar breakdown was offered in all the annual reports from 1895 to 1936.

70 Henry Waddy (1863–1926) was called to the Bar in 1885; he was Recorder in Scarborough 1913–1917 and Police Court Magistrate at Tower Bridge from 1917 to 1926.

Chapter 4

1 Fenner Brockway was something of a political radical who became concerned with the treatment of crime after spending twenty-eight months in jail as a conscience objector during the First World War. He was to become an active member of the Howard League for Penal Reform.

2 Le Mesurier (1935) quotes from the 1934 Probation Directory that there were 831 probation officers at the time, 503 men and 328 women. About one-third were full-time and 148 of the full-time officers belonged to one of the voluntary societies who received a grant to cover 50 per cent of their salary from the Home Office (Le Mesurier 1934: 38).

3 *See HO45/13386 Development of Probation.*

4 Leo Page (1890–1951) was appointed a JP in Berkshire in 1925. He served on a number of Home Office committees including the Advisory Committee on Probation.

5 Home Office memo dated 19 September 1926 in *HO45/20104 Nottinghamshire Combined Probation Areas 1926–8.*

6 Article held in *HO45/22904 Bury Combined Probation Area Order 1929 – Difficulties in Appointing a Probation Officer.*

7 Again from the *Bury Times* of 4 May 1929 held in *HO45/22904*.

8 Letter dated 7 May 1929 held in *HO45/22904*.

9 Again see *HO45/22904*. By December 1929 the Finance Committee at Bury Council had agreed to appoint a probation officer in line with the Home Office scheme.

10 Article in the *Exeter Express and Echo* dated 6 October 1928 and held in
    HO45/24106 Devon – Combined Probation Area Order.

11 Letter from Magistrates at Great Torrington, Devon to the Home Office dated 28
    January 1929, held in *HO45/24106*.

12 Letter from Magistrates at Stanborough and Coleridge to Home Office, early 1929
    held in *HO45/24106*.

13 Home Office Minute dated 12 March 1929 held in *HO45/24106*.

14 See *HO45/20460 County of Warwick – Combined Probation Areas 1929–42*.

15 Home Office Minute dated 21 October 1929 in *HO45/24112 Higher Courts
    Probation Arrangements 1929–50*.

16 Letter from Clerk to the Court at Leamington Spa to the Home Office dated 13
    January 1930 held in *HO45/20460*.

17 See *HO45/21162 Flintshire Combined Probation Area 1941–7*.

18 Letter from the Clerk of the Court Flint Magistrates dated 14 August 1941 held in
    HO45/21162.

19 Home Office Minute dated 18 August 1941 held in *HO45/21162*.

20 Home Office (1927) p. 59. The previous review of probation (Home Office 1922)
    had stressed religious zeal and particularly force of character as the main methods
    of reforming offenders rather than anything that could be taught at an academic
    institution.

21 Letter from the Howard League for Penal Reform dated 15 June 1927, contained in
    HO45/13403 Treatment of Young Offenders 1927–9.

22 See *HO45/13403*.

23 Quoted in *HO45/13403*.

24 Dr Arthur Norris (born 1875) was appointed Medical Inspector of Industrial and
    Reformatory Schools in 1914, shortly after which he joined the army and was
    decorated during the war. He returned in 1917 to succeed C. E. B. Russell as Chief
    Inspector of Reformatory and Industrial Schools, a post he held well into the 1930s.
    The Memos are held in *HO45/13403* and are dated September and October 1927,
    shortly after the publication of the Report.

25 Dr Arthur Norris in *HO45/13403*.

26 Contained within *HO45/13403*.

27 Letter contained within *HO45/21804*.

28 Letter contained within *HO45/21804*.

29 Oliver Stanley (1896–1950) was a Conservative MP with aristocratic connections.
    In 1932 he was at the early stage of what was to be a successful political career. He
    was a member of Cabinet for most of the war years.

30 *Hansard Commons*, Vol. 261, col. 1168, 1931–1932.

31 *Hansard Commons*, Vol. 261, col. 1179, 1932–1933.

32 *Hansard Commons*, Vol. 267, col. 2086, 1931–1932.

33 Mr Rhys Davies on 12 February 1932 contained in *Hansard Commons*, Vol. 261, col. 1188, 1931–1932.

34 *See HO/317/12,13 and 14 – Children and Young Persons Bill House of Commons – Vols 1 and 2, Children and Young Person Bill – House of Lords.*

35 HO/317/12, p. 26.

36 As we have already seen, Harris and Norris had discussed the possibility of establishing probation hostels approved by the Home Office. A general condition to reside at any home, such as a rescue home and the like, had been queried with the Home Office by a Court as early as 1908, see *HO144/1023/163781*. A section of the *Criminal Justice Administration Act of 1914* allowed the insertion of general conditions of residence to a probation order; however, the Home Office had come to disapprove of the powers for the reasons stated.

37 Sydney Harris in a Home Office memo sometime in 1930. See *HO45/317/12*, p. 117.

38 *HO45/317/12*, p. 221.

39 *HO45/317/12*, p. 242.

40 Letter is held in *HO317/12*.

41 *HO317/12*, p. 331.

42 Again see *HO317/12*.

43 *Howard Journal*, Vol. 3, No. 3, 1930–1933, 1933, Editorial p. 12.

44 Memo to Cabinet by Herbert Samuel, dated 12 January 1932 contained in *HO317/12*.

45 See *HO45/16213 Joint Universities Council for Social Studies – Training for Future Probation Officers.* The group included Professor Carr Saunders of Liverpool University (later to be Director of the LSE), C.M. Lloyd of the LSE, Miss Snodgrass from Glasgow University and Miss Devon from Birmingham University. The JUC was formed in 1917 and Macadam was a member even then (see J.U.C.S.S. 1918, Yelloly 1980).

46 See *HO45/16213*.

47 The register is held in *HO45/13715 Probation Officers – Register of Applicants for Appointment*. Harris's Minute is dated 12 November 1923.

48 Minutes of the Advisory Committee on Probation and After Care meeting held November 1929 in *HO45/16213*.

49 Minutes of the Advisory Committee on Probation and After Care, meeting held 20 February 1930 in *HO45/16213*.

50 William Clarke-Hall to NAPO Conference, 1931. Quoted in *Probation*, Vol. 1, No. 8, July 1931.

51 Home Office Minute dated sometime in mid-1930, in *HO45/16213*.

52 Selection Committee Minutes which sat 3 October 1930, in *HO45/16213*.

53 The replies were collated by the Home Office and are held in *HO45/16213*, dated July 1932.

54 William Clarke-Hall writing in *Probation*, No. 1, July 1929, p. 7.

55 *Probation*, No. 1, July 1929, p. 10.

56 Editorial, *Probation*, Vol. 1, No. 2, December 1929, p. 20.

57 See *Probation*, Vol. 1, No. 3.

58 Dr Charles Burns, *Probation*, Vol. 1, No. 3, July 1930.

59 Dr Bennett, 'Hysteria', *Probation*, Vol. 1, No. 6, January 1931.

60 H. Crichton-Miller, 'Causes of Crime', *Probation*, Vol. 1, No. 7, April 1931, p. 99.

61 William Clarke-Hall quoted in *Probation*, Vol. 1, No. 9, October 1931.

62 See for instance *Probation*, Vol. 1, No. 10, January 1932.

63 Earl of Feversham, 'Probation today', *Probation*, Vol. 1, No. 10, January 1932, p. 147.

64 See *Probation*, Vol. 1, No. 12, July 1932, p. 179.

65 W. H. Chinn, 'Investigations by the Probation Officer', *Probation*, Vol. 1, No. 13, October 1932, pp. 199–200.

66 Basil Henriques at NAPO Conference 1933 quoted in *Probation*, Vol. 1, No. 17, October 1933, pp. 269–271. Henriques (1890–1961) founded the Jewish Settlement in London in 1914, was also vice-chair of the National Association of Boys Clubs and president of the London Federation of Boys Clubs. He was chair of the East London Juvenile Court from 1936 to 1955.

67 S. Clement-Brown, 'Is delinquency an individual or a family problem?', *Probation*, Vol. 1, No. 19, April 1934, p. 299.

68 Elizabeth Macadam, 'The intellectual Background of Probation Work', *Probation*, Vol. 2, No. 9, July 1937, p. 139.

69 Reported in *Probation*, Vol. 2, No. 7, January 1937, p. 102.

70 *42nd Annual Report of the London Police Court Mission* (1934) pp. 9 and 12.

71 *41st Annual Report of the London Police Court Mission* (1933) p. 4.

72 *41st Annual Report of the London Police Court Mission* (1933) p. 6.

73 Dorothy Eyres, 'Probation over the London border', *Probation*, Vol. 1, No. 3, July 1930, p. 74.

74 Dr Grace Pailthorpe qualified in 1914 and worked as medical officer and ran a mobile ambulance unit in the First World War. She was the originator of the ISTD (see below) and later in life an abstract artist of some note.

75 The Howard League for Penal Reform was also sceptical (*Howard Journal*, Vol. 3, No. 4, 1933, p. 99).

76 There is also an element of eugenics in her work when she advocates the segregation and even sterilization of mental defectives, as mentioned above.

77 Dr Edward Glover was born in 1888 and after his medical training went to Germany in 1920 where he studied psychoanalysis. He returned to England where he was particularly instrumental in introducing the work of Freud and applying it to the young offender via his work at the ISTD and the British Psychoanalytical Society, which he left in 1944. The clinic he and Dr Pailthorpe founded in 1934 is now known as the Portman Clinic and continues to treat young offenders. (Biographical Sketch by Kubic contained in ISTD Archive.)

78 *I.S.T.D. Annual Report for 1935*, held in ISTD Archive.

79 *I.S.T.D. Annual Report for 1937*, p. 11, held in ISTD Archive.

80 *I.S.T.D. Annual Report of 1934*, held in ISTD Archive.

81 ISTD Scientific Committee Minutes, 9 November 1932.

82 ISTD Scientific Committee Minutes, 6 November 1934.

83 ISTD Scientific Committee Minutes, 2 July 1935.

84 See 'Is Delinquency an Individual or a Family Problem?', *Probation*, Vol. 1, No. 18, January 1934, pp. 299–300.

85 See for instance *Probation*, Vol. 2, No. 3, January 1936. The notice also refers to a probation officer who had recently completed the course.

86 Cohen (1985) discusses this concept in detail from a modern perspective.

87 All quotes are from Sidney Harris's speech to the NAPO Conference of 1932 as reported in *Probation*, Vol. 1, No. 13, October 1932, pp. 193–194.

88 Minute by Chief Commissioner dated 9 March 1936 in *MEPO2/4228 Juvenile Criminality in London 1935*.

89 Letter from Sidney Harris to Chief Commissioner dated 22 May 1936 in *MEPO2/4228*.

90 Report by the Statistical Branch dated September 1937, in *HO45/18118 Increase in Juvenile Crime 1937–8*.

91 Chief Commissioner of Metropolitan Police, Minute dated 3 March 1937 in *MEPO2/4252 Juvenile Crime – Suggested Reasons for Increase 1937–8*.

92 Lord Merrivale was the peer in question, see *HO45/17080 Social Services Committee*.

93 Home Office Minute, undated, by Sidney Harris sometime in 1935 in *HO45/17080* referring to the issues of probation funding, the training scheme which was in difficulty at the time and the wide variations in probation use around the country.

94 *42nd Annual Report of the London Police Court Mission*, 1934, p. 4.

95 *42nd Annual Report of the London Police Court Mission*, 1934, p. 8.

96 *44th Annual Report of the London Police Court Mission*, 1936, p. 8.

97 Feversham, president of NAPO and also a member of the committee reviewing probation in *Probation*, Vol. 2, No. 5, July 1936, p. 73.

98 *MEPO2/4585 Chief Constables Association of England and Wales – Statement of Evidence of Representatives Giving Evidence to Social Services Committee*.

99 Both quotes are noted in *MEPO2/4585*.

100 Home Office Minute sometime in 1936 in *HO45/17080*.

101 *44th Annual Report of the London Police Court Mission*, 1936, p. 4.

102 *44th Annual Report of the London Police Court Mission*, 1936, p. 5.

103 London Police Court Mission Committee, minutes of meeting held on 7 May 1936.

104 Minutes of Meeting held in *HO45/17080*.

105 Letter to the Home Office from the Archbishop of Canterbury dated 24 October 1936 in *HO45/17080*.

106   Home Office Minute dated 24 June 1937 in *HO45/17080*.
107   See *HO45/17080*.
108   Minutes of the London Police Court Mission Committee meeting held on 12
      October 1937.
109   Bernard Joseph Reynolds (born 29 November 1891) joined the Civil Service in
      1911. He transferred to the Home Office in 1914 and after war service returned
      working his way up the clerical grades to join the Higher Grades in 1922. He also
      had key responsibility for the Probation Officers Superannuation Fund (before
      1937) as part of his work at the Home Office. He does not appear to have had a
      public school or Oxbridge education.
110   Doris Rosling, born 3 October 1900, graduated with a BA in London and rose to
      be an assistant secretary in the Children's Department at the Home Office in 1947.
      She was also joint secretary to the Curtis Committee which reviewed the whole
      social services in 1945–1946.

Chapter 5

1   Memo to Secretary of State dated 1 March 1938 held in *HO144/22447 Report of
    Departmental Committee on Corporal Punishment 5*.
2   Harris's notes of the Conference are full and appear to be contemporaneous though
    they are actually undated. They are held in *HO144/22447*.
3   Home Office Minute dated 19 May 1938 held in *HO144/22447*.
4   Memo to Cabinet dated 16 June 1938 held in *HO144/22447*.
5   Sir Samuel Hoare in the Commons on 19 November 1938, in *Hansard Commons*,
    Vol. 342, col. 272. Viscountess Astor added immediately 'and lazy fathers'.
6   Hoare's description of the proposed new orders is contained in *Hansard Commons*,
    Vol. 342, col. 274–5.
7   *Howard Journal*, Vol. 5, No. 3, 1938–1940, p. 146.
8   *Howard Journal*, p. 149.
9   *Hansard Commons*, Vol. 353, col. 408. 9 November 1939.
10 *The Howard Journal*, Vol. 5, No. Spring 4, 1940, Editorial, p. 225.
11 Readers are referred to other works such as Mannheim (1940, 1941) or more
    recently Calder (1969), Smithies (1982) and Thomas (2003).
12 The figures are taken from *Probation Bulletin No. 1*, a copy of which is held in
    HO45/24261 Probation Bulletin No.'s 1–6, 1946–1950.
13 The figures quoted relate to sentences in the Magistrates Courts between 1938 and
    1946. They are taken from Smithies (1982: 199–200).
14 B. J. Reynolds in a Home Office Minute, undated but sometime in 1936. Held in
    HO45/18514 Appointment of PPO for Metropolitan Police Court District.

15 Alexander Paterson, Prison Commissioner and in charge of the Borstals had recommended Clutton-Broch.

16 Letter from Clutton-Broch to the Probation Branch dated 8 May 1939 held in *HO45/18514*.

17 H. E. Norman, *Probation*, Vol. 3, No. 3, November 1938.

18 Home Office Minute dated 11 July 1939 held in *HO144/22452 Probation Officers-Various Issues*.

19 See *HO144/22452*.

20 H. E. Norman *N.A.P.O. Report – Wartime Problems*, dated 29 May 1940. Held in *HO144/22473 Various Probation-Including N.A.P.O. Report on Wartime Problems Encountered by Probation Officers*.

21 See *HO144/22473*, included in a Minute made sometime in 1942.

22 *HO45/20730 War Time Social Work Notes by Principal Probation Officers 1945/6*.

23 See *HO45/22473*.

24 Home Office Minute by B. J. Reynolds dated 14 March 1940 held in *HO144/22453 Conscientious Objectors as Probation Officers*.

25 Home Office Minute by B. J. Reynolds dated 16 March 1940 in *HO144/22453*.

26 See *HO144/22453*.

27 H. E. Norman, 'The War and Probation', *Probation*, Vol. 3, No. 8, 1939, p. 113.

28 Editorial, *Probation*, Vol. 3, No. 8, 1939, p. 114.

29 *Probation,* Vol. 3, No. 9, 1940, p. 130.

30 Basil Henriques on Birching, *Probation*, Vol. 3, No. 13, 1941, p. 180.

31 Editorial, *Probation*, Vol. 3, No. 15, 1941, p. 207.

32 *Probation*, Vol. 3, No. 14, 1941, pp. 194–196.

33 *Probation,* Vol. 3, No. 15, 1941, p. 213.

34 *Probation*, Vol. 3, No. 15, 1941, p. 216.

35 *Probation*, Vol. 3, No. 17, 1942, p. 236.

36 J. R. Kennedy, 'Mother and Child', *Probation*, Vol. 3, No. 16, p. 225.

37 G. May Wilcox, Reminiscences, *Probation*, Vol. 4, No. 4, pp. 33–34.

38 Claud Mullins (1887–1968) was a Barrister and later a Metropolitan Police Court Magistrate between 1931–1947. He was also a councillor and Vice-President of the Family Planning Association.

39 Dr Edward Glover in the Introduction to Mullins (1943) p. xiv.

40 *Howard Journal*, Vol. 6, No. Autumn 2, 1942, p. 123.

41 See *Probation*, Vol. 4, No. 4, 1943, p. 59.

42 Taken from Minutes of Council Meeting held on 29 January 1942. The social worker appointed was G. May Wilcox who is quoted above.

43 W. G. Minn was a former probation officer in London who had recently been appointed as Probation Inspector at the Home Office.

44 The quote and other information are taken from the Minutes of ISTD Council Meeting held on 12 March 1942.

45 ISTD Minutes of Council Meeting held 1 June 1943.

46 Taken from ISTD Minutes of Council Meetings held on 5 August 1942 and 19 January 1944.

47 ISTD Minutes of Council Meeting held on 21 March 1945.

48 ISTD Minutes of Council 29 July 1942.

49 ISTD Minutes of Council 14 October 1942. It was usually Dr Friedlander or Dr Glover who gave these lectures. Incidentally, by this time Dr Grace Pailthorpe had left the ISTD; she returned briefly to work at the ISTD between 1948 and 1952 (Saville and Rumney 1991).

50 As already mentioned Doris Rosling was a former Police Court Missionary appointed as an Inspector in the Probation Branch in 1936.

51 Reynolds' speech is reported in *Probation* Vol. 4, No. 5, 1943, p. 54, which is where these quotes are taken from.

52 Report by Probation Inspector on a visit to Cheshire on 11, 13, 23 and 30 May 1938, p. 1 held in *HO45/23839 Probation 1938–1949*.

53 Report by Miss Hutchinson and Mr Morton of the Home Office dated May and June 1947, held in *HO45/23839*.

54 *Claud Mullins* in a letter to Sidney Harris dated 8 July 1943 held in *HO45/23176*.

55 Home Office Minute dated 2 June 1949 held in *HO45/23176 London Probation Committee 1936–49*. Winifred Goode (born 10 March 04) was a graduate of London University and a barrister before becoming a Factory Inspector in 1930. In 1936 she joined the Children's Branch and in 1947 she was appointed Principal and later Assistant Secretary in the Probation Division.

56 Home Office Minute dated January 1943 held in *HO45/25000 Probation Advisory Committee-Reconstitution 1937–48*.

57 Final draft of *Probation Work in England and Wales*, prepared in 1937 and held in *HO45/21873 Training of Probation Officers*. Macadam was still teaching on the Home Office three-month training in 1945.

58 See *HO45/18832 Probation Officer Trainees-Position in Event of War 1939–41*.

59 Taken from a Home Office Minute dated 2 February 1945 in *HO45/21873*.

60 Ministry of Labour and National Service (1945: 59), the exact publication date of this was February 1945.

61 Elizabeth Glover joined probation from the London Police Court Mission in 1931. She was a former Deputy Principal Probation Officer in London and worked as Probation Inspector through the war.

62 Home Office Memo dated December 1945 by E. Glover, who by this time was also secretary to the Probation Training Board. In *HO45/21874 Training of Probation Officers*.

63 See *HO45/21874*.

64 J. H. Cottam, 'Causes and Treatment of Delinquency', *Probation*, Vol. 4, No. 5, 1943, p. 72.

65 Marjorie Craig, Probation Officer in Bootle writing in *Probation*, Vol. 4, No. 10, 1945, p. 103.

66 J. A. Vigor, 'First impressions of juvenile delinquency', *Probation*, Vol. 4, No. 10, 1945, p. 115.

67 *Probation*, Vol. 5, No. 7, 1947, p. 93.

68 Taken from 'What kind of probation officers do we need?' by A. G. Rose, *Probation*, Vol. 5, No. 12, 1947, pp. 166–167.

69 The contrary view was expressed by Elizabeth Glover, discussed above, who wrote 'Our best youth clubs are probably one of the biggest social assets of this country at the present time' (Glover 1949: 131).

70 Samuel Hoare was by then Lord Templewood and President of the Howard League for Penal Reform, who also make the same claim as Rose (1961) in their Annual Report of 1947/8.

71 *Report of the Administration of Justice Standing Committee Sub-Committee on Compulsory Attendance Centres* dated 7 December 1945 and held in *HO45/20729*.

72 Minutes of the meeting of the above Committee held on 26 October 1945 held in *HO45/20729*.

73 Both quotes are taken from the Minutes of the meeting held with Principal Probation Officers on 2 November 1945, held in *HO45/20729*. Henriques (1950) also saw great practical difficulties with the proposed centres.

74 *Report of Sub-Committee of Standing Committee on Administration of Justice*, held in *HO45/20729*.

75 *Criminal Justice Bill 1948 s3(1).*

76 *Criminal Justice Bill 1948 s4(1).*

77 See *Criminal Justice Bill 1948 S3(2).*

78 *Criminal Justice Bill 1948 Schedule 5 s6.*

79 *Hansard Commons*, Vol. 443, col. 2196, 1947–1948.

80 Criminal Justice Act 1948 Sec. 19(2).

81 Criminal Justice Act 1948 Sec. 48.

82 *Probation*, Vol. 5, No. 14, p. 185.

83 See *Probation*, Vol. 5, No. 16, p. 216.

84 Criminal Justice Act 1948 *clause 56.*

85 The report on Chuter Ede's speech is contained in *Probation*, Vol. 5, No. 21, pp. 269–271.

86 See *Probation*, Vol. 5, No. 23, p. 293.

87 The figures and quote are taken from *Report of the Children's Branch and Probation Branch at the Home Office 1946–1952* held in *HO45/25198 Report on Children's Branch and Probation Branch 1946–1952*.

Chapter 6

1   *Probation*, Vol. 5, No. 4, p. 53. By this time Feversham had been President of NAPO for nearly twenty years.
2   *Probation*, Vol. 5, No. 21, p. 273.
3   Feversham's speech is reported in *Probation*, Vol. 5, No. 22, p. 282.
4   *Probation*, Vol. 5, No. 5, p. 67.
5   Reported in *Probation*, Vol. 5, No. 1, p. 5.
6   The conference is reported in *Probation*, Vol. 5, No. 20, p. 258.
7   Peter Duncan Scott (1914–1977) was a forensic psychiatrist who after working at Stamford House took up a joint post at the Maudsley Hospital and Brixton Prison as a psychiatrist. He was a teacher of note in his field though not wedded to a particular theoretical approach (DNB).
8   The account is in *Probation*, Vol. 5, No. 22, p. 286.
9   *Probation*, Vol. 5, No. 23, p. 298.
10 See *Probation*, Vol. 5, No. 17, p. 231.
11 *Probation*, Vol. 5, No. 16, p. 218.
12 These notices are all included in *Probation*, Vol. 5, No. 24.
13 *Probation*, Vol. 5, No. 13, p. 180.
14 *Probation*, Vol. 9, No. 4, pp. 47–49.
15 *Probation*, Vol. 12, No. 2, p. 37.
16 *Probation*, Vol. 5, No. 6, p. 71.

Bibliography

Aichorn, August (1925/1951) *Wayward Youth*. London: Imago Publishing.

Anderson, Sir Robert (1907) *Criminals and Crime: Some Facts and Suggestions*. London: James Nisbet and Co.

Annison, Jill (2009) 'Delving into the *Probation Journal*: Portrayals of women probation officers and women offenders', *Probation Journal*, Vol. 56, No. 4, pp. 43–50.

Attlee, C. R. (1920) *The Social Worker*. London: G. Bell and Sons Ltd.

Ayscough, H. H. (1923) *When Mercy Seasons Justice – A Short History of the Work of the Church of England in the Police Courts*. Westminster: CETS.

Bagot, J. H. (1941) *Juvenile Delinquency – A Comparative Study of the Position in Liverpool and England and Wales*. London: Jonathon Cape.

Bailey, Victor (1987) *Delinquency and Citizenship – Reclaiming the Young Offender*. Oxford: Claranden Press.

Barrett, Rosa M. (1900) 'The Treatment of Juvenile Offenders together with statistics of their number', *Journal of The Royal Statistical Society*, Vol. LXIII, No. 2, pp. 183–271.

Belchem, James (1990) *Class, Party and the Political System in Britain*. Oxford: Basil Blackwell Ltd.

Bennett, James (1981) *Oral History and Delinquency – The Rhetoric of Criminology*. Chicago: University of Chicago Press.

Benney, Mark (1936) *Low Company – Describing the Evolution of a Burglar*. London: Peter Davies.

Board of Education (1920) *Report by the Juvenile Organisations Committee of the Board of Education on Juvenile Delinquency*.

Bochel, Dorothy (1962a) 'A brief history of N.A.P.O. Part I – The Edridge era', *Probation*, Vol. 10, No. 3, pp. 33–31.

———. (1962b) 'A brief history of N.A.P.O. Part II – A time of growth', *Probation*, Vol. 10, No. 4, pp. 53–55.

———. (1976) *Probation and After-Care – Its Development in England and Wales*. Edinburgh: Scottish Academic Press.

Bosanquet, Helen (1914/1973) *Social Work in London 1869–1912*. London: John Murray.

Bowlby, John (1947) *Forty-Four Juvenile Thieves: Their Characters and Home-Life*. London: Bailliere, Tindall and Cox.

Brake, M. and Hale, C. (1992) *Public Order and Private Lives*. London: Routledge.

Bray, Reginald (1907) *The Town Child*. London: T. Fisher Union.

———. (1908) 'The Family', *Pan Anglican Papers S. A.*, Vol. 3f, pp. 32–36.

———. (1912) *Labour and the Churches*. London: Constable and Company Ltd.

Briggs, Asa and Macartney, Anne (1984) *Toynbee Hall – The First Hundred Years.* London: Routledge and Kegan Paul.

Burt, Cyril (1925) *The Young Delinquent.* London: University of London Press.

———. (1944) *The Young Delinquent.* London: University of London Press.

Calder, Angus (1969) *The People's War – Britain 1939–45.* London: Jonathon Cape.

Cannadine, David (1990) *The Decline and Fall of the British Aristocracy.* New Haven, CT: Yale University Press.

Cassady, S. (2001) 'Frederic Reiner: The founder of Probation', *Probation*, Vol. 48. No. 4, pp. 287–289.

Chapman, Cecil (1932) *From the Bench.* London: Hodder and Stoughton.

Chapman, Richard A. and Greenaway, J. R. (1980) *The Dynamics of Administrative Reform.* London: Groom Helm.

Children and Young Persons Act 1933.

Clarke-Hall, William (1917) *The State and the Child.* London: Headley Bros.

———. (1926) *Children's Courts.* London: George Allen and Unwin.

Clement-Brown, S. (1970) 'Looking Backwards – Reminiscences 1922–46', *British Journal of Psychiatric Social Work*, Vol. X, pp. 161–169.

Coddington, F. J. O. (1950) 'The probation system under the Criminal Justice Act', in L. Radzinowicz and J. W. C. Turner (eds) *The Journal of Criminal Science Vol II.* London: Macmillan and Co.

Cohen, Stanley. (1979) 'The Punitive City – Notes on the dispersal of social control', *Contemporary Crises* Vol. 3, Issue 4, Oct. 1979, pp. 339–363.

———. (1985) *Visions of Social Control.* Cambridge: Polity Press.

Conservative Party (1946) *Youth Astray – A Report on the Treatment of Young Offenders.* London: The Conservative Party.

Courtenay-Orchard, H. (1931) *The Police Court Missionary's Story.* Walsall: Christian Worker's Armoury.

Criminal Justice Act 1925.

———. 1948.

———. 1991.

Criminal Justice Bill 1924.

———. 1938.

———. 1947.

Crowther, Anne (1988) *British Social Policy 1914–1939.* London: MacMillan Education Ltd.

Cumming, Sir John (1935) *A Contribution Towards a Bibliography Dealing with Crime and Cognate Subjects.* London: Police College.

Dangerfield, George (1966) *The Strange Death of Liberal England.* London: MacGibbon and Kee.

Dark, Sidney (1939) *Inasmuch.... Christianity in the Police Courts.* London: Student Christian Movement Press.

Davies, Andrew (1998) 'Youth gangs, masculinity and violence in late Victorian Manchester and Salford', *Journal of Social History*, Vol. 32, No. 2, pp. 349–369.

Davin, Anna (1978) 'Imperialism and Motherhood', *History Workshop*, No. 5, Spring 1978, pp. 9–65.

Davis, Jennifer (1980) 'The London Garotting Panic of 1862: A Moral Panic and the creation of a Criminal Class in mid-Victorian England', in V. A. C. Gatrell et al (eds), *Crime and the Law: The Social History of Crime in Western Europe since 1500*, pp. 190–213. London: Europa Publications.

——. (1984) 'A poor mans system of justice: The London Police Courts in the second half of the nineteenth century', *Historical Journal*, Vol. 27, No. 2, pp. 309–335.

Dawtry, Frank (1957/8) 'Whither Probation?' *British Journal of Delinquency*, Vol. XIII, pp. 180–187.

Deering, J. et al (1996) 'Individual Supervision and Reconviction: An Experimental Programme in Pontypridd', *Probation*, Vol. 43, pp. 43–70.

Devon, James (1912) *The Criminal and the Community*. London: John Lane The Bodley Head.

Dictionary of National Biography (various editions) Oxford: Oxford University Press.

Donald, Thomas (2003) *An Underworld at War – Spivs, Deserters, Racketeers and Civilians in the Second World War*. London: John Murray.

Downes, David and Morgan, Rod (1994) ' "Hostages to Fortune?" The Politics of Law and Order in Post-War Britain', in M. Maguire et al (eds), *The Oxford Handbook of Criminology*. Oxford: Clarendon Press.

DuCane, Edward (1893) 'The decrease of crime', *The Nineteenth Century*, Vol. 33, March, pp. 480–492.

Elkin, Winifred A. (1938) *English Juvenile Courts*. London: Kegan Paul, Trench, Trubner and Co Ltd.

Ellison, Mary (1934) *Sparks Beneath The Ashes – Experiences of a London Probation Officer*. London: John Murray.

Emsley, Clive (1996) *Crime and Society in England 1750–1900*. London: Longman.

Fenner Brockway, F. (1928) *A New Way with Crime*. London: Williams and Norgate Ltd.

Folkard, Steven et al (1966) *Studies in the Causes of Delinquency and the Treatment of Offenders*. London: Home Office Research Unit.

Foucault, M. (1991) *Discipline and Punish – The Birth of the Prison*. London: Penguin.

Friedlander, Kate (1947) *The Psycho-Analytical Approach to Juvenile Delinquency. Theory: Case Studies: Treatment*. London: Routledge and Kegan Paul.

Galton, Francis (1869/1978) *Hereditary Genius*. London: Julian Friedman Publishers Ltd.

——. (1907) *Inquiries into Human Faculty and Its Development*. London: J. M. Dent and Sons Ltd.

Gamon, Hugh (1907) *The London Police Court, Today and Tomorrow*. London: Dent and Co.

Gard, Raymond (2009) *The End of the Rod – A History of the Abolition of Corporal Punishment in the Courts of England and Wales*. Boca Raton, FL: BrownWalker Press.

Garland, David (1985) *Punishment and Welfare*. Aldershot: Gower.

———. (1988) 'British Criminology before 1935', *British Journal of Criminology*, Vol. 28, No. 2, pp. 1–19.

———. (1996) 'The Limits of the Sovereign State', *British Journal of Criminology*, Vol. 36, No. 4, pp. 445–471.

———. (2001) *The Culture of Control*. Oxford: Oxford University Press.

Gatrell, V., Lenamn, B. and Parker, G. (eds) (1980) *The Social History of Crime in Western Europe since 1500*. London: Europa Publications.

Gibson, Ian (1978) *The English Vice – Beating, Sex and Shame in Victorian England and After*. London: Duckworth.

Gillis, John R. (1981) *Youth and History*. London: Academic Press.

Glover, Elizabeth (1949) *Probation and Re-Education*. London: Routledge and Kegan Paul.

Glover, Edward (1960) *The Roots of Crime – Selected Papers on Psychoanalysis, Vol. 2*. London: Imago.

Goring, Charles (1913) *The English Convict – A Statistical Study*. London: HMSO.

Guilfoyle, Mike (2013) 'Transforming rehabilitation: the end of the probation service', *Criminal Justice Matters*, Vol. 92, pp. 38–39.

Haldane, J. B. (1911) *The Social Worker's Guide – A Handbook of Information and Counsel for All Who Are Interested in Public Welfare*. London: Sir Isaac Pitman and Sons Ltd.

Hamblin Smith, M. (1922) *The Psychology of the Criminal*. London: Mathuen and Co. Ltd.

Harris, Jo (1937) *Probation – A Sheaf of Memories – Thirty Four Years Work in Local Police Courts*. England: M. F. Robinson and Co. Ltd.

Harris, S. W. (1937) *Probation and Other Social Work of the Courts – Third Clarke-Hall Lecture*. London: Clarke-Hall Fellowship.

Hay, D. (1975) 'Property Authority and the Criminal Law', in D. Hay et al (eds), *Albion's Fatal Tree*, pp. 17–64. London: Penguin.

Hay, J. R. (1975) *The Origins of the Liberal Welfare Reforms 1906–1914*. London: MacMillan Press Ltd.

Henriques, Basil (1950) *The Indiscretions of a Magistrate*. London: The non-fiction book club.

Hobsbawm, E. J. (1969) *Industry and Empire*. Middlesex: Pelican.

Holmes, Thomas (1900) 'Youthful Offenders and Parental Responsibility', *The Contemporary Review*, pp. 845–854.

———. (1901) 'The Police Court and its problems – An interview with Mr Thomas Holmes', *The Young Man*, Vol. 15, pp. 325–328.

———. (1908) *Known to the Police*. London: E. Arnold.

Home Office (1891) *Probation of First Offenders Act – Return Relating to the Probation of First Offenders Act (HC 231).*

———. (1895) *Report from the Departmental Committee on Prisons (C7702).*

———. (1896) *Report to Her Majesties Commissioners of Prisons on the Operation of Discharged Prisoners Aid Societies (C8299).*

———. (1900) *Probation of First Offenders Act – Returns relating to the Probation of First Offenders Act (HC 348).*

———. (1903) *Probation of First Offenders Act – Returns relating to the Probation of First Offenders Act (HC 281).*

———. (1906) *Probation of First Offenders Act – Returns relating to the Probation of First Offenders Act (HC 307).*

———. (1907a) *Probation of First Offenders Bill.*

———. (1907b) *Treatment of Youthful Offenders (HC 667).*

———. (1908) *Memorandum Issued by the Secretary of State for the Home Department with Reference to the Probation of Offenders Act 1907 (Cd 3981).*

———. (1910a) *Report of the Departmental Committee on the Probation of Offenders Act 1907 (CD 5001).*

———. (1910b) *Report of the Departmental Committee on the Probation of Offenders Act 1907 – Minutes of Evidence (CD 5002).*

———. (1913) *Confidential Report of the Departmental Committee on the Remuneration of Probation Officers in the Metropolitan Police Court District.*

———. (1922) *Report of the Departmental Committee on the Training and Payment of Probation Officers Cmd 1601.*

———. (1923) *First Report of the Work of the Children's Branch.*

———. (1924) *Second Report of the Work of the Children's Branch.*

———. (1925) *Third Report of the Work of the Children's Branch.*

———. (1927) *Report of the Departmental Committee on the Treatment of Young Offenders (Cmd 2831).*

———. (1928) *Fourth Report of the Work of the Children's Branch.*

———. (1932) *Report of the Departmental Committee on Persistent Offenders (Cmd 4090).*

———. (1936) *Report of the Departmental Committee on the Social Services in Courts of Summary Jurisdiction (Cmd 5122).*

———. (1938a) *Report of the Departmental Committee on Corporal Punishment (Cmd 5684).*

———. (1938b) *Fifth Report of the Work of the Children's Branch.*

———. (1959) *Penal Practice in a Changing Society (Cmnd 645).*

———. (1962) *Report of the Departmental Committee on the Probation Service (Cmnd 1650).*

———. (1966) *Report on the Work of the Probation and After Care Department 1962–65 (Cmnd 3107).*

———. (1988) *National Standards for the supervision of Community Service Orders.*
London: H.M.S.O.

———. (1992) *National Standards for the Supervision of Offenders in the Community.*
London: H.M.S.O.

Hood, R. (2004) 'Hermann Mannheim and Max Gruenhut – Criminological pioneers
in London and Oxford', *British Journal of Criminology*, Vol. 44, No. 4, pp. 1–27.

Howard Association (1881) *Annual Report.*

———. (1898) *Juvenile Offenders – A Report.*

Howard League for Penal Reform (1921–1943) *The Howard Journal.*

———. (1947) *Lawless Youth – A Challenge for the New Europe.* London: George Allen
and Unwin.

Humphries, Stephen (1981) *Hooligan or Rebels? – An Oral History of Working-Class
Childhood and Youth 1889–1939.* Oxford: Basil Blackwell.

Hynes, Samuel (1968) *The Edwardian Turn of Mind.* Princeton, NJ: Princeton
University Press.

———. (1976) *The Auden Generation – Literature and Politics in England in the 1930s.*
London: The Bodley Head.

Ignatieff, Michael (1978) *A Just Measure of Pain – The Penitentiary in the Industrial
Revolution 1750–1850.* London: MacMillan.

Jarvis, F. V. (1972) *Assist and Befriend – A History of the Probation and After-Care
Service.* London: National Association of Probation Officers.

Jeyes, S. H. and How, F. D. (1912) *The Life of Sir Howard Vincent.* London: George Allen
and Unwin.

Joint University Council for Social Studies (1918) *Social Study and Training at the
Universities.* London: P. S. King and Son Ltd.

Jones, A. E. (1945) *Juvenile Delinquency and the Law.* Middlesex: Pelican.

Keith-Lucas, Bryan and Richards, Peter G. (1978) *A History of Local Government in the
Twentieth Century.* London: George Allen and Unwin.

Kelsall, R. K. (1955) *Higher Civil Servants in Britain from 1870 to the Present Day.*
London: Routledge and Kegan Paul.

King, Joan F. S. (1958) *The Probation Service.* London: Butterworth and Co. Ltd.

Le Mesurier, L. (1935) *A Handbook of Probation and Social Work of the Courts.* London:
National Association of Probation Officers.

Leeson, Cecil (1914) *The Probation System.* London: P. S. King and Son.

———. (1917) *The Child and the War.* London: P. S. King and Son.

Lieck, Albert (1922) *The Justice at Work.* London: Butterworth and Co.

Macadam, Elizabeth (1910) 'Training for Social Work', *Charity Organisation Review*,
Vol. 28, No. 163, July, pp. 72–82.

———. (1925) *The Equipment of the Social Worker.* London: George Allen and Unwin.

———. (1945) *The Social Servant in the Making.* London: George Allen and Unwin.

MacLeod, Roy (ed.) (1988) *Government and Expertise – Specialist Administrators and
Professionals, 1860–1919.* Cambridge: Cambridge University Press.

Macrae, F. J. (1957/8) 'The English Probation Training System', *British Journal of Delinquency*, Vol. XIII, No. 3, pp. 210–215.

Mair, George and Burke, Lol (2012) *Redemption, Rehabilitation and Risk Management. A History of Probation*. Oxford: Routledge.

Mangan, James A. (1986) *Athleticism in the Victorian and Edwardian Public School*. London: The Falmer Press.

Mannheim, H. (1940) *Social Aspects of Crime in England Between the Wars*. London: George Allen and Unwin Ltd.

———. (1941) *War and Crime*. London: Watts and Co.

Martin, J. P. (1988) 'The Development of Criminology in Britain 1948-60', *British Journal of Criminology*, Vol. 28, No. 2, pp. 35–44.

Martinson, R. (1974) 'What Works? – Questions and Answers about Prison Reform', *The Public Interest*, Spring, No. 5, pp. 22–54.

Masterman, C. F. G. (ed.) (1901/1973) *The Heart of the Empire*. London: T. Fisher Union.

———. (1911) *The Condition of England*. London: Methuen and Co. Ltd.

Maxwell, Sir Alexander (1948) *The Home Office – Its Functions in Relation to the Treatment of Offenders – Second Annual Lecture on Criminal Science Delivered at Cambridge University on Oct. 31st 1947*. London: Stevens and Sons Ltd.

May, T. (1991) *Probation – Politics, Policy and Practice*. Milton Keynes: Oxford University Press.

———. (1994) 'Probation and Community Sanctions', in M. Maguire et al (eds) *The Oxford Handbook of Criminology*. Oxford: Oxford University Press.

McGuire, J. and Priestly, P. (1985) *Offending Behaviour – Skills and Stratagems for Going Straight*. London: B. T. Batesford Ltd.

McWilliams, William (1983) 'The Mission to the English Police Courts 1876–1936', *Howard Journal*, Vol. 22, No. 3, pp. 129–147.

———. (1985) 'The Mission Transformed', *Howard Journal*, Vol. 24, No. 4, pp. 257–272.

———. (1986) 'The English Probation System and the Diagnostic Ideal', *Howard Journal*, Vol. 25, No. 4, pp. 241–260.

Meacham, Standish (1972) 'The Sense of Impending Clash – English working – Class unrest before the First World War', *The American Historical Review*, Vol. 75, Part 5, pp. 1343–1364.

Melossi, Darrio and Pavarini, Massimo (1981) *The Prison and The Factory – Origins of the Penitentiary System*. London: MacMillan Press.

Ministry of Labour and National Service (1945) *Social Work – Careers for Men and Women, No. 39 – a Detailed Description of Qualifications, Training and Prospects of Employment*.

Minn, W. G. (1948) 'Training for the work of a probation officer in England and Wales', *Journal of Criminal Science*, Vol. 1, pp. 163–172.

Morgan, A. E. (1939) *The Needs of Youth*. London: Oxford University Press.

Morris, Terence (1988) 'British Criminology 1935–48', *British Journal of Criminology*, Vol. 28, No. 2, pp. 20–34.

Morrison, W. D. (1892) 'The Increase of Crime', *The Nineteenth Century*, Vol. 31, June, pp. 951–957.

Mullins, Claude (1943) *Crime and Psychology*. London: Methuen and Co.

National Association of Probation Officers (1929–1965) *Probation – The Journal of N.A.P.O.*

——. (2007) *Changing Lives- An Oral History of Probation*. London: N.A.P.O.

Newsam, Sir Frank (1954) *The Home Office*. London: George Allen and Unwin.

Newton, George (1956/7) 'Trends in Probation Training', *British Journal of Delinquency*, Vol. XII, No. 2, pp. 123–135.

Norwood-East, W. (1927) *An Introduction to Forensic Psychiatry in the Criminal Court*. London: J. and A. Churchill.

——. (1942) *The Adolescent Criminal – A Medico-Sociological Study of 4000 Male Adolescents*. London: J. and A. Churchill Ltd.

Nuttall, C. et al (1998) *Reducing Offending: An Assessment of Research Evidence on Ways of Dealing with Offending Behaviour – Home Office Research Study 187*. London: Home Office Research and Statistics Directorate.

Page, Leo (1937) *Crime and the Community*. London: Faber and Faber.

Page, Martin (1992) *Crimefighters of London – A History of the Origins and Development of the London Probation Service 1876–1965*. London: Inner London Probation Service.

Pailthorpe, Grace, W. (1932) *Studies in the Psychology of Delinquency*. London: HMSO/ Medical Research Council.

Paterson, A. (1911) *Across the Bridges or Life by the South London River Side*. London: Edward Arnold.

Pearson, Geoffrey (1983) *Hooligan – A History of Respectable Fears*. London: The MacMillan Press.

——. (1989) 'A Jekyll in the Classroom, a Hyde in the Street: Queen Victoria's Hooligans', in D. Downes (ed.), *Crime and the City*. Basingstoke: Macmillan.

Pease, Ken (1999) 'The Probation Career of Al Truism', *Howard Journal*, Vol. 38, No. 1, pp. 2–16.

Pellew, Jill (1982) *The Home Office 1848–1914 – From Clerks to Bureaucrats*. London: Heinemann.

Pick, Daniel (1989) *Faces of Degeneration – A European disorder, c.1848–c.1918*. Cambridge: Cambridge University Press.

Pitts, John (1988) *The Politics of Juvenile Crime*. London: Sage.

Platt, Anthony M. (1969) *The Child Savers*. Chicago, IL: University of Chicago Press.

Plowden, Alfred C. (1903) *Grain or Chaff? – The Autobiography of a Police Magistrate*. London: T. Fisher Union.

Probation of First Offenders Act 1887.

Probation of Offenders Act 1907.

Quinton, R. F. (1910/1984) *Crime and Punishment in England 1850–1922*. New York, NY: Garland Publishing.

Radzinowicz, L and Hood, R. (1986) *A History of English Criminal Law and its Administration from 1750. Volume 5 – The Emergence of Penal Policy*. London: Stevens and Sons.

Rhodes, E. C. (1939) 'Juvenile Delinquency', *Journal of the Royal Statistical Society*, Part 3, pp. 384–405.

Richmond, Mary E. (1917/1965) *Social Diagnosis*. New York, NY: Free Press.

Rose, Gordon (1961) *The Struggle for Penal Reform*. London: Stevens and Sons Ltd.

Rose, Nikolas (1985) *The Psychological Complex – Psychology, Politics and Society in England 1869–1939*. London: Routledge and Kegan Paul.

Rowbotham, Judith (2009) 'Turning away from criminal intent', *Theoretical Criminology*, Vol. 13, No. 1, pp. 105–128.

Russell, C. E. B. (1910) *Young Goal Birds*. London: MacMillan and Co. Ltd.

———. (1917) *The Problem of Juvenile Crime*. London: Oxford Univesity Press.

Russell, C. E. B. and Rigby, L. M. (1906) *The Making of the Criminal*. London: MacMillan and Co. Ltd.

———. (1932) *Lad's Clubs – Their History Organisation and Management*. London: A. & C. Black Ltd.

Samuel, Viscount (1945) *Memoirs*. London: The Crescent Press.

Saville, E. and Rumney D. (1991) *A History of the I.S.T.D.* London: I.S.T.D.

Searle G. R. (1971) *The Quest for National Efficiency – A Study in British Political Thought 1899–1914*. Oxford: Basil Blackwell.

Semmel, Bernard (1960) *Imperialism and Social Reform – English Social-Imperial Thought 1895–1914*. London: George Allen and Unwin Ltd.

Smith, D. F. (1994) 'Juvenile Delinquency in the British Zone of Germany, 1945–51', *German History*, Vol. 12, No. 1, pp. 39–63.

Smithies, Edward (1982) *A Social History of Crime in World War 2*. London: George Allen and Unwin.

Solicitor (1932) *English Justice*. London: George Routledge and Sons Ltd.

Springhall, J. O. (1972) 'The Boy Scouts, class and militarism in relation to British youth movements 1908–1930', *International Review of Social History*, Vol. 17, pp. 125–158.

———. (1977) *Youth, Empire and Society*. London: Groom Helm.

Stack, John A. (1994) 'Reformatory and industrial schools and the decline of child imprisonment in mid-Victorian England and Wales', *History of Education*, Vol. 23, No. 1, pp. 59–73.

Stanton, Walter (1935) *Sidelights on Police Court Mission Work*. Worcester: The Trinity Press.

Stedman-Jones, Gareth (1971) *Outcast London – A Study in the Relationship between Classes in Victorian Society*. Oxford: Clarendon Press.

Stevenson, John (1984) *British Society 1914–45*. Middlesex: Penguin.

Stocking, George W. Jr. (1987) *Victorian Anthropology*. New York, NY: Free Press.

Stokes, Sewell (1950) *Court Circular*. London: Michael Joseph.

Storch, Robert (1981) 'The Plague of the Blue Locusts: Police Reform and Popular Resistance in Northern England, 1840–57' in M. Fitzgerald et al (eds), *Crime and Society*. London: Routledge.

Summers, Anne (1977) 'Militarism in Britain before the Great War', *History Workshop*.

Taylor, A.J.P. (1975) *English History 1914–1945*. Oxford: Oxford University Press.

Taylor, Howard (1998) 'The politics of the rising crime statistics of England and Wales – 1914–60', *Crime, History and Societies*, Vol. 2, No. 1, pp. 5–28.

Thorpe, Andrew (1992) *Britain in the 1930's*. Oxford: Blackwell.

Timasheff, N. S. (1941) *One Hundred Years of Probation 1841–1941 (Part One)*. New York, NY: Fordham University Press.

———. (1943) *One Hundred Years of Probation 1841–1941 (Part Two)*. New York, NY: Fordham University Press.

Timms, Noel (1964) *Psychiatric Social Work in Great Britain 1939–62*. London: Routledge and Kegan Paul.

Tobias, J. J. (1972) *Crime and Industrial Society in the Nineteenth Century*. London: B. T. Batsford Ltd.

Todd, Marjory (1963) *The Probation Officer and His World*. London: Victor Gollancz Ltd.

———. (1964) *Ever Such a Nice Lady*. London: Victor Gollancz Ltd.

Troup, Sir Edward (1925) *The Home Office*. London: G. P. Putnam's Sons Ltd.

Valier, Claire (1998) 'Psychoanalysis and Crime in Britain during the inter-war years', *British Criminology Conferences: Selected Proceedings*, Vol. 1: Emerging Themes in Criminology.

Vanstone, Maurice (2003) 'A History of Groups in Probation Work: Part One – From "Clubbing the Unclubbables" to Therapeutic Intervention', *The Howard Journal*, Vol. 42, No. 1, pp. 69–86.

———. (2007) *Supervising Offenders in the Community – A History of Probation Theory and Practice*. Aldershot: Ashgate.

Vincent, Howard (1883) 'Discharged Prisoners: How to Aid Them', *The Contemporary Review*, Vol. 43, March 1883, pp. 325–331.

Waddy, Henry T. (1925) *The Police Court and It's Work*. London: Butterworth and Co.

Watson, A. F. (1942) *The Child and the Magistrate*. London: Jonathon Cape.

Webb, Molly et al (2001) 'Entering Probation Training during the 1950s and 1960s', *Probation Journal*, Vol. 48, No. 4, pp. 281–286.

West, D. J. (1988) 'Psychological Contributions to Criminology', *British Journal of Criminology*, Vol. 28, No. 2, pp. 77–92.

Whitehead, Philip and Statham, Roger (2006) *The History of Probation – Politics and Cultural Change 1876 – 2005*. Kent: Shaw and Sons Ltd.

Who Was Who Vols 2, 3, 4 and 5. London: A. and C. Black.

Wiener, Martin (1987) 'The march of penal progress?', *Journal of British Studies*, Vol. 26, No. 1, pp. 83–96.

Wiener, Martin, J. (1990) *Reconstructing the Criminal – Culture, Law and Policy in England 1830–1914*. Cambridge: Cambridge University Press.

Wilkinson, Paul (1969) 'English Youth Movements 1908–1930', *Journal of Contemporary History*, Vol. 4, No. 2, pp. 3–23.

Woodroofe, Kathleen (1962) *From Charity to Social Work*. London: Routledge and Kegan Paul.

Worrall, A. (1997) *Punishment in the Community – The Future of Criminal Justice* London: Longman.

Yelloly, Margaret (1980) *Social Work Theory and Psychoanalysis*. London: Van Nostrand Reinhold Company.

Young, A. F. and Ashton, E. T. (1956) *British Social Work in the Nineteenth Century*. London: Routledge and Kegan Paul.

Young, Peter (1976) 'A sociological analysis of the early history of probation', *British Journal of Law and Society*, Vol. 3, No. 1, pp. 44–58.

Index

26009051R00150

Printed in Poland
by Amazon Fulfillment
Poland Sp. z o.o., Wrocław